That Recipe Sleeps with the Fishes

A collection of Italian family recipes kept under lock and key for generations

That Recipe Sleeps with the Fishes

A collection of Italian family recipes
kept under lock and key
for generations

James Desiderio

ISBN: 0692070206
ISBN-13: 978-0692070208

Printed by CreateSpace, An Amazon.com Company

Dedication

This book is dedicated to my beautiful daughters, Amanda and Jenna (below), who make me happy each and every day...

...and to the memories of my parents, Victor and Estelle Desiderio (below left) and of my in-laws, Lucio and Coradina Prado (below middle/right)

Contents

Pignoli cookies

1 1/2 C sugar
4 eggs
1/4 tsp grated lemon rind
2 1/2 C cake flour
2 tables

Biscotti

350° oven
20 min
cut and bake 15 min

3 1/4 C flour
2 1/2 teaspoon B.P.
6 eggs
1 C sugar
5 tablespoon butter
1 bottle of Anise extract

Pittsella

in one bowl

6 eggs
1 C melted butter
1 1/4 C sugar
1 bottle almond or anise ext
4 teasp B.P.
3 1/4 C flour
mix altogether

(1 tblsp anise seed optional)

use waffle iron

Canoli Shells

1 1/2 cups flour
1 tablespoon cocoa
1 tablespoon sugar
1/4 teaspoon salt

Mix flour, sugar, salt
work in the spry or crisco
Knead well. Take a piece
the size of nickle and roll
very thin. Place loosely
a canoli tube, overlap opposite
ends after wetting the ends
with egg yolk lightly beaten - pinch
ends.
When
carefully
Carefully
gently so
shells.
(over)

Cream Cheese Cake

soften 3 - 8 oz pkgs of cream cheese
Beat until creamy
add 5 eggs one at a time beating
after each egg (for 3 min each)
add 1 C sugar - beat
add 2 teasp vanilla
pour over graham cracker
crust - consisting of 3 tablespoons
melted butter + 1/4 C of sugar -
Butter pan heavily so crumbs

Foreword

This book is more than 15 years in the making. In part because of the need to record, test, re-test and photograph each recipe, but mostly due to the time it took to gather the nerve to unveil sacred family recipes before entering the Witness Protection Program. Seriously, if my grandmother (may she rest in peace) knew I was revealing her recipe for what we, as kids, used to call "bed sheet ravioli," I would have the permanent imprint of her gnocchi roller on my forehead! More on that later.

The roots of my immediate family are in the boroughs of New York City. Prior generations hail from various towns in southern Italy, mostly in and around Naples. Each generation has managed to preserve various traditions and customs from the prior generation, especially those related to food – all aspects of food – growing it, preserving it, cooking it, eating it!

In the spirit of full transparency, many of the recipes herein are for the widely enjoyed classics, like lasagna. Now, obviously, there is nothing "secret" about a recipe for lasagna – you can find hundreds of them on the internet. The reason such recipes have been included in this collection of family recipes has more to do with the subtle tweaks made to the classic versions, either in technique or ingredients, that make them special. These are some of the things that make "good" lasagna into "great" lasagna – MOM'S lasagna! Then there other recipes, like "pasta che taddi," that are fantastic, rustic dishes commonly found on dinner tables throughout many regions in southern Italy but, for one reason or another, are completely absent from Italian cuisine as we know it in the US. Pity, but I think much of that has to do with the market availability of fresh ingredients. Take, for example, my favorite lettuce, called "cichoriuni" in Sicily. The name refers to a specific type of lettuce, as well as to the salad from which it's made. Cichoriuni is in the chicory family but much more delicate – both in flavor and texture. So much so that, once picked, cichoriuni will wilt into a lifeless mass of leaves within about an hour unless kept in cold water awaiting spiritual transformation into one of the best salads you'll ever eat. Given that characteristic, it's easy to understand why cichoriuni isn't next to the Iceberg lettuce at your local Stop 'n Shop. The solution – grow your own – it's easy!

Finally, also in the spirit of full transparency, I should say that I am not a professional chef – never have been, probably never will be. In fact, to the best of my knowledge, no one in my family has ever been a professional chef, a fact that I find sadly ironic given the quality (and immense quantity) of food that has surrounded me since birth! I like to cook and I like to eat; put those together with the freshest of ingredients, a little creativity and a few pots and pans and that's all it takes! Buon appetito!

Opposite: Just a sample of my mother's hand-written recipes that I have kept for decades. She would write them down on whatever paper was handy at the moment - index cards, envelopes, old greeting cards - whatever. Most were in English. Some, like older ones from my grandmother, Maria Spirito, required translation from Italian. Unfortunately, neither my mother nor grandmother kept many written recipes for anything other than desserts and baked goods. Nothing else seemed to require the measuring of ingredients - cooking was guided solely by the senses. That was the main challenge for me - converting what I learned into "instructions" that I could pass on in writing to others.

Weights and Measures

VOLUME

1 teaspoon (t) = 5 mL
1 tablespoon (T) = 13 t = 5 mL
1 fluid ounce (oz) = 2 T = 30 mL
1/4 cup = 2 oz = 4 T = 60 mL
1/3 cup = 80 mL
1/2 cup = 4 oz = 120 mL
2/3 cup = 160 mL
3/4 cup = 6 oz = 180 mL
1 cup = 8 oz = 1/2 pint = 240 mL
1 pint = 2 cups = 16 oz
4 cups = 2 pints = 1 quart (q)
4 q = 1 gallon

WEIGHT

1/4 oz = 7 grams (g)
1 oz = 28.4 g
4 oz = 1/4 pound (lb) = 113.4 g
8 oz = 1/2 lb = 227 g
16 oz = 1 lb = 454 g

LENGTH

1 inch (in) = 2.54 centimeters (cm)
12 in = 1 foot (ft)

Appetizers

• Peperoni da Palazzolo •
Palazzolo Peppers

• Fichi Freschi con Prosciutto e Gorgonzola •
Prosciutto-Wrapped Fresh Figs with Gorgonzola

• Melanzane Sott'olio •
Marinated Eggplant in Olive Oil

• Vongole Origanate •
Baked Clams Oreganato

• Pepperoncini Ripieni •
Stuffed Hot Cherry Peppers

• Funghi Ripieni con Salsiccia •
Sausage Stuffed Mushrooms

• Peperoni Arrostiti •
Fire-Roasted Sweet Peppers

• Caponata alla Siciliana •
Sicilian Eggplant Caponata

• Cozze alla Diavola •
Mussels in Spicy Tomato Sauce

• Bruschetta •
Grilled Italian Bread with Assorted Toppings

• Calamari Fritti •
Fried Calamari

Peperoni da Palazzolo

Palazzolo Peppers

Palazzolo peppers are the best sweet frying peppers in existence – bar none! The heirloom seeds propagated within my extended family are named for the town of Palazzolo Acreide, Sicily, Italy, about 20 miles due west of Siracusa and the birthplace of my mother-in-law, Coradina Prado.

I have been propagating Palazzolo pepper seeds in my garden for many years. My search for a comparable, commercially available pepper led me to a variety known as "Jimmy Nardello" peppers, the seeds for which can be purchased through any number of seed supply companies. I've grown both varieties side-by-side and found them to be nearly indistinguishable with respect to frying characteristics and taste. The plants themselves, however, have some subtle differences, in that Jimmy Nardello plants seem (to me, at least) to be a bit smaller in stature and slightly lighter green in color. Interestingly, Jimmy Nardello peppers apparently also originated from Southern Italy and were brought to Connecticut with the immigration of the Nardello family in the late 1800s. So – for all I know – Palazzolo peppers and Jimmy Nardello peppers might indeed be one and the same! You'll still have to grow your own, however - I've never seen them in food markets here in the U.S.

Ingredients

Approximately 2 lbs freshly picked Palazzolo peppers

High temperature oil, like safflower oil, for frying

2 cloves garlic chopped

2 T olive oil

1 to 1 1/2 cups jarred San Marzano tomatoes in their juice, or prepared marinara sauce

Salt to taste

Directions

1. Using a paring knife, cut approximately 1/2" off the top of each pepper. You will see a small seed pod, which you can scoop out with the paring knife (if you prefer) or just leave it in.
2. Heat approximately 2 T safflower oil in a large frying pan or wok until very hot.
3. Carefully drop peppers in pan, working in batches so as not to over-crowd; they should immediately smoke and sizzle. Place a pan lid over the peppers as they fry. [Note: I typically fry these peppers outdoors using a propane burner, because of the amount of smoke, and just 'because it's fun].
4. Turn peppers with metal tongs until the skin begins to char all over, and peppers are somewhat pliable.
5. Removed peppers from pan and place in large bowl, covered with foil.
6. Repeat with additional batches of peppers, adding more safflower oil to the pan as needed.
7. Once all peppers are fried, lower heat to medium/low and add olive oil to the pan.
8. Add garlic and cook for 15 seconds.
9. Add tomatoes and cook 2-3 minutes, stirring.
10. Remove from heat and pour over peppers, tossing to coat.
11. Add salt to taste.

Top: Fried Palazzolo peppers ready for serving

Bottom Left: Palazzolo pepper plant

Middle right: Palazzolo peppers sizzling in the frying pan

Bottom right: Tomato sauce ready to be mixed with the fried Palazzolo peppers

Opposite: Jenna with a bag full of freshly picked Palazzolo peppers (and a cucuzza)

Fichi Freschi con Prosciutto e Gorgonzola

Prosciutto-Wrapped Fresh Figs with Gorgonzola and Balsamic Glaze

Fig trees have been cultivated by man for thousands of years; evidence for which has been found in archaeological sites as far back as 5000 B.C. Fig trees are indigenous to the Mediterranean region, but are found in most temperate and subtropical climates around the world. There are hundreds of fig varieties, each with subtle yet distinct variations in appearance, texture, taste. If you're lucky enough to live in a warm weather climate, maintaining fig trees is fairly easy. In colder climates – where temperature can reach below freezing in winter months – growing figs can be challenging (but not impossible). Having said that, I've long since abandoned trying to maintain fig trees in the ground where I live. Instead, I grow them in large containers that I can move to protected areas for over-wintering. Trees grown in this way can still reach 10 ft in height and produce plenty of fresh figs. Of course, if you can't grow your own, many food markets stock fresh figs during the harvest season.

Ingredients

Fresh figs

Prosciutto di Parma

Gorgonzola cheese

Balsamic glaze (see note)

Directions

1. Cut figs into 4-6 wedges each, depending on their size
2. Wrap a piece of prosciutto di Parma around each wedge
3. Top with crumbled gorgonzola cheese. I prefer the longer-aged gorgonzola piccante for this recipe, as it is more firm and crumbly. Alternatively, you may use gorgonzola dolce, which is sweeter and softer.
4. Drizzle balsamic glaze and serve.

Note: You can use store-bought balsamic glaze for this recipe or you can make your own. Start with a good quality, "tradizionale" balsamic vinegar. Stir together 1 cup of balsamic vinegar and 1/4 cup honey in a sauce pan. Bring to boil, then reduce heat to simmer until reduced by half. Allow to fully cool to room temperature.

Top: Fichi freschi con prosciutto e gorgonzola
Right: Young fig tree in my greenhouse
Below: Figs ready for harvest
Opposite: Freshly picked figs

Melanzane Sott'olio

Marinated Eggplant in Olive Oil

Eggplant marinated in olive oil is one of those pure and simple dishes that embellishes a great antipasto, yet I'm amazed at the number of recipes that just get it so wrong! First off, there is no need to "cook" the eggplant in boiling water in order to remove bitterness - fresh, young eggplant aren't bitter! Secondly, no need to salt and then squeeze the moisture out of an eggplant - you'll just end up with a grayish brown mass that's unpleasant both to the eye and palate. This family recipe preserves the creamy white color and delicate flavor of fresh eggplant, against a background of acidity from a brief stay in vinegar, balanced by a hint of mint and, of course, garlic. Try some on a sandwich or just enjoy with some crusty Italian bread.

Ingredients

2 eggplant

8 cups water

6 cups apple cider vinegar

5 T salt

12 fresh mint leaves chopped

1 t dried oregano

3 cloves garlic, sliced thin

1 t crushed red pepper flakes

Approximately 2 cups extra virgin olive oil

Directions

1. Place water and salt in a pot and heat just until the salt dissolves. The water should be hot but not near boiling temperature.
2. Pour the salted water into a large bowl and add the cider vinegar.
3. Trim the ends off the eggplant and completely peel using a potato peeler.
4. Working quickly to avoid oxidation (browning) of the eggplant, first cut the eggplant in half lengthwise. Lay the cut side down on a cutting board and slice the eggplant cross-wise into "half moon" slices no thicker than 1/8 inch. Immediately place the sliced eggplant into the bowl of vinegar/water. Repeat with the remaining eggplant.
5. Lay a piece of plastic wrap on the surface of the marinating eggplant, making sure that each slice is in contact with the liquid. Refrigerate overnight.
6. Strain the eggplant but do not rinse, and do not squeeze the eggplant. Return the eggplant to the bowl and add the mint, oregano, garlic, red pepper and olive oil. Mix well.
7. At this point, I typically transfer the eggplant to 1-quart mason jars, topping each with a little extra olive oil to cover. If you can resist the urge to consume the eggplant immediately, an additional 24 hours in the marinade will allow the flavors to blend and further soften the eggplant.

Eggplant 101 - Botanically speaking, an eggplant is technically a fruit - that is, a seed-bearing structure that develops from the ovary of a flowering plant. Further, an eggplant plant can produce two different "types" of eggplant, derived from cross-pollinating male and female flowers. This has caused some confusion, leading some to label an eggplant either "male" or "female," which isn't exactly accurate. However, if you take a look at the bottom of the eggplant, you will notice a "scar." If the scar is round, the eggplant was derived from a male flower and if it's more like a flattened disc, from a female flower. This is really only important if you're concerned about minimizing the number of seeds in your eggplant recipe - eggplant derived from female flowers tend to have more seeds than those from males flowers. Personally, I'm not that concerned. Plus, if you harvest eggplant early enough, seeds will be fewer in number.

Above: Black Beauty (left) and Florida Highbush (right) eggplant in my garden
Below: Melanzane sott' olio

Vongole Origanate

Baked Clams Oreganato

Access to an over-abundance of wild, locally-harvested hard shell clams was part of growing up on Long Island. Atlantic hard shell clams (*Mercenaria mercenaria*) harvested from the inter-tidal sand flats surrounding Long Island can range from 1.5 to 4 inches across. Technically, all hard shell clams can be called "quahogs" (pronounced *coe-hogs*), although the name is typically applied to the largest (*i.e.*, oldest) clams. Littleneck clams are the smallest - approximately 7 to 10 per pound, and the size that I prefer for most clam recipes, including this one.

Baked clams oreganato is an Italian-American version of the Italian appetizer, "fasolari grantinati." Fasolari are hard shell clams of the Mediterranean, similar in size to Littleneck clams but with a smoother shell.

Whichever marine mollusk you choose, make sure you use the freshest available for this tasty appetizer!

Ingredients

24 Littleneck clams (see note)

3 T olive oil

1/2 medium onion, diced

1/2 stalk celery, diced

2 cloves garlic, mined

2 T fresh Italian oregano, chopped

1 T fresh Italian parsley, chopped

1/2 t coarse black pepper

1/2 t crushed red pepper

1/2 c dry white wine

Approximately 1 1/2 c bread-crumbs

Grated zest from half a lemon

Approximately 1 cup filtered clam liquor (see Note)

Directions

1. Scrub clams well and soak them as described below (see note).
2. Open the clams over a bowl to catch the clam liquor. Scrape the contents to one half-shell, discarding the other half-shell.
3. Heat olive oil over medium heat, and cook onion and celery until just softened (2-3 minutes)
4. Add garlic, parsley, oregano, and red and black pepper and cook another minute.
5. Add wine and cook until reduced by half.
6. Remove pan from heat, add lemon zest and filtered clam liquor (see note).
7. Add breadcrumbs and mix well. The stuffing should be moist enough to hold together - not too wet and not too dry
8. Preheat oven to 350°C
9. Divide stuffing among the 24 clams on the half-shell
10. Bake clams approximately 15 minutes until stuffing is golden brown.

Note: Live, fresh clams in their shell should have some weight to them. Discard any clams that are not fully closed, feel too light in weight, or sound "hollow" when the shell is tapped. To clean live clams, place them in a sink or other container, cover them with cold water, and allow to sit for 20 minutes. They will purge themselves of most of the sand and other debris as they "breathe."

The reserved clam liquor can be filtered to remove any remaining debris using double-thickness cheesecloth or (if you're patient) by using a coffee filter.

Above left: Stuffing ready for clams

Above right: Freshly picked oregano

Right: Freshly opened Littleneck clams and unfiltered reserved liquor

Below: Vongole origanate

Peperoncini Ripieni

Stuffed Hot Cherry Peppers

Cherry peppers are perfect little vessels for stuffing. They are easy to core and have relatively thick walls that enable them to hold their shape well. I prefer hot cherry peppers for this appetizer but feel free to substitute sweet cherry peppers if you prefer.

I grow and pickle my own cherry peppers, but store-bought, jarred cherry peppers can be used in a pinch. The advantage of growing your own (aside from freshness, of course) is that you can select a seed variety bred to produce larger peppers – 1 ½- 2" in diameter, which are ideal for stuffing. I also like my pickling recipe better than the store-bought version. Lastly, I like to pick both green and red peppers from the vine to make the appetizer more colorful and, when served on a white platter, reminds me of the old *tricolore italiano*.

Ingredients

2 dozen pickled hot cherry peppers

Aged provolone cheese, cut into ½" cubes (one per pepper)

Prosciutto di Parma (1/2 slice per pepper)

Breadcrumbs (1 t per pepper)

Extra virgin olive oil

Dried oregano

Directions

1. Remove seed pod from cherry peppers by cutting a circle around the stem with a sharp paring knife. If the entire seed pod doesn't come out attached to the stem, you can use a spoon (or your finger) to remove the rest – don't worry about leaving a few seeds behind.
2. Arrange the peppers on a flat surface and place 1 t of breadcrumbs in each pepper, followed by a little drizzle of olive oil.
3. Wrap a cube of provolone cheese in a piece of Prosciutto di Parma and stuff into each pepper.
4. Arrange the stuffed peppers on a plate, top with another little drizzle of olive oil, sprinkle on oregano and serve

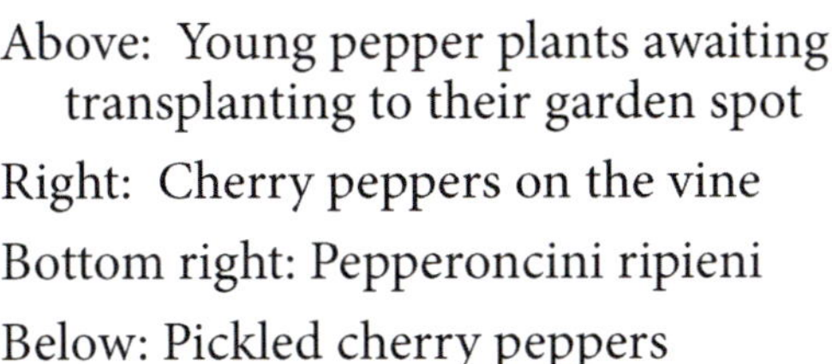

Above: Young pepper plants awaiting transplanting to their garden spot

Right: Cherry peppers on the vine

Bottom right: Pepperoncini ripieni

Below: Pickled cherry peppers

Funghi Ripieni con Salsiccia

Sausage Stuffed Mushrooms

Stuffed mushrooms make for a great appetizer. There are countless ways to stuff a mushroom, but my favorite has to be this one that incorporates Italian sausage into the stuffing. Of course, I always use homemade sausage from this recipe, but feel free to substitute – just as long as it's good sausage!

Ingredients

2 dozen whole, large, white mushrooms, approx. 2 inches in diameter

4 links (approximately 1 lb) of Italian sausages

3 T olive oil

1 stalk celery, chopped

1/4 c chopped onion

2 cloves garlic, finely chopped

1/4 c parsley, chopped

1/4 c grated Pecorino Romano cheese

3/4 c bread crumbs

1/2 t dried oregano

1/2 c dry white wine

Salt and pepper to taste

Directions

1. Carefully remove stems from mushrooms. Clean mushroom caps with a damp cloth to remove any debris. Cut the bottom off of each stem and discard. Coarsely chop the remaining stems or pulse briefly in a food processor.
2. Remove the sausage from the casing and brown in 1 T olive oil, breaking up the sausage into small pieces. Remove from pan and set aside.
3. Add another 1 T oil to the pan, add the chopped stems and a little salt and pepper and sauté until the stems loose half their moisture, about 10 minutes. Remove from pan to a separate bowl.
4. Add the remaining 1 T oil to the pan and sauté the celery and onion for 2 minutes. Add the garlic and sauté another 30 seconds.
5. Add the mushroom stems back to the pan, add the white wine and cook until the wine has reduced by half.
6. Remove the pan from the heat, add the sausage back to the pan along with the remaining ingredients. Mix well.
7. Fill mushroom caps with a generous amount of stuffing, place them on a shallow baking tray and bake, uncovered, at 350ºF until browned, about 40 minutes.

Mushroom factoids:

Mushrooms, of course, are fungi. That is, neither plant nor animal. They contain no chlorophyll and, therefore, cannot make their own "food" as plants can. Mushrooms are saprophytes, which means they must derive their nutrition from decaying organic matter, like a rotting tree stump or a Massachusetts congressman (just kidding).

A fact that most people don't appreciate is that the common white or "button" mushroom, the crimini or "baby bella" mushroom and the portobello mushroom are one and the same species, *Agaricus bisporus*. The only difference between the three is the stage of maturity, with the white mushroom being least mature and the portobello most mature. I prefer to use large white mushrooms for this recipe because the caps seem to hold their shape better in the oven.

Above: Funghi ripieni con salsiccia

Below: White, Baby Bella and Portobello mushrooms - same mushroom, different stage of maturity

Peperoni Arrostiti

Fire-Roasted Sweet Peppers

Roasted peppers are a staple component of any good antipasto. They are relatively easy to prepare but a couple of pointers are worth mentioning to get the most flavor out of your peppers; foremost - the type of pepper! My preferences are Giant Marconi or Corno di Toro peppers. These are large (7-10"), full-bodied, thick-walled varieties (see photo) with tons of flavor, which the roasting process only enhances.

Ingredients

A dozen or so fresh, Italian style peppers

2 cloves garlic, chopped

1 t dried oregano

Extra virgin olive oil

Salt and coarse ground black pepper to taste

Directions

1. Double up a brown paper shopping bag and stand it on a baking tray next to your grill.
2. Place whole peppers directly over a hot flame (gas grill, white hot coals, wood fire, etc) until the skin begins to char. Turn peppers to get a good char over the entire skin.
3. Using tongs, remove the charred peppers from the grill and place them into the brown paper bag. When all of the peppers are done, close the bag to trap the steam inside and allow to cool until the peppers can be handled.
4. Working with one pepper at a time, tear the pepper open and remove the seed pod and stem, then peel off the charred skin. Don't try to remove every last bit of char.
5. Tear the peeled pepper into strips about 1/2 inch thick and place in a bowl. Repeat with remaining peppers.
6. Add the garlic, oregano and enough oil to coat all of the peppers well; about a quarter cup (see photo).
7. Add salt and pepper to taste. Mix and serve with crusty Italian bread.

Note: Of course, I grow my own Marconi and Corno di Toro peppers, but I've seen them in food markets, especially in Italian neighborhoods. They are green peppers that turn red when fully mature. I like to pick both green and red peppers to make the dish more colorful. The peppers need to be charred over high heat - you don't want to "bake" them to a mushy consistency. This can be done over an open flame on a stove top burner, in a gas grill, or over white-hot coals. I prefer the coals as this method imparts a nice smokiness to the peppers. NEVER rinse the peeled peppers - it washes away a lot of the flavor from the tiny bits of charred skin. Finally, ignore all other recipes that include vinegar as an ingredient. Vinegar is for pickled – not roasted – peppers!

Clockwise from above:
Freshly picked peppers ready for roasting
Roasted peppers ready to peel and seed
Peppers roasting over hot coals
Peperoni arrostiti ready to serve
Giant Marconi pepper plants starting out

Caponata alla Siciliana

Sicilian Eggplant Caponata

Caponata is one of those Sicilian dishes for which every town (or even home) has their own version. The one element common to all caponata recipes is the sweet-and-sour (*agrodolce*) undertone. The "sour" is almost always derived from wine vinegar, while the "sweet" can come from sugar, cinnamon (yuk), honey, raisins, even figs (my preference is honey). Chopped nuts - either pignoli or almonds - are common ingredients for caponata, but I omit nuts altogether - there are plenty already in my family.

Caponata can be served warm or at room temperature (my preference), just in a bowl or as a topping for bruschetta (also my preference). Again, freshness of ingredients is the key. I like to make caponata in the summertime when I'm able to use vegetables right from my garden - makes a world of difference. I even prefer my own fermented green olives to the jarred variety, but the latter is fine in a pinch.

Ingredients

2 lbs (about 3 medium) Italian style eggplant, unpeeled and cut into about 3/4 inch dice (see note)

1/2 c plus 2 T extra virgin olive oil

1 medium onion, chopped

2 or 3 inner, tender stalks of celery, leaves included, chopped

1 clove garlic, chopped

6 vine-ripened San Marzano tomatoes, chopped (or substitute 1 1/2 c canned San Marzano tomatoes, crushed)

6 basil leaved, chopped

1 c pitted Sicilian green olives (Castelvetrano style), coarsely chopped

2 T capers

1⁄3 c red wine vinegar

3 T honey

Coarse ground black pepper to taste

Sea salt to taste

Directions

1. Fry the eggplant in two batches. Place 1/4 c of the olive oil in a large frying pan and heat to shimmering. Drop in half of the eggplant, stir quickly to coat, and fry until eggplant is softened and browned, about 12 minutes. Repeat with the remaining eggplant. Remove eggplant from pan and set aside.
2. Add the remaining 2 T olive oil to the pan along with the celery and onion and cook about 5 minutes.
3. Add the garlic , olives and capers and cook about 2 minutes.
4. Add the tomatoes, basil, vinegar and honey. Mix well.
5. Add back the eggplant, mix, and cook until thickened and most of the liquid has evaporated.
6. Add salt and pepper to taste.
7. Transfer caponata to a serving platter to serve warm or allow to cool to room temperature. Serve with crusty Italian bread, or on bruschetta.

Note: Some recipes call for salting the eggplant to remove moisture and make it more "dense" prior to frying. The fact is that over-ripened eggplant can be "spongy" and porous and they tend to soak up a lot of oil in the frying process. If you select younger, more firm eggplant, you can skip the salting step.

Above: Cubed eggplant browning for caponata

Right: Caponata alla Siciliana on bruschetta

Below: Caponata finishing in the pan

Cozze alla Diavola

Mussels in Spicy Tomato Sauce

Cozze alla diavola (or "mussels fra diavolo") has to be one of my favorite appetizers. Typically, this dish is prepared by making a spicy tomato sauce in a pan, perhaps with some wine and other ingredients, and then dropping in whole mussels in their shell. The mussels cook in the sauce and, when they open, the whole thing is poured into a large serving dish and enjoyed with some crusty Italian bread. I've had it that way many times, and it's very good, but I do something a bit different for my version of cozze alla diavola. I actually open each raw mussel (it's very easy) and scrape the meat to one half of the shell, discarding the other half. I then spoon some spicy marinara sauce directly on top of each mussel and place them under a broiler to cook. I think cooking them in this manner concentrates the flavors of both the mussels and the marinara sauce to produce an incredibly tasty dish.

You can choose to eat them with a fork, or do what I do and just pick one up and slide it into your mouth - after all, it already comes in its own little "spoon!" Yum.

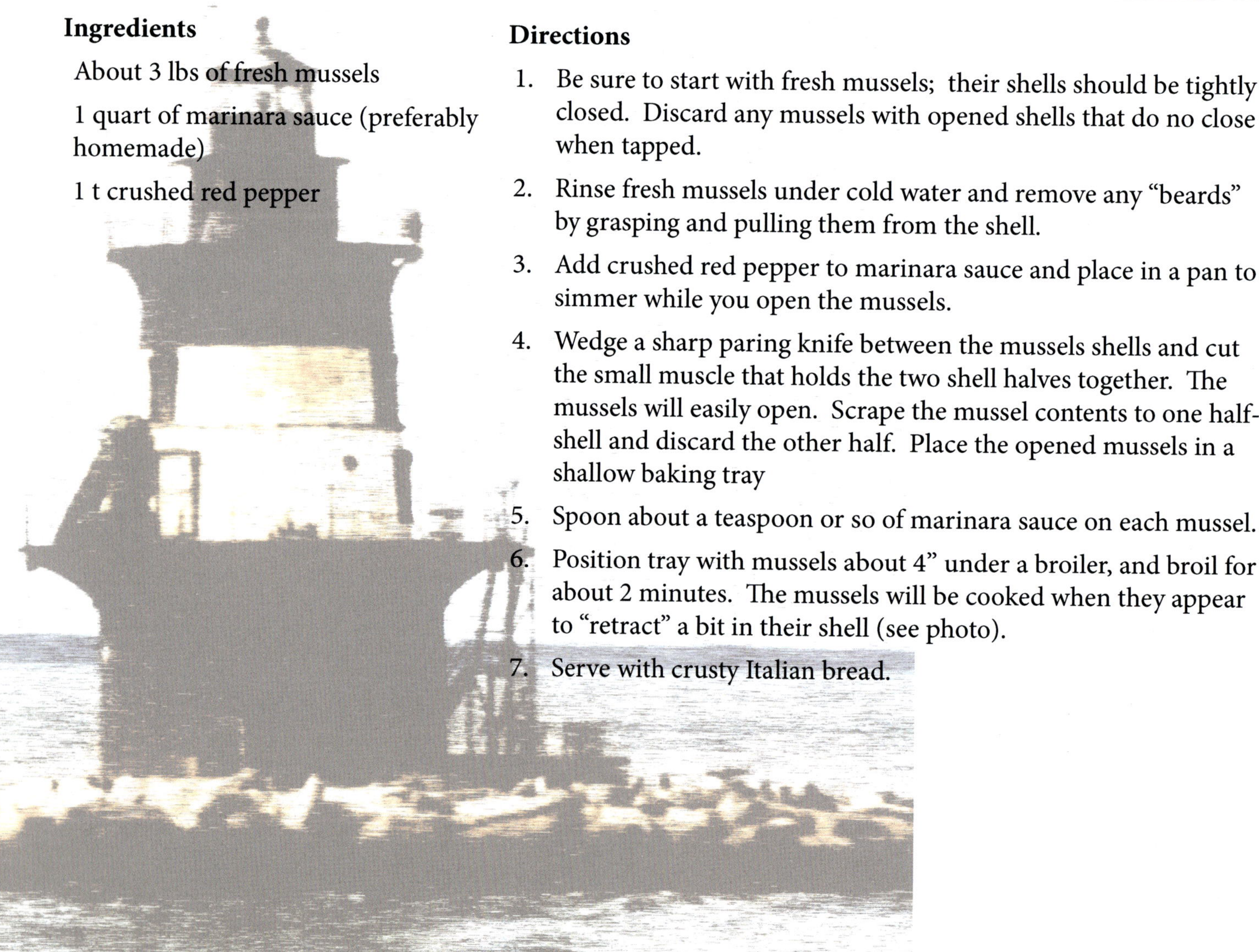

Ingredients

About 3 lbs of fresh mussels

1 quart of marinara sauce (preferably homemade)

1 t crushed red pepper

Directions

1. Be sure to start with fresh mussels; their shells should be tightly closed. Discard any mussels with opened shells that do no close when tapped.
2. Rinse fresh mussels under cold water and remove any "beards" by grasping and pulling them from the shell.
3. Add crushed red pepper to marinara sauce and place in a pan to simmer while you open the mussels.
4. Wedge a sharp paring knife between the mussels shells and cut the small muscle that holds the two shell halves together. The mussels will easily open. Scrape the mussel contents to one half-shell and discard the other half. Place the opened mussels in a shallow baking tray
5. Spoon about a teaspoon or so of marinara sauce on each mussel.
6. Position tray with mussels about 4" under a broiler, and broil for about 2 minutes. The mussels will be cooked when they appear to "retract" a bit in their shell (see photo).
7. Serve with crusty Italian bread.

Above: Cozze alla diavola

Below Left: Fresh mussels

Below right: Opened mussels on the half shell, ready for the marinara topping

Bruschetta

Grilled Italian Bread with Assorted Toppings

Rule #1: you're not allowed to serve bruschetta unless you pronounce it correctly! It's pronounced broo-SKET-ah, not broo-SHET-ah. The latter drives me absolutely crazy, especially when I hear it in so-called "Italian" restaurants. In Italian, "*che*" is a hard "k" sound. Think "Schenectady."

There are many options for bruschetta toppings; a few of my family's favorites are listed below. The amounts given below will make about 8 slices, depending on the size of the slices and how much of the topping you put on each – feel free to adjust accordingly. If you're not using homemade bread, choose a good quality, rustic loaf (semolina or ciabatta bread work well).

The classic tomato and basil

About 3 cups assorted cherry tomatoes, halved or coarsely chopped

1 T extra virgin olive oil

Several fresh basil leaves coarsely chopped

Sea salt and coarse ground pepper to taste

Mix all ingredients in a bowl and top bread

Plum and prosciutto heaven

12-16 slice of Prosciutto di Parma

Taleggio cheese, room temperature

About 4 ripe Italian prune plums

Olive oil for drizzling

Spread taleggio on each piece of bread, top with coarsely torn prosciutto and chopped plums; drizzle olive oil

The Mediterranean (Jenna's favorite)

About 6 oz of jarred artichoke hearts marinated in oil

About 4 oz pitted, oil-cured black olives

About 4 oz crumbled gorgonzola cheese

Olive oil for drizzling

Coarsely chop olives and artichoke hearts; top bread then top with gorgonzola; drizzle olive oil

Directions

1. Prepare favorite topping from the examples shown (or invent your own).
2. Lightly brush bread slices with olive oil and toast both sides, either under a broiler or on a grill (I prefer the latter). The objective is to get the bread a little crispy but chewy – like a good pizza crust – and not *croccante* (hard and crunchy).
3. Rub each slice with the cut garlic clove and top with your favorite topping.

Beans and sun-dried tomatoes

About 4 oz canned white cannellini beans, rinsed

About 4 oz sun-dried tomatoes in olive oil, chopped

1 sprig fresh oregano, chopped

Red pepper flakes to taste (optional)

Olive oil for drizzling

Mix together ingredients and top bread; drizzle olive oil

Arugula and anchovies

About 4 oz fresh arugula

1T olive oil

1 T lemon juice

1 tin anchovies wrapped in capers

Coarse ground pepper to taste

Toss arugula with lemon, oil and pepper; top bread, then top with anchovy-wrapped capers

Clockwise from top:

Classic tomato and basil
Prosciutto, plum and taleggio
Artichoke, oil-cured olives and gorgonzola
Arugula and anchovies
Cannellini beans and sun-dried tomatoes

Calamari Fritti

Fried Calamari

Calamari fritti, or fried calamari, is another of my favorite appetizers, but there are a couple of absolute requirements, for my taste: (i) the tentacles must be included. Eating calamari without the tentacles is liking eating lobster without the claws; (ii) the coating needs to be light in order for the calamari to stand on its own and "shine" - there's nothing worse than making your way through a heavy batter of eggs and breadcrumbs to try to find the calamari; and (iii) a marinara dipping sauce is fine, but a generous squeeze of fresh lemon is the way to go. Pairing fried calamari with pickled hot banana peppers just elevates the dish to a whole new level, especially if you grow and pickle your own peppers! This is my "never fail/go to" recipe for calamari fritti. Like I always say...a few, simple, fresh ingredients will never do you wrong.

Ingredients (serves 6-8)

2 lbs cleaned calamari, body and tentacles (see Note)

2 cups all-purpose flour

2 cups semolina flour

2 T salt

2 T coarse ground black pepper

1T dried oregano

1 lemon cut into 8 wedges

12 oz pickled hot banana pepper ring

Canola oil for deep frying

Directions

1. Cut the squid body into rings about a half inch thick; leave tentacles whole.
2. In a large bowl, mix the flour, salt, pepper and oregano.
3. Fill a pot with 2-3 inches of oil and heat to 375°F (use a deep-fry thermometer attached to the side of the pot).
4. Working with small batches at a time (about a handful), drop the squid pieces into the flour mixture and toss to coat.
5. Shake off excess flour (a separate colander works well here) and carefully drop the squid into the oil.
6. Fry for 1-2 minutes until golden brown; remove and set aside on a baking tray lined with paper towels. Repeat with the remaining squid, adjusting the heat to keep the oil temperature as close to 375°F as possible.
7. Transfer the calamari to a serving platter, mix in the hot peppers, add extra salt and pepper to taste, and serve with lemon wedges.

I prefer fresh squid as opposed to cleaned and frozen (or "previously frozen") squid. The downside, of course, is that you have to clean the squid yourself. If you don't feel up to the task, go ahead and use the cleaned/frozen option.

Note: To clean fresh squid...(i) lay the squid on a flat surface and grab a firm hold of the head with one hand, as close to the body as you can, and near the end of the body with your other hand, (ii) pull the head from the body - the rest of the "guts" (sorry) should come out attached to the head, (iii) with a sharp knife, cut the tentacles as close to the eyes as possible, and discard everything from the eyes back, (iv) remove and discard the "beak" (the small hard structure) from the center of the tentacles by just popping it out, (v) now on to the body...remove the fin-like structures by pulling them from the body; (vi) remove the outer "skin." While the skin is completely edible, I find that the coating will stick better after frying if the skin is removed, (vii) feel around inside the tube for the long piece of cartilage. Remove it and any other remaining "innards" that you might come across. You're done - do not rinse the squid under water.

Above: Calamari fritti ready for serving
Right: Fresh calamari
Below right: Cleaned calamari
Below: Hot banana peppers plants in my garden

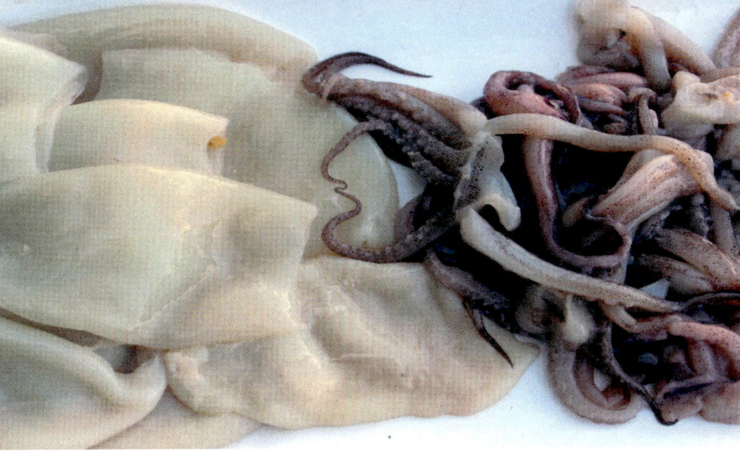

Salads

• Cichoriuni •
Italian Chicory and Lemon Salad

• Insalata di Patate •
Italian Potato Salad

• Insalata di Caprese •
Tomato, Mozzerella and Basil Salad

• Insalata di Pomodori •
Tomato Salad

• Insalata di Baccala •
Salt Cod Salad

• Insalata di Arance alla Siciliana •
Sicilian Orange Salad

• Insalata di Fagiolini •
Green Bean Salad

• Insalata di Pere e Gorgonzola •
Pear and Gorgonzola Salad

• Insalata di Tarasaco •
Dandelion Salad

• Insalata di Bresaola e Parmigiano •
Bresaola and Parmesan Salad

Cichoriuni

Italian Chicory and Lemon Salad

Cichoriuni is - by far - my favorite salad. The term "cichoriuni" is used in Southern Italy to refer to both the type of lettuce and to the salad from which it's made. I would describe cichoriuni as a cross between a chicory and loose-leaf type of lettuce; the leaves being much more delicate and "softer" than a classic chicory type. This is one lettuce that you'll *have* to grow in your garden in order to enjoy. Its characteristics are such that the leaves wilt rapidly following harvest unless kept in cold water. This is the reason why, unfortunately, you won't see this variety in food markets.

Cichoriuni is very easy to grow. The seeds I use were brought to America from Sicily by my in-laws. I have since propagated them from one season to the next for many, many years. Several years back, I came across a picture in a seed catalog of what looked remarkably like cichoriuni, and purchased a pack to evaluate alongside my own seeds. The seeds were for a lettuce called "Italienischer," from Territorial Seed Co., Cottage Grove, OR. The plants they produced were, indeed, very similar to cichoriuni. Not exact, but very similar enough to make me think that there is common ancestry between the two varieties.

So, if you want to enjoy a fantastic summer salad and revel in the fact that you grew it yourself, get a pack of those seeds and start planting. It's worth it - trust me!

Ingredients (Serves 6)

1 or 2 heads of cichoriuni (depending on size)

1 lemon

1 medium onion, sliced thinly

Few shakes of dried oregano

Coarse ground black pepper and sea salt, to taste

Extra virgin olive oil

Directions

1. Rinse cichoriuni in cold water and coarsely tear the leaves, keeping them in cold water. When you are ready to prepare the salad, spin the leaves dry in a salad spinner and place in a bowl.
2. Slice the lemon in half and then slice one of the halves in half again (see photo).
3. Using a hand juicer, extract the juice from 3/4 of the lemon, reserving the remaining 1/4; pour the lemon juice over the cichoriuni.
4. Slice the remaining lemon quarter as thinly as possible to produce wedges as shown at left; add them to the cichoriuni.
5. Drizzle a generous amount of olive oil over the salad, add onion, oregano, black pepper and salt; toss well.
6. Serve immediately with crusty Italian bread.

Note: I assume - and this is a complete guess on my part - that the word "cichoriuni" was derived from the botanical genus *cichorium*, which encompasses many types of chicory and endive varieties.

Above: Cichoriuni salad
Right: Young plants in early spring
Below: Mature plant ready for harvest
Opposite: Rinsing/refreshing in ice cold water

Insalata di Patate

Italian Potato Salad

Potato salad is one of my favorite summer side dishes. I love all kinds of potato salad, but this recipe - popular across Southern Italy - is a family favorite. The main difference, of course, between American style and Italian potato salad is the substitution of olive oil for mayonnaise. Beyond that, the splash of tomato, onion, olives and capers really elevates this to a flavor-packed dish that can be served warm, cold or at room temperature (my preference).

I used to make this salad with unpeeled, new red potatoes (still my preference), but since my kids don't like unpeeled potatoes for some reason, I have since used peeled all-purpose potatoes. Still good, but if I had my choice, I would go for the unpeeled red potatoes!

Ingredients (Serves 8)

Approximately 4 lbs all purpose potatoes, peeled and cut into 1" pieces

1 T salt, plus additional for seasoning

3/4 cup white Prosecco vinegar

1 T capers in vinegar

1/4 cup oil-cured black olives, pitted and coarsely chopped

1/2 cup Sicilian green olives, pitted and coarsely chopped

1/2 cup fresh grape tomatoes, halved

1/3 cup red onion, peeled and thinly sliced

Several sprigs of parsley, chopped

Few shakes of dried oregano

Coarse ground black pepper, to taste

1/2 cup extra virgin olive oil

Directions

1. Place peeled and cut potatoes in a large pot; add salt and water to cover by at least 1 inch.
2. Bring to a boil and cook potatoes until they are just barely fork tender. Do not over-cook; they will continue to "steam" in the following step.
3. Drain potatoes in a colander and return them to the pot. Add 1/2 cup of the Prosecco vinegar, cover the pot and give it a shake to mix the vinegar. Set aside, covered, until cooled to near room temperature.
4. While potatoes are cooling, place the sliced onion in a small bowl. Sprinkle with a little salt and add the remaining 1/4 cup vinegar. Allow to "pickle" until the potatoes are cooled.
5. Transfer the cooled potatoes to a large bowl; add the onion and the rest of the ingredients.
6. Gently toss and adjust salt and pepper to taste.
7. Serve at room temperature with an extra drizzle of olive oil. If you want to get fancy, you can serve on top of a few leaves of Romaine or Radicchio.

Insalata di Caprese

Tomato, Mozzerella and Basil Salad

Insalata di Caprese ("Caprese salad"), as the name might imply, is said to have originated on the Isle of Capri, off the coast of Naples. It is nothing short of simple perfection - a cinch to assemble - yet so often disappointing in restaurants. The main reason? Omission of the key ingredient..freshness! Like so many Italian dishes composed of just a few simple ingredients, "freshness" is paramount. So grab some FRESH tomatoes, FRESH mozzerella, FRESH basil and the best quality extra virgin olive oil you can find and slap 'em together. Try to resist the urge to drizzle Balsamic vinegar on your Caprese salad, as is common practice here in America - the authentic version employs only olive oil.

Naturally, I grow my own tomatoes and basil, and make my own mozzerella, in order to address the "freshness" requirement. I haven't yet tried to press my own olive oil, but it's in the back of my mind. Anyway...go for the highest quality ingredients and you can't go wrong.

Ingredients (Serves 6)

6-8 vine-ripened salad tomatoes

1 lb fresh mozzerella

A dozen or so fresh basil leaves, coarsely chopped

Coarse ground black pepper and sea salt to taste

Extra virgin olive oil

Directions

1. Slice tomatoes and mozzerella 1/4 to 1/2" thick, and arrange them in alternating order on a plate.
2. Scatter basil over the top.
3. Sprinkle with black pepper and salt to taste.
4. Drizzle with a generous amount of olive oil
5. Serve at room temperature or slight chilled, keeping in mind that olive oil will solidify if too cold.

Left: Caprese salad ingredients

Opposite top: Classic Insalata di Caprese, reflecting the colors of "Il Tricolore" (the flag of Italy)

Opposite bottom: Twist on the classic, using home-grown heirloom yellow tomatoes (treasonous, but still yummy)

Insalata di Pomodori

Tomato Salad

There's nothing that screams "summertime!" to me more that a tomato salad with vine-ripened, freshly-picked San Marzano tomatoes. You can go to your local market and find the ripest tomatoes they offer and they wouldn't even come close to the flavor and freshness of these tomatoes - which is why you need to *grown your own!*

Ingredients (Serves 6)

About 2 dozen or so vine-ripened San Marzano tomatoes (or substitute the best possible Italian plum tomatoes that you can find)

1 small onion, sliced into rings

1 Italian hot finger pepper (see photo) or substitute similar

1 t dried oregano

Coarse ground black pepper

Sea salt

Extra virgin olive oil

Directions

1. Rinse tomatoes and slice them crosswise about 1/2" thick (see photo).
2. Slice hot pepper into thin rings and add to tomatoes, using as much (or as little) as you prefer. I typically use about a third to half a pepper.
3. Add sliced onion and oregano.
4. Add black pepper and sea salt to taste.
5. Add a generous amount of olive oil to coat tomatoes. Don't worry about over-doing it - you can sop up the excess with crusty Italian bread, which should be served with this salad.
6. Mix and serve at room temperature or slightly chilled; the olive oil will solidify if too cold.

Clockwise from top:

Insalata di pomodori

Unripened San Marzano tomatoes on the vine

A bowl of freshly picked San Marzano tomatoes

Opposite:

Italian hot finger peppers on the vine (left)

Onion plant seed pods (right)

Insalata di Baccalá

Salt Cod Salad

For most Italian families, Christmas eve would be incomplete without Insalata di Baccalá as part of *La Festa dei Sette Pesci* (the Feast of the Seven Fishes). Of course, this salad can be enjoyed at any time of the year if you're willing to take the time required to prepare the baccalá.

The key to a great dish, of course, is in the quality of ingredients. Look for baccalá sold in whole filets - not the chopped up pieces sold in those small wooden boxes. The fish should be light in color and at least a half inch thick at the anterior (head) end. Rehydrated baccalá should have a clean, ocean-fresh smell - not "fishy."

Ingredients (Serves 6-8)

Approximately 2 lbs of rehydrated salt cod (see seafood chapter for directions for hydrating)

3 lemons

1/2 cup red onion, sliced thin

2 cloves garlic, minced

1 cup Italian black olives (not the salt-cured kind), or substitute Kalamata olives, coarsely chopped

2 T capers in vinegar

1/2 cup hot banana pepper rings, coarsely chopped

1/4 cup celery, chopped

1/2 cup Italian flat leaf parsley, coarsely chopped

1/2 cup extra virgin olive oil, plus extra for drizzling

Sea salt and coarse ground black pepper to taste

Directions

1. Place the rehydrated baccalá in a sauce pan large enough to accommodate the pieces.
2. Cover the fish with cold water. Slice one lemon in half, squeeze the juice into the pan and drop in the lemon halves.
3. Heat the pan until it just comes to a simmer and poach the baccalá for 5 minutes.
4. Remove fish from pan and place into a bowl to cool. I typical cover the bowl with foil.
5. When cooled to room temperature, flake the fish using a fork (see photo).
6. Add the juice and zest of the remaining 2 lemons and toss well.
7. Add the onion, garlic, olives, pepper rings, celery and parsley and toss.
8. Add the olive oil and toss well.
9. Add salt and pepper to taste.
10. Allow salad to sit a room temperature for 30 minutes for flavors to meld prior to serving. You can serve as is, or on a few of your favorite lettuce leaves. Drizzle a little extra olive oil and don't forget the crusty Italian bread.

Above: Insalata di Baccalá
Right: Baccalá right from the fish market
Below left: Hydrated baccalá
Below right: Flaking the baccalá after poaching

Insalata di Arance alla Siciliana

Sicilian Orange Salad

Insalata di arance alla Siciliana is one salad that everyone has to try at least once - and once you do, you'll be hooked for good! I remember thinking that the combination of oranges, onions and olive oil is just WRONG, but in fact, it's an incredible combination of savory and sweet that hits every taste bud group on one's tongue; and the gentle sprinkle of red pepper flakes just puts it over the top.

There are a number of different variations of this salad - some include shaved fennel, olives, mint, and other components. My view is that the oranges are the star of the dish and, therefore, should take center stage. Blood oranges are, of course, popular in Sicily and they certainly make for a great orange salad, but my personal preference is for a simple salad with conventional navel oranges. Serve this salad just slightly chilled so the olive oil stays fluid. Alternatively, do what I do and keep the salad at room temperature and serve it on ice cold salad plates.

Ingredients (Serves 6)

6 navel oranges, peeled and cut into bite-sized pieces (see note below)

About 1/3 cup red onion, sliced thin

Sprinkle of sea salt

1/2 t crushed red pepper flakes

1/4 cup extra virgin olive oil

Directions

1. Place orange pieces in a bowl and add onion, salt and red pepper.
2. Add olive oil and toss well.
3. Allow to sit a room temperature for 30 minutes for flavors to meld. Toss again prior to serving.

Note: The key to a classic Sicilian orange salad is in the way the oranges are peeled and pieced. Leaving a generous portion of the pith attached to the orange is the way the salad is prepared in Italy. The pith is the white, fleshy part between the outer peel and the juicy pulp. The pith gives the orange pieces more structure, some "bite," and just a little bit of bitterness that helps balance the super-sweetness of the orange pulp. So remove the peel with a paring knife and leave behind a good amount of pith, piecing the orange such that each piece has a bit of pith attached. By the way...the orange pith is higher in fiber and vitamin C, by weight, than the pulp itself!

Above: Classic Insalata di Arance alla Siciliana, my favorite
Below: Sicilian orange salad made with blood oranges, also very yummy

Insalata di Fagiolini

Green Bean Salad

There's just something so refreshing about a cold bean salad on a hot summer day, especially when the beans were picked just minutes before.

I typically grow a few different varieties of pole beans each year in my garden, and all are great to use in this simple salad recipe. A few of my favorites are (i) Trionfo Violetto, which are purple on the vine but turn green upon cooking, (ii) Romano, a thick, flat, green bean, and (iii) a standard green bean variety like Blue Lake or Kentucky Wonder (pictured opposite).

Pole beans are just about the easiest vegetable to grow, and very prolific. The plants can be trellised (pictured opposite) or, if you have limited space, grown around a single pole (thus the name). Either way, you'll be hooked - supermarket beans can't compared to the freshness and flavor of beans picked right from the vine!

Ingredients (Serves 6)

Approximately 2 lbs of fresh green beans

1/2 to 1 cup red onion, sliced thin

Several sprigs fresh Italian oregano, chopped

Approximately 6 T extra virgin olive oil

3 T Balsamic vinegar

Salt and coarse ground black pepper to taste

Directions

1. Rinse beans and trim off stems. Cut into 2-3" lengths.
2. Place several inches of salted water in a pot large enough to hold the beans, and bring to a low boil.
3. Add the beans to the pot, cover, and cook for several minutes (tossing occasionally) until the beans have softened slightly but still firm; careful not to over-cook. Strain and refresh under cold water.
4. Transfer the beans to a serving bowl and add the remaining ingredients. Allow to marinate for 30 minutes, tossing occasionally.
5. Serve at room temperature or chilled (my preference).

Opposite top: Insalata di fagiolini

Opposite bottom: A trellis of green beans in my garden

Right: Fresh Italian oregano

Insalata di Pere e Gorgonzola

Pear and Gorgonzola Salad

When one thinks of the key agricultural crops of Italy, the things that first come to mind are tomatoes, olives, grapes, maybe figs - pears not so much. The fact is that Italy supplies about 70% of the world's pear crop, mostly from the region of Emilia-Romagna. The Abate Fetel pear is the signature variety; its flesh is firm enough to cut into thin wedges, yet much softer than, say, a Bosc pear. The Abate Fetel has a very rich, sweet, honey-like flavor - a perfect counter-balance to the rich saltiness of gorgonzola. Abate Fetel pears can be hard to find in the US; but I've seen them on occasion in my local Whole Foods market. Use these, if possible, for this recipe, otherwise choose a ripe, sweet variety of your liking.

The other thing that makes this family recipe particularly special is the grappa-soaked raisins. Grappa, of course, is the Italian brandy made from the pomace (i.e., the pulp, skins, seeds, and stems) left over from pressing wine grapes.

I prefer a soft lettuce for this salad, like an Italian Lattua lettuce, which (of course) I grow in my garden. A good substitute would be something like Boston lettuce.

Ingredients (Serves 6)

1 bunch of lettuce of the green leaf variety (Boston lettuce, curly green leaf lettuce, etc)

1/4 of a red onion, finely diced

3 ripe pears

1/3 C golden raisins

1/3 C grappa

6 oz gorgonzola cheese

4 T extra virgin olive oil

2 T balsamic vinegar

1 T honey

1 t prepared mustard

1/4 t sea salt

Coarse ground pepper to taste

Directions

1. Soak raisins in grappa for at least 1 hr, then remove from grappa and set aside.
2. Prepare dressing by whisking together oil, vinegar, mustard, honey, salt and pepper.
3. Wash and thoroughly dry the lettuce, and tear into bite-sized pieces.
4. Slice pears in half lengthwise and remove the core. You may peel the pears or leave them unpeeled. Slice pears lengthwise into thin slices.
5. Toss lettuce and onion with about half of the dressing to lightly coat.
6. Divide lettuce among serving plates, top with pear slices, and golden raisins.
7. Crumble the gorgonzola and divide among the salad servings.
8. Drizzle on the remaining dressing and serve immediately.

Above: Insalata di pere e gorgonzola
Right: Grappa-soaked golden raisins
Below left: A wedge of mountain gorgonzola
Below right: Abate Fetel pears

Insalata di Tarasaco

Dandelion Salad

I have a love-hate relationship with dandelions. That is, I love them in a my salad, but hate them on my lawn. There was a time when I enjoyed foraging for dandelion leaves, but nowadays - given the widespread use of pesticides, herbicides, fertilizers, etc - I turn to my local food market for cultivated dandelion greens. Or, of course, they're easy to grow from seed.

Dandelions are in the same family as chicory. Like many types of chicory, dandelion leaves have a distinct bitterness to them, which I particularly like in salads. From a nutritional perspective, you can't do much better than dandelion greens. They are loaded with vitamins (A, B, C and K) and essential elements (calcium, iron, magnesium, phosphorous and copper). They are high in fiber and have been shown to stimulate the release of bile, which aids in digestion.

I love a good dandelion salad at the end of a meal (that's right, I said "end"). I realize that most Americans enjoy salads as a first course, but in Italian homes, salads are typically served at the end of a meal, as a refreshing finale and digestive aid. Either way, pick up (or grow) some dandelion greens and enjoy this family recipe.

Ingredients (Serves 6)

1 bunch of dandelion leaves, about 10-12 oz

A 1/2 inch thick piece pancetta (about 5 oz), cut into small cubes

About a quarter of a red onion, sliced thinly

4 T extra virgin olive oil

2 T balsamic vinegar

1 t prepared mustard

1/2 t dried oregano

1/2 t sea salt

1/2 t coarse ground black pepper

Shaved Parmigiano Reggiano

Directions

1. Wash dandelion leaves well and pat (or spin) dry. Chop the leaves into 2- to 3-inch pieces. You may wish to discard a few inches of the tougher lower stems, but I typically use the entire bunch.
2. Cook the pancetta over low/medium heat until rendered and nicely browned (see photo). Remove pancetta from pan and transfer to paper towels to absorb excess grease.
3. In a small bowl, whisk together the oil, vinegar, mustard, oregano, salt and pepper to make a dressing.
4. In a salad bowl, toss the dandelion greens and onion with the dressing to coat.
5. Add the pancetta and Parmesan and toss lightly. Serve immediately.

Clockwise from top:

Insalata di tarasaco

Pancetta prior to cooking

Pancetta, nicely rendered and browned

Dandelion leaves in a colander

Insalata di Bresaola e Parmigiano

Bresaola and Parmesan Salad

Bresaola is in the top five of my most favorite cured meats, alongside prosciutto, capocolla and sopressata. What differentiates bresaola from the other aforementioned delicacies is, of course, that bresaola is made from beef. Making your own homemade bresaola is a great way to go (see page 257), but a good quality bresaola from an Italian deli will do just fine for this salad.

This recipe combines just a few ingredients that work perfectly together to produce one of the best salads you'll have, Try it as a starter course for dinner or a perfect lunch salad. As always, high quality, fresh ingredients make the dish.

Ingredients (Serves 6)

3/4 lb bresaola sliced very thin

8 oz fresh arugula

About 6 oz shaved aged Parmigiano Reggiano cheese

1 lemon (juice and zest)

4 T extra virgin olive oil

Coarse ground black pepper and Mediterranean sea salt to taste

Directions

1. Mix the juice of 1 lemon with the olive oil.
2. Toss together the arugula, lemon/oil mixture, lemon zest, Parmigiano and salt and pepper.
3. Place about half of the dressed arugula on a serving platter. Scatter sliced bresaola on top and then top with the remaining arugula.
4. Sprinkle with additional ground pepper and an extra drizzle of olive oil (optional) and serve with a lemon slice.

Note: The salad can be prepared on a large serving platter or as smaller, individual plates (as shown).

Above: Insalata di bresaola e parmigiano
Right: Finished bresaola in my curing cabinet
Below: Slicing open a fully cured bresaola

Soups

• Scarola e Fagioli alla Napoletana •
Naples Style Escarole and Bean Soup

• Stracciatella •
Italian Egg Drop Soup

• Trippa alla Siciliana •
Sicilian Style Tripe

• Pasta che Taddi •
Sicilian Squash Leaf Soup

• Pasta che Cucuzza •
Pasta with Sicilian Squash

• Pasta e Fagioli •
Pasta and Bean Soup

• Zuppa di Lenticchie •
Lentil Soup

• Zuppa di Tacchino al Collo •
Turkey Neck Soup

• Zuppa di Ceci Neri •
Black Chickpea Soup

Scarola e Fagioli alla Napoletana

Naples Style Escarole and Bean Soup

Escarole is in the endive family and makes a great salad, but it's also sturdy enough to stand up to cooking. This classic recipe combines a few simple ingredients to make a hearty and delicious soup. There are lots of different variations of escarole and beans, but this is the traditional recipe that's enjoyed in and around Naples, and the one that I grew up loving as a kid. Don't forget the crusty Italian bread!

Ingredients (Serves 6):

1 large head of escarole, approximately 1 1/2 lbs

1/4 cup extra virgin olive oil

2 15-oz cans of cannellini beans, drained and rinsed

1/2 medium onion, chopped

Few sprigs fresh oregano, chopped

1 clove garlic chopped

Crushed red pepper flakes (to taste)

1/2 t coarse ground black pepper

Sea salt (to taste)

Grated Pecorino Romano cheese

Directions:

1. Separate the head of escarole into individual leaves an wash well.
2. Coarsely tear leaves (see photo).
3. Bring 4 quarts of water plus 2 t salt to a slow boil in a large pot.
4. Add escarole leaves and cook for about 10 minutes. Remove leaves with a straining ladle to a separate bowl, RESERVING COOKING LIQUID!
5. In a separate soup pot, cook onions in olive oil until just translucent. Add garlic and cook another 30 seconds.
6. Add cannellini beans, oregano, black pepper and crushed red pepper; bring to simmer for 2 minutes.
7. Add escarole leaves and enough reserved cooking liquid to cover all ingredients.
8. Stir and adjust salt, as needed.
9. Cover pot and simmer until the thickest parts of the escarole leaves are fork tender, about 20 minutes.
10. Serve with a sprinkle of Pecorino Romano and an extra drizzle of olive oil.

Note:: Some recipes for this soup call for chicken stock in place of the escarole cooking liquid. Using chicken stock makes for a richer soup, but I prefer sticking with the escarole cooking liquid so as not to mask the subtle, rustic flavor of the greens and beans.

Above: Scarola e fagioli alla Napoletana

Right: Pot of finished soup ready for serving

Below right: Torn escarole leaves ready for cooking

Below left: A head of escarole ready to be picked from my garden

Stracciatella

Italian Egg Drop Soup

You'd be hard-pressed to find a better "comfort" food than stracciatella. One bowl on a cold rainy day or when a cold has got you down does wonders for your inner well-being.

Stracciatella is the original Italian wedding soup, traditionally served as part of a multi-course Italian wedding dinner. The word "stracciatella" is derived from *stracciare*, which means "to tear" or "to shred." The strands of egg that are produced during the preparation of this soup have the appearance of finely shredded paper.

I typically use my chicken stock recipe (shown here) as a starting point for this soup.

Ingredients (Serves 6-8):

1 whole fresh chicken, approximately 4 lbs

1 medium onion (peel left on)

1 parsnip

1 small turnip

2 carrots

1 stalk celery

6-8 sprigs flat leaf parsley (reserve one for garnish)

2 bay leaves

1 T whole black peppercorns

1 T salt

5 eggs

Parmigiano Reggiano (optional)

Directions:

1. Prepare the base chicken stock by placing all ingredients except the eggs in an 8-quart stock pot.
2. Add approximately 3-4 quarts water; enough to cover the chicken by a couple of inches. Bring to a low boil and then reduce to simmer - the longer the better, but at least 3 hrs.
3. Remove from heat and with a large slotted spoon, remove the chicken and vegetables to a large platter and allow to cool enough to handle.
4. Strain the stock through a fine mesh sieve and return to the cleaned pot.
5. Bring the stock back to a simmer.
6. Scramble the eggs in a bowl and then add them to the stock in a fine drizzle with continuous gentle stirring (see photo). The eggs will cook in strands as they hit the stock.
7. Break up the cooked carrots and add them back to the soup, along with the chopped fresh parsley garnish.
8. Adjust the salt if necessary, and serve with a sprinkle of Parmigiano.

Note: I'm a purist, so I prefer to use only the chicken stock to make stracciatella, in the traditional way. For a heartier soup, you can add back some of the cooked chicken, but try to resit that temptation. I save the cooked chicken for my appreciative dog!

Above: Stracciatella
Right: Adding the eggs to the soup
Below: Chicken stock in progress

Trippa alla Siciliana

Sicilian Style Beef Tripe

Tripe is a dish that everyone needs to try at least once – if only to dispel the preconception that anything made from a cow's stomach should not be on a dinner plate! Truth be told…if not prepared correctly, tripe can indeed be tough, rubbery and most unpleasant. It's probably the main reason why people, having tried tripe for the first time, are tuned off forever. Properly prepared, however, tripe is soft and tender, with a mild, almost "buttery" flavor.

Tripe is enjoyed all over Italy, but particularly in Southern Italy, with some slight variations in preparation across the southern regions. This particular family recipe is the one that I stick with.

Ingredients (Serves 6-8)

Approx 2 lb of beef tripe, prepared as described (opposite)

3 T olive oil

1 medium yellow onion, sliced

1 clove garlic, chopped

Few sprigs of parsley, chopped

4 bay leaves

½ c dry white wine

2 quarts jarred San Marzano tomatoes and the juice (or substitute canned Italian tomatoes)

3 baking potatoes, peeled and cut into pieces of 1-2"

1 t red pepper flakes

Mediterranean sea salt and coarse ground black pepper

Grated Pecorino Romano cheese

Directions

1. Heat the oil in a large frying pan; add the onion and cook for 1-2 minutes.
2. Add the garlic and cook another 30 seconds.
3. Add the prepared tripe (see opposite) and sauté another 5 minutes.
4. Add the wine and cook another 2 minutes.
5. Add the jarred tomatoes, parsley, bay leaves, potatoes and red pepper.
6. Cover pan and simmer for 30 minutes until the potatoes are fork tender.
7. Adjust seasoning with salt and pepper to taste.
8. Serve with grated Pecorino Romano cheese and some crusty Italian bread.

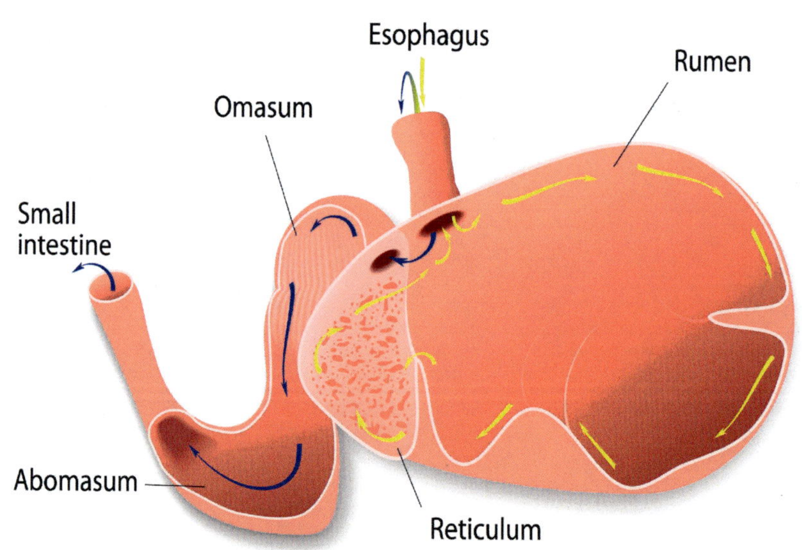

Opposite: Trippa alla Siciliana

Right: Illustration of a ruminant stomach showing location of the reticulum

About tripe:

Tripe! Where to begin? How 'bout at the beginning, with some ruminant anatomy! Ruminant animals (cattle, sheep, goats, deer, etc) have a four-chamber stomach. In bovine species (or "cows" for the sake of simplicity), the stomach chambers are the rumen, reticulum, omasum, and abomasum. Tripe is derived from the innermost lining of the cows' stomach, and each chamber produces its own unique type of tripe. However, the most common and desirable tripe is the honeycomb variety, obtained from the reticulum (see illustration, opposite).

Preparing tripe for cooking:

Tripe found in most meat markets nowadays comes "pre-washed." Look for tripe that is white to very pale cream in color. Even pre-washed tripe requires some preparation prior to cooking. This begins with rinsing the meat thoroughly under cold running water, removing any remaining debris trapped among the honeycomb structure. Also trim off any excess fat and connective tissue that may be present. Some cooks rub rock salt over the tripe during the initial cleaning, which acts as an abrasive to help "scour" the meat clean, a step that I personally find unnecessary, unless you buy tripe that is not pre-washed. Place the washed tripe (whole) in a large pot and cover with cold water and add about 4 T baking soda (note: the baking soda might also be totally unnecessary, but since that's the way my grandmother did it, I don't want to take any chances). The thought is that the baking soda (sodium bicarbonate) raises the pH of the water, which aids in tenderizing the meat – who knows! Cover the pot, bring to a low boil, and then reduce heat to simmer for about 2 hours. Remove the tripe to a bowl, give it a quick rinse of fresh water and allow to cool enough to handle. Cut the tripe into bite-sized pieces; I usually cut strips that are about 2" long and ½" wide, but you don't need to be precise. The tripe is now ready for the recipe.

Pasta che Taddi

Sicilian Squash Leaf Soup

There is probably no soup more rustic than this one. "*Taddi*" (in Sicily) or *tenerumi* (in other parts of Southern Italy) are the tender, young, terminal leaves and tendrils of the cucuzza plant. If grown on a support trellis, the cucuzza plant is a vigorous climbing vine and can grow as much as 2 feet in a single day under optimum conditions. One plant can produce many cucuzze (plural) squash, which are enjoyed in a variety of Italian dishes. The *taddi,* too, are completely edible and form the basis of this simple, yet delicious, Sicilian soup.

Unfortunately, *taddi* are hard to find unless you are fortunate enough to live near an Italian specialty produce shop. Alternatively, the plants are very easy to grow - give it a try!

Sicilians look upon this soup as a *digestiva* - a kind of digestive aid - because it's light, refreshing, and the *taddi* are said to provide a laxative-like property.

Ingredients (Serves 6-8)

About 2 lbs cleaned taddi

1 medium yellow onion, coarsely chopped

4 T extra virgin olive oil

2 potatoes, peeled and cut into bite-sized chunks

2 ripe tomatoes

About 1/2 lb dry ditalini pasta

Crushed red pepper flakes

Grated Pecorino Romano cheese

Salt and coarse ground pepper to taste

Directions

1. In a large pot, bring 4 quarts of water plus 2 t salt to a simmer.
2. Place the whole tomatoes in the water for 1 minute, then remove and refresh under cold water. Peel, seed and coarsely chop the tomatoes; set aside.
3. Place the taddi in the water and simmer until they're just tender, about 10 minutes.
4. Meanwhile, in a separate soup pot, sauté the onion in olive oil until translucent. Add the potatoes, tomatoes and red pepper flakes (to taste).
5. Remove the taddi from the water using tongs or a spoon strainer and transfer to the other soup pot; do not discard the water.
6. Ladle a sufficient amount of water from the first pot to cover the contents of the soup pot by about an inch. Cover the soup pot and simmer.
7. In a separate pot, bring salted water to a boil and cook the pasta until just barely cooked - about 7 minutes.
8. Transfer a desired amount of pasta to the soup pot, along with additional water from the cooked taddi to achieve a soup consistency (see photo right).
9. Continue simmering until potatoes are fork tender; add salt/pepper to taste.
10. Serve with Pecorino cheese, a drizzle of olive oil an additional red pepper flakes (if desired).

Above left: Cucuzza vine growing in my garden

Above right: Terminal leaves and tendrils cut from the cucuzza vine

Right: Young cucuzza leaves; tendrils and stems removed

Below: Pasta che taddi

Pasta che Cucuzza

Pasta with Sicilian Squash

Pasta che cucuzza is another rustic dish comprised of a few simple, fresh ingredients. The soup makes a great standalone lunch, or a first course dinner plate. Again, you might have to seek out an Italian produce store to find cucuzze, or you can grow your own (much preferred). I've experimented with substituting other squash with disappointing results; cucuzze seem to be the only variety that retains its firmness in a soup. For a heartier version of this dish, you can substitute chicken or vegetable stock for the pasta water, but my preference is for the traditional version.

Ingredients (Serves 4-6)

1 cucuzza, approximately 2 lbs

1 medium onion, chopped

1 clove garlic, chopped

1 T tomato paste

1/2 lb dry campanelle pasta

2 T extra virgin olive oil plus more for drizzling

Crushed red pepper

Salt and ground black pepper to taste

Grated Pecorino Romano cheese

Directions

1. In a large pot, bring 4 quarts of water plus 2 t salt to a boil.
2. Peel and seed the cucuzza and chop into 1 inch chunks.
3. In a separate soup pot, sauté the onion in olive oil until translucent - about 2 minutes.
4. Add the cucuzza pieces, garlic and crushed red pepper and sauté another 2 minutes.
5. Add the tomato paste, mix and remove from heat.
6. Cook the pasta in the boiling water until barely al dente, approximately 7 minutes.
7. Transfer the pasta to the soup pot along with a sufficient amount of pasta water to achieve a soup consistency (see photo right).
8. Simmer on low until the cucuzze are fork tender.
9. Add salt and black pepper to taste.
10. Serve with Pecorino cheese, a drizzle of olive oil an additional red pepper flakes (if desired).

About cucuzze:

The cucuzza is technically a gourd, but is grown and used like a summer squash in a variety of Italian dishes. The cucuzza plant is a vigorous, climbing vine that can produce many cucuzze, which if allowed to grow hanging from a vine, can reach more than 6 feet in length. Alternatively, the plant can be allowed to grow across the ground, like a zucchini plant, in which case the cucuzze take on a somewhat twisted, serpent-like shape, giving the squash its alternative name - *zucchetta serpente di Sicilia.* Under optimum growth conditions, cucuzze can grow as much as 8-10 inches a day. The saying in Italian is: *crescono davanti ai tuoi occhi* (they grow right before your eyes). Unless you are cooking with very young cucuzze (less than 12 inches in length), you will have to peel the outer skin, which becomes thick and inedible as the cucuzze grow larger.

Above: Pasta che Cucuzza
Right: Coradina with freshly harvested cucuzze
Below: Cucuzze on the vine in my garden

Pasta e Fagiole

Pasta and Bean Soup

Pasta e fagiole is another one of those rustic Italian dishes for which many regional variations exist. The one common thread, as the name would imply, is that all include beans of one variety or another and some kind of pasta. Some recipes include pancetta; others, like this one, omit the pork.

This family recipe includes two classic Italian bean varieties - white cannellini beans and ceci (chickpeas). You can use dried beans, but of course they have to be rehydrated first. Alternatively, good quality canned beans are fine and enables one to throw this dish together in minutes.

Ingredients (Serves 6)

2 T olive oil

1 stalk celery, chopped

1 medium onion, chopped

2 cloves garlic, chopped

1/2 t fresh thyme leaves

Few springs of parsley, chopped

1t fresh oregano, chopped

1 t red pepper flakes

2 cups chicken stock (preferably homemade)

1 qt crushed San Marzano tomatoes

1 15-oz can white cannellini beans, drained

1 15-oz can ceci, drained

1 1/2 cups dried ditalini pasta

Salt to taste

Grated Parmigiano Reggiano

Directions

1. Heat olive oil in an 8-qt pot and sauté celery, onion and red pepper.
2. Add ceci, cannellini, oregano, thyme, parsley and garlic and cook for 2 minutes with gentle mixing.
3. Add chicken stock and tomatoes.
4. Add salt to taste, cover and bring to a simmer.
5. Meanwhile, in a separate pot, boil salted water and add ditalini, cooking until just *al dente*, about 7 minutes.
6. Strain ditalini and add to soup.
7. Continue to simmer for another 10 minutes the remove from heat.
8. Serve with grated Parmigiano and plenty of crusty Italian bread.

Opposite top: Pasta e Fagiole
Right Fresh Italian oregano in my garden

Zuppa di Lenticchie

Lentil Soup

Lentils have been part of the human diet for millennia, and are believed to have originated in the Mediterranean basin. They are an excellent source of protein, fiber, essential minerals (copper, iron, molybdenum, manganese) and B vitamins – all with virtually no fat. Lentils come in many varieties, spanning various shapes, sizes and colors.

For this recipe, I prefer the traditional brown lentils because they are among the most "plump" and cook to the right consistent for soup. Pancetta is much more commonly used in Italian dishes than is bacon, but the smokiness of bacon really complements the "earthiness" of the lentils, so I start off by rendering some bacon just for the fat; the bacon itself isn't included in the soup. My younger daughter will happily consume the unused bacon. For a vegetarian version, you can omit the meat entirely (but it won't be as good)

Lentil soup is commonly served as part of a "good luck" tradition to ring in the New Year in Italy, typically with cotechino, a type of Italian pork sausage.

Ingredients (Serves 6-8)

1 lb dried brown lentils

4 strips of regular bacon

4 oz pancetta, chopped

1 stalk celery, chopped (approx 1/2 cup)

1 medium onion, chopped (approx 1/2 cup)

1 carrot, chopped (approx 1/2 cup)

1 clove garlic, chopped

4 bay leaves

1 T fresh thyme, chopped

1 t coarse black pepper

1 t red pepper flakes

12 cups water

4 t salt

3 oz tomato paste

2 T balsamic vinegar

Olive oil for drizzling

Directions

1. Rinse the lentils in a colander and remove any debris (tiny pebbles, etc) that can sometimes be present.
2. In a 6-quart stock pot, cook the bacon under low/medium heat until rendered. Remove bacon, reserving the fat in the pot.
3. Add the pancetta and cook under low/medium heat until rendered. Remove pancetta and reserve aside.
4. Add the celery, carrot and onion to the pot and sauté for 2-3 minutes. Add the garlic and sauté for another 30 seconds.
5. Add the dried, rinsed lentils and cook for about 1 minute, stirring to coat the lentils in the fat.
6. Add the water and remaining ingredients stir until tomato paste is dispersed.
7. Increase heat and cook until soup is near boiling, and then reduce to simmer on low heat, stirring periodically, until lentils are tender, approximately 1 – 1 ½ hours.
8. Serve in individual bowls and drizzle with a little olive oil. For those who want an extra "kick," add a chopped up hot cherry pepper.

Opposite, clockwise from top/left:
Zuppa di lenticchie
Rendering pancetta
Sautéed vegetable ingredients

Fun Facts:

- The botanical name for the brown lentil plant is *Lens culinaris*. The modern day word for the optical "lens" is derived from this Latin name, based on the lentil's convex shape.
- Lentils were one of the first domesticated crops; they have been uncovered at archaeological sites in the Middle East dating back 8000 years.
- Lentils are technically not considered beans, but rather, among the "pulse" crops, those harvested solely for the dry seed (unlike green beans, for example).

Zuppa di Tacchino al Collo

Turkey Neck Soup

Turkey is not nearly as popular in Italy as it is in the U.S., and Thanksgiving as we know it here isn't celebrated in Italy. Italian-Americans do, of course, celebrate Thanksgiving because - hey - any holiday that brings together an ungodly amount of food and every relative within a 100-mile radius is a good enough reason to celebrate.

I can remember Thanksgiving holidays as a child when my mother would bring home a freshly killed turkey from Zorn's, a local poultry farm. Of course, that was before Long Island was overtaken by suburban sprawl. Every part of the turkey was used for Thanksgiving dinner; wasting food in my home was a mortal sin! My mother would place the turkey neck in the roasting pan and cook it alongside the turkey - it was my father's favorite part.

To this day, I still use the entire turkey. The neck, however, I reserve for turkey neck soup. In fact, my family loves this soup so much that I sometimes pick up turkey necks in the food market just to make this soup. Though it's not mandatory, roasting the necks and vegetables briefly under a broiler before preparing the soup really brings an added depth of flavor.

Ingredients (Serves 6-8):

Several fresh turkey necks, approximately 3-4 lbs

1 T olive oil

1 medium onion, peeled

1 parsnip

1 small turnip

2 carrots

1 stalk celery

1 whole tomato

6-8 sprigs flat leaf parsley (reserve one for garnish)

4 bay leaves

1 T whole black peppercorns

2 whole allspice berries

4 t salt

Approximately 1/3 - 1/2 lb of dried soup pasta (fideo, acini di pepe, or similar)

Directions:

1. Place turkey necks, onion, parsnip, turnip, carrot, celery and tomato in a shallow roasting pan or on a baking tray and drizzle with olive oil. Roast under a broiler until the vegetables begin to brown (see photo).
2. Transfer turkey necks and vegetables to a 12-quart stock pot along with the remaining ingredients (except pasta).
3. Add water to cover the ingredients by about 1 to 2 inches (note, the 12-quart stock pot will only be a little more than half full at this point).
4. Bring to a low boil and then reduce to simmer - the longer the better, but for at least 3 hrs.
5. Remove from heat and allow to cool enough to handle. Using a large slotted spoon, remove the turkey necks and vegetables to a large platter.
6. Strain the stock through a fine mesh sieve and transfer to a smaller (e.g., 8-quart) pot. Bring the stock back to a simmer and add the pasta and cook to package directions (5 to 7 minutes).
7. Remove the meat from the turkey necks and return it to the pot. Coarsely mash the carrots and return to pot, along with the fresh parsley garnish.
8. Adjust the seasonings if necessary, and serve.

Above: Zuppa di tacchino al collo
Below left: Fresh turkey necks
Below right: Roasted soup components

Zuppa di Ceci Neri

Black Chickpea Soup

Black chickpeas are very popular in India, but also found in many Mediterranean regions, particularly in the Middle East and in parts of Southern Italy. They are smaller in size than their cream-colored cousins, and have a greater depth of richness and flavor, in my opinion. Though they're commonly referred to as "black" chickpeas, they can range in color from brown to reddish brown to nearly black. Black chickpeas make for a fantastic rustic soup, along the lines of a black bean soup - but much better! If you're fortunate enough to live near an Italian produce market, you can usually find black chickpeas (*ceci neri*). Alternatively, they're easy to find on-line. Look for ceci neri imported from the Basilicata region of Southern Italy.

Ingredients (Serves 6-8)

2 cups dried black chickpeas

2 T olive oil plus more for drizzling

1 stalk celery, chopped

1 medium onion, chopped

2 cloves garlic, chopped

2 t salt

1 t coarse ground black pepper

4 bay leaves

1 sprig rosemary, finely chopped (about 2 t)

1 T balsamic vinegar

1 T tomato paste

Crushed red pepper flakes to taste (optional)

Directions

1. Rinse dried chickpeas and then soak overnight in 8 cups of cold water (do not discard the water).
2. In a 6-quart stock pot, sauté the celery and onion in 2 T olive oil over medium heat until translucent. Add the garlic and sauté an additional 30 seconds.
3. Add the tomato paste and cook for another minute, with stirring.
4. Transfer the chickpeas and soaking water to the pot.
5. Add the bay leaves, rosemary, vinegar, salt and pepper and bring to a low boil; cover soup and continue to cook on low heat approximately 2 hrs until the chickpeas are tender and partially broken down.
6. You will need to add another 2 cups of water during the cooking process as the chickpeas cook and absorb water.
7. Adjust seasonings and serve with a sprinkle of crushed red pepper (optional), an extra drizzle of olive oil (optional) and some crusty Italian bread.

Note: For a thicker soup, I sometimes use an immersion blender for a few seconds near the end of the cooking process, until some of the chickpeas are broken down. Be sure not to puree the entire soup; leave a sufficient amount of whole chickpeas for texture.

Above: Zuppa di ceci neri
Below: Comparison of black and conventional dried chickpeas
Opposite: Young rosemary plant in my herb garden

Pasta

• Ravioli di Lenzuolo •
"Bedsheet" Ravioli

• Lasagna al Forno •
Baked Lasagna

• Pasta alla Puttanesca •
Pasta "Prostitute" Style

• Linguine alla Vongole in Bianco •
Linguine in White Clam Sauce

• Pasta alla Bolognese •
Pasta with Bolognese Style Meat Sauce

• Bucatini all' Amatriciana •
Bucatini with Guanciale, Fresh Tomatoes and Pepperoncini

Spaghetti alla Carbonara •
Spaghetti with Guanciale, Eggs and Parmesan Reggiano

• Linguine Aglio e Olio •
Linguine with Garlic and Oil

• Lumachoni Farciti •
Stuffed Shells

• Gnocchi al Pesto •
Gnocchi with Pesto Sauce

• Pasta con le Sarde •
Pasta with Sardines

• Pasta cui Cavuli •
Cavatelli Pasta with Kohlrabi

Ravioli di Lenzuolo

"Bedsheet" Ravioli

When I was very young, my grandmother, Maria Campo, lived in Santa Barbara CA and would visit us in New York a couple of times a year and stay for about a week or two on each visit. She would almost always visit during the Christmas holiday and take charge of making one of the (seemingly endless) dinner courses for Christmas dinner - usually the pasta course. Now, making ravioli to feed the number of family members that typically came to our home for Christmas dinner was no small feat. For one thing, our kitchen table was not large enough to lay out the staggering number of fresh ravioli that needed to "set up" a bit before cooking. So....my grandmother would take a fresh clean *lenzuolo* (bedsheet) and throw it over my parents' bed. As she painstakingly prepared the fresh ravioli - each one by hand - she would spread them on the bedsheet to set up. Picture in your mind a bed covered from headboard to footboard with a single-layered sea of fresh ravioli! Each time grandma would visit, we asked if she was going to make "bedsheet ravioli." In case you're wondering, no - there were no leftovers, incredible as that seems.

Ingredients (Serves 8)

Two recipes fresh pasta dough (see pg 245)

Filling:

2 lbs whole milk ricotta cheese

1/2 lb whole milk mozzerella, finely chopped

4 eggs

2 cloves garlic, minced

1/2 cup grated Pecorino Romano cheese

1/4 cup grated Parmesan cheese

Approx 1/2 cup chopped fresh parsley

Approx 1/3 whole nutmeg, grated

2 t salt

1 t coarse ground black pepper

Directions

1. Prepare filling by mixing together all filling ingredients in a large bowl. Note - filling can be prepared a day in advance, if kept refrigerated.
2. Roll pasta dough into long, thin sheets. If using a pasta maker like the one pictured (opposite), pass the dough through the rollers, gradually decreasing the thickness setting until the final pass is done through the next to last setting on the machine.
3. Lay the sheet of pasta on a floured work surface and place about a tablespoon of filling along the length of the sheet, spacing them about 2 inches apart.
4. Cover the filling with another pasta sheet and press it down against the bottom sheet, shaping the pasta around each mound of filling. If the pasta dough is the right consistency, there is no need to use an egg wash to "seal" the pasta sheets together, but that's certainly optional.
5. Cut the ravioli into individual pieces with a cutting wheel.
6. Bring a large pot of salted water to a boil, drop the ravioli in, and cook for 4 or 5 minutes. The ravioli will float to the surface as they cook. Strain and serve with your favorite tomato sauce.

Note: There are a few different ways to shape ravioli. Various ravioli forms are available in which a thin sheet of pasta dough is laid onto the form. Filling is then spooned into the wells of the form, which is then covered by another sheet of pasta. A quick pass of a rolling pin cuts the individual ravioli. Special "ravioli rollers" are also available that basically work the same way, without using a form. I typically use the hand-cut method in which a sheet of pasta is laid on a floured work surface and a spoonfuls of filling are placed in a line about 2 inches apart along the length of the sheet. This is then covered with another sheet of pasta and individual ravioli are cut either with a cutting wheel or ravioli stamp, which can be round or square.

Above: Ravioli di lenzuolo
Right: Rolling out the pasta dough
Below: Shaping and cutting ravioli

Lasagna al Forno

Baked Lasagna

Lasagna is truly an ancient Italian classic. So old, in fact, that there is still some uncertainty as to its origin. Personally, I don't care where it came from, I'm just totally indebted to the inventor! In my family, lasagna is the pasta course that traditionally precedes a holiday dinner celebration, but every once in a while, I would make lasagna as a standalone dinner. The problem is that one wouldn't typically prepare lasagna for four people, so unless I'm cooking for visiting family members, I would end up giving most of the lasagna to my (very appreciative) neighbors.

As you might imagine, there are wide variations in lasagna recipes across Italy. My preference is for the southern Italian versions in which tomato sauce is king. For this recipe, the starting point is a traditional, slow-cooked, San Marzano tomato sauce (page 277) containing meatballs and sausage. However, since my oldest daughter is not a fan of any type of meat, I use only the sauce to build the lasagna - a sort of pseudo "vegetarian" version. If I had my way, I would scatter some chunks of coarsely broken up sausage and meatballs from the cooked sauce over each of the ricotta cheese layers as you construct your lasagna - MUCH better! I would encourage you to follow that approach.

Ingredients (Serves 12)

For the filling:

3 lbs whole milk ricotta cheese

1 lb whole milk, low moisture mozzerella (not fresh mozzerella)

6 large eggs

3 cloves garlic, minced

1/2 cup grated Pecorino Romano cheese

1/2 cup grated Parmesan cheese

Approx 1 cup chopped fresh parsley

Approx 1/3 whole nutmeg, grated

3 t salt

1 t coarse ground black pepper

For the lasagna:

24 oz boxed lasagna pasta

Approximately 6 cups cooked tomato sauce (page 277)

Directions:

1. Slice about a dozen very thin slices from the block of mozzerella and set aside. These are for topping the final layer. Shred or finely dice the rest of the mozzerella.
2. In a large bowl, mix together the ricotta, shredded mozzerella, eggs, garlic, parsley, nutmeg, salt, pepper, Romano and Parmesan cheeses.
3. Bring a large pot of salted water to a boil. Add about a tablespoon of olive oil to the water and place the lasagna pasta into the pot, one at a time such that they are not completely on top of each other in the water. Cook pasta for only about 7 minutes. The pasta will be slightly undercooked, which can be checked by pinching a piece between your fingernails. If the center of the pasta is still white, it's just right. Drain the pasta and transfer to a bowl of cold water to stop further cooking.
4. In a large baking tray, approximately 10 x 16 inches and about 2 1/2 inches deep, begin by spreading about a cup of tomato sauce over the bottom, then place a layer of pasta, overlapping the edges so that the entire bottom of the tray is covered.
5. Cover evenly with about a third of the cheese mixture and then about 2 cups of tomato sauce. Repeat for two more layers, aligning the pasta perpendicular to the pasta layer below it. You should end up with a layer of pasta on top, which you will cover with the thinly sliced mozzerella and a coating of tomato sauce.
6. Loosely cover with foil and bake for about 1 hr at 375ºF, removing the foil during the final 15 minutes to slightly brown the top layer.

Above: Lasagna al forno
Right: Ricotta mixture for lasagna
Below: A tray of lasagna fresh from the oven

Pasta alla Puttanesca

Pasta "Prostitute" Style

Pasta alla puttanesca, or simply *puttanesca* as I knew it growing up, is one of my favorite pasta sauces because of its intense flavor. Most agree that the sauce originated around Naples, but the stories vary widely about how the rather interesting name came about. I tend to believe that the history of sauce really has nothing to do with ladies of the night, but rather the alternative, "slang" usage of *puttanata* in Italy, which basically translates to "crap" as it's used in the U.S. So, for example, one might say "*dovresti essere in prigione per questa puttanata!*" (you should be in jail for that kind of crap!). In that sense, I think the term *puttanesca* came about because the quick and easy sauce was thrown together with whatever "crap" happened to be in the kitchen at the time. Whatever the origin, *puttanesca* is truly is an incredibly flavorful sauce that can be whipped up in no time and served over your favorite pasta.

Traditionally, *puttanesca* is served over spaghetti, bucatini or linguine, but feel free to use your favorite pasta shape.

Ingredients (Serves 4-6)

1 medium onion, chopped

4 T extra virgin olive oil

2 quart jars of fresh San Marzano tomatoes

1 6-oz can of tomato paste

Salt and coarse ground black pepper

Approximately 2 oz anchovies in oil (preferably white anchovies), chopped

4 garlic cloves, minced

1/2 t crushed red pepper

2 T capers in vinegar

1/2 to 1 cup pitted Kalamata olives

Few leaves basil, chopped

Few springs of parsley, chopped

1 t fresh oregano, chopped

1 lb dry pasta (thick spaghetti, bucatini or your favorite)

Directions

1. Sauté onion, garlic, anchovies and red pepper in olive oil for several minutes.
2. Add tomatoes, paste and the remaining sauce ingredients; mix well to distribute the tomato paste.
3. Cook sauce on medium low for about 20 minutes.
4. In the meanwhile, bring a pot of salted water to a boil and cook spaghetti for approximately 7 minutes, until just barely *al dente*.
5. Transfer a generous amount of the *puttanesca* sauce to a large pan and add the spaghetti, tossing several minutes to finish cooking in the sauce.
6. Serve immediately with extra sauce on the side and plenty of crusty Italian bread.

Opposite above: Pasta alla puttanesca

Opposite below: Puttanesca ingredients; olives, oregano, garlic, capers and white anchovies

Linguine alla Vongole in Bianco

Linguine in White Clam Sauce

Linguine alla vongole is one of my favorite pasta dishes. A couple of things about that....first, this dish is much better as a "white" sauce rather than the "red" version. As much as I love tomato sauce, I find that tomatoes overwhelm the delicate flavor of young, sweet clams. Second, avoid at all cost the use of canned, chopped clams, unless you're particularly fond of that tinny, preservative flavor on your pasta.

The "purest" would prepare this dish with only whole, young clams in their shell. Having said that, using only whole clams is just not enough "clam" for my liking. The solution that I have landed on is to supplement the dish with whole baby clam meat - but ONLY the kind that comes frozen in plastic packaging, containing nothing but whole baby clam meat in their natural juice (see note below). The combination of whole Littleneck clams and whole baby clam meat makes for a clam "explosion" that puts this dish over the top.

Timing is everything with this dish. Linguine cooks to *al dente* in about 8 minutes, but you want to finish cooking it in the clam broth. The clams themselves will fully open after about 5 minutes. When they do, gently remove them to a separate bowl so you can finish the pasta in the broth.

Ingredients (Serves 4-6)

5 lbs Littleneck clams

1 16-oz package of whole baby clam meat with their juice (see Note)

1/2 cup extra virgin olive oil, plus more for drizzling

4 cloves garlic, chopped

1/2 medium onion, sliced thin

1 cup dry white wine

2 t red pepper flakes

Several sprigs of fresh Italian parsley, chopped

Directions

1. Wash clams thoroughly in cold water. Discard any that are partially open, suspiciously light in weight, or that sound "hollow" when tapped.
2. Bring a pot of salted water to a boil for the pasta.
3. Sauté the onion in olive oil until translucent. Add the garlic and red pepper and cook for 30 seconds.
4. Add the Littlenecks, baby clam meat and wine. Cover and cook on medium heat until the clams fully open, about 5 minutes.
5. At the time the clams are added to the pot, place the linguine in the boiling water, stirring occasionally.
6. When the clams have opened, transfer them with a slotted spoon to a bowl (leave behind the baby clam meat). At this point, the pasta should be approaching the *al dente* stage.
7. Drain the pasta and then add it, along with the parsley, to the clam broth. Continue cooking for a minute or two, until the linguine absorbs some of the clam broth.
8. Transfer pasta and remaining broth to a large serving bowl and top with the Littleneck clams.

Note: Whole baby clam meat is available from a number of sources. I typically use a product from a local distributor, PanaPesca USA. The clams are farm raised and supplied in 1-pound plastic pouches. They contain only whole clams in their natural juice - no preservatives or additives.

Above: Linguine alla vongole in bianco

Below: Whole Littleneck clams added to the pot

Pasta alla Bolognese

Pasta with Bolognese Style Meat Sauce

Bolognese sauce is said to have originated in the northern Italian city of Bologna. It is a rich, thick, meat sauce that is typically served over large pasta shapes, which tend to stand up better to hearty sauces. Though there are variations across Italy, the classic Bolognese sauce (particularly in southern Italy) has to include pancetta as one meat ingredients. Beyond that, it's not uncommon to include beef, pork and/or veal. Milk is another required ingredient in a true Bolognese sauce, adding to its richness and tempering the tomatoes, which provide more of a subtle, background flavor in this sauce. Finally, there's the wine - most recipes call for a dry white wine, but I have always used Marsala. I think it gives just a hint of sweetness that really compliments the meat.

Ingredients (Serves 4-6)

1 lb ground pork (see note)

1 lb ground beef

6 oz pancetta, 1/4" dice

6 oz prosciutto, 1/4" dice (see note)

1 T olive oil

1 T butter

1/2 cup diced celery

1/2 cup diced carrot

1/2 cup diced onion

1/2 cup Marsala wine

14-16 oz jarred tomatoes in their juice

3 T tomato paste

1 1/2 cups whole milk

Salt and black pepper to taste

1 lb pasta (e.g., tagliatelle, bucatini or pappardelle)

Freshly grated Pecorino Romano

Directions

1. In a large sauce pot, cook pancetta in 1 T olive oil over medium heat until rendered and browned; remove with a slotted spoon and set aside.
2. Add the prosciutto and fry for a few minutes until browned; remove and set aside with the pancetta.
3. Add half of the ground pork and fry until browned; remove and set aside; repeat with the remaining half.
4. Repeat step 3 with the ground beef.
5. Pour off the fat from the pot and add 1 T butter; sauté vegetables for 2 minutes.
6. Add the Marsala wine to deglaze pot.
7. Add back the meat to the pot, along with the tomatoes and tomato paste; mix well and add salt and pepper to taste.
8. Add the milk, mix well, reduce heat, cover and simmer for about 2 hrs, stirring occasionally.
9. When sauce is ready, cook pasta until just *al dente* in a large pot of boiling salted water.
10. Transfer several ladles of sauce to a large frying pan over medium heat; drain pasta well and add to the sauce to finish cooking the pasta for a minute or so.
11. Top with additional sauce to taste, and serve with grated Pecorino.

Note: Instead of store-bought ground pork, I like to get a small pork butt (the same cut that I use for homemade sausage) and coarse-grind my own pork for this recipe - much better. You can always save the excess for other recipes. Also, you can typically find the end cuts of prosciutto in the deli case (or ask your butcher to save them for you). They are great for all sorts of recipes, including this one, and you can usually pick them up at a fraction of the cost of shaved Prosciutto di Parma. Dice them up, vacuum seal and freeze them.

 This sauce recipe is actually sufficient for 2 lbs of pasta, though 1 lb of pasta will typically serve 6.

Above: A steaming hot platter of Pasta alla Bolognese with bucatini pasta

Below left: The four different meats that make up the Bolognese sauce (clockwise from top: diced prosciutto, coarse-ground pork butt, ground beef and diced pancetta

Below right: A serving of Pasta alla Bolognese with homemade tagliatelle pasta

Bucatini all' Amatriciana

Bucatini with Guanciale, Fresh Tomatoes and Pepperoncini

With just a few ingredients, there aren't a whole lot of different ways to make this rustic dish of bucatini all'amatriciana. What makes it special, therefore, is the highest quality and freshest ingredients. The sauce is named after the Italian town of Amatrici, in the northern Lazio region. It's said that dish was a staple among shepherds in the Apennine mountains because the ingredients were inexpensive and readily available - pasta, tomatoes and the less desirable cuts of pork that didn't make it to the market.

Guanciale, or cured pork jowl, is the star of this dish. It's high fat content gives a unique flavor and rich silkiness to the pasta. Curing your own, as described on "Guanciale" on page 253 elevates it to worlds unknown!

Ingredients (Serves 4-6)

1 lb dried bucatini pasta

1 T extra virgin olive oil

6-8 oz guanciale, 1/2" dice

1 medium onion, chopped

2 cloves garlic, chopped

14-16 oz jarred tomatoes in their juice (or substitute 1 15-oz can whole, peeled San Marzano tomatoes)

Crushed red pepper flakes (to taste)

Freshly grated Pecorino Romano

Directions

1. Bring a pot of salted water to a boil for the pasta.
2. Heat olive oil over medium heat in a pan and add diced guanciale. Cook guanciale on medium low heat until the fat is rendered and the pieces are nicely browned. Remove from pan with a slotted spoon, leaving the fat in the pan.
3. Add the onion and red pepper flakes and cook, stirring, until the onion is just translucent.
4. Hand-crush the tomatoes and add them, with their juice, to the pan along with the browned guanciale. Cook on low/medium heat for about 15 minutes, uncovered.
5. Meanwhile, add the pasta to the boiling water and cook for a couple of minutes less than the package directions indicate. You want them less than "al dente" to allow the final cooking to take place in the sauce.
6. Drain the pasta, reserving about a half cup of the pasta water.
7. Add the pasta to the sauce and toss, allowing the pasta to soak up the sauce and cook until just al dente. You may add a little of the pasta water only if needed to maintain the sauce consistency.
8. Remove from heat and add a generous amount of Pecorino Romano - at least a half cup.
9. Serve immediately with extra crushed red pepper and Pecorino.

Opposite:

Above: The final few minutes of bucatini all' amatriciana, cooked outdoors at a campsite; the tossed pasta soaking up the sauce goodness!

Below left: Home-cured and sliced guanciale

Below right: Jarred home-grown tomatoes

Spaghetti alla Carbonara

Spaghetti with Guanciale, Egg and Cheese

Spaghetti alla carbonara, as with so many classic Italian pasta dishes, is composed of only a few principal ingredients – pasta, eggs, cheese and pork. The key – as always – is to use the highest quality ingredients that you can get your hands on. Guanciale is the pork component that's traditionally used for carbonara, and the only choice for me. I cure my own guanciale so I always have some on hand, because it can be hard to find unless you have access to a good Italian meat market - like there's any other kind! If you absolutely must, you can substitute pancetta, or even stoop as low as bacon, but these won't give you the same result. Just please don't add cream to your carbonara as is done in so many American restaurants. The "creaminess" in carbonara comes from the emulsification of the fat from the guanciale, eggs and a splash of pasta water.

Spaghetti alla carbonara is easy to prepare, but your undivided attention is needed during the final minutes when this glorious dish comes together. My daughter calls this dish "bacon and eggs" pasta.

Ingredients (Serves 4-6)

1 lb dry spaghetti

1 T olive oil

6-8 oz guanciale, 1/2" cubed

3 large, fresh eggs

Freshly coarse ground black pepper

1/2 cup grated Pecorino Romano cheese

Directions

1. In an 8-quart pot, bring to a boil 6 quarts of water and 2 T salt.
2. Add the olive oil to a large frying pan and fry the guanciale over low heat until rendered and nicely browned. Turn off heat, leaving the guanciale and rendered fat in the pan (see note).
3. Mix the eggs and cheese together in a bowl.
4. Just when the pasta is cooked to *al dente* (about 7 minutes), return the guanciale to low heat, reserve 1 cup of the pasta water, and then drain the pasta in a colander.
5. Add the pasta the guanciale along with about a quarter cup of the, pasta water. Toss until the water is absorbed by the pasta. Remove the pan from the heat.
6. Add a few tablespoons of the pasta water to the egg mixture to help temper it, then add the mixture to the pasta. Quickly toss the pasta. The heat of the pasta will cook and thicken the egg mixture. Avoid letting the egg mixture collect at the bottom of the pan, where it might turn into scrambled eggs. If the sauce appears too thick, you can add a bit more of the reserved pasta water. You're looking for a smooth, creamy texture to the sauce (see photo).
7. Add a generous amount of freshly ground black pepper and serve immediately.

Note: With some practice, you'll be able to time things right so that the pasta is done to *al dente* at the same time the guanciale is rendered, so you can turn of the heat on the guanciale and move directly to adding the drained pasta.

Above: Spaghetti alla carbonara
Below left: Rendering the guanciale
Below right: Home-cured guanciale

Linguine Aglio e Olio

Spaghetti with Garlic and Oil

Linguine *aglio e olio* (or just "*aglio e olio*") is the quintessential rustic pasta dish. *Aglio e olio* (garlic and oil) is said to have originated in Naples and is enjoyed all over Italy. Its preparation couldn't be simpler - pasta...oil...garlic...mix - but some attention is needed to get it just right, and of course, use of the highest quality ingredients is key.

Ingredients (Serves 4-6)

1 lb dry linguine

8 cloves garlic, whole

1/2 cup extra virgin olive oil

3 dried pepperoncini (small hot peppers) chopped, or substitute about 1 t of crushed red pepper flakes

Grated Pecorino Romano cheese (optional)

Directions

1. In a large pot, bring 6 quarts of water plus 2 T salt to a boil. Add pasta, stirring occasionally.
2. While the pasta is cooking, prepare the sauce. Heat oil to medium/low in a pan large enough to hold a pound of cooked pasta
3. Add pepper and garlic, and cook until garlic is browned (see note)
4. Just before the pasta is cooked to al dente, drain it (reserving about 1/4 cup of pasta water) and add the pasta to the pan with the garlic and oil
5. Increase heat, add the reserved pasta water, and toss until the pasta finished cooking to al dente, and is coated well with the sauce.
6. Transfer immediately to a platter for serving. If desired, feel free to drizzle a little extra oil over the pasta along with grated Romano cheese

Note: Some recipes call for thinly sliced or chopped garlic, and only lightly browned. The way my family has always made *aglio e olio* is to use whole cloves of garlic and to cook them long enough over medium/low heat to brown them very well (see photo). I think this gives the perfect, distinctive, flavor to the oil, which really makes the dish.

Lumachoni Farciti

Stuffed Shells

Lumachoni pasta is an alternative shape to the better-known "jumbo shells" that are more commonly used for stuffing. The pasta is in the shape of snail shells (*lumache* in Italian is "snails") as opposed to the traditional seashell shape. The reason I like lumachoni pasta has nothing at all to do with flavor, as both pasta shapes taste the same (assuming they're both high quality products). Rather, the shape and size of lumachoni pasta result in the perfect pasta-to-cheese ratio for my liking. Plus, the lumachoni pasta has an interesting shape that's more visually appealing on the plate - hey, call me crazy! Anyway… choose your favorite pasta for stuffing, and make sure to double-down with some great homemade tomato sauce (page 277).

Ingredients (Serves 12)

For the filling:

Use the same filling as for lasagna (see page 71)

For the pasta:

Two 1-lb. bags of dried l*umachoni giganti* pasta

Approximately 6 cups cooked tomato sauce (page 277)

Directions:

1. Bring a large pot of salted water to a boil. The pot should be large enough to easily accommodate the 2 lbs of pasta with plenty of water to cover. Add about a tablespoon of olive oil to the water and cook the lumachoni pasta for about 2 to 3 minutes less than the package directions. The pasta will be slightly undercooked, which can be checked by pinching a piece between your fingernails. If the center of the pasta is still white, it's just right. Drain the pasta and transfer to a bowl of cold water to stop further cooking. Keep pasta in water.
2. Grab an extra large (15" x 21") baking sheet pan and begin by spreading about a cup of tomato sauce in the pan.
3. Remove one shell at a time, shake off excess water and stuff with a tablespoon or so of the cheese filling. Place the stuffed shell on the sheet pan. Repeat with the remaining shells until the pan is full. Avoid over-crowding. Note - you may find that a number of shells are broken and not suitable for stuffing. Just discard the broken shells - the 2 lbs that you made will give you a sufficient number of intact shells for the amount of cheese filling.
4. Spoon tomato sauce over the shells (see photo), loosely cover with foil and bake for about 40 minutes at 375ºF, removing the foil during the final 15 minutes to slightly brown the edges of the shells.
5. Serve with extra tomato sauce, grated Pecorino Romano cheese, and crusty Italian bread.

Above: A serving of lumachoni farciti
Left: Filling the partially cooked lumachoni pasta
Below: Covered with sauce and ready for the oven
Opposite: Dried lumachoni pasta

Gnocchi al Pesto

Gnocchi with Pesto Sauce

Gnocchi are enjoyed all over Italy and in many different ways. One of my favorites is the classic potato gnocchi popular in northern Italy. Prepared incorrectly, gnocchi can be dense and heavy, or even mushy. Properly prepared, gnocchi are light and airy; fluffy little pillows of goodness! Then there's the accompanying sauce - the classic marinara is always a winner, but every once in a while I mix it up with a freshly prepared pesto, especially in mid-summer when my basil crop is at its peak.

Ingredients (Serves 4)

2 lbs russet potatoes

1 cup flour

2 eggs, beaten

For the pesto:

Leaves from 1 large bunch of fresh basil

2 oz pignoli nuts

3 cloves garlic

Parmigiano Reggiano

Extra virgin olive oil

Directions

1. Bring about 4 quarts of lightly salted water to a boil. Peel and halve the potatoes and boil until just barely cooked, until the tip of a knife can be inserted into the potato.
2. Remove the potatoes with a slotted spoon, reserving the water (you will cook the gnocchi in it). While the potatoes are still hot, pass them through a potato ricer. I like to use the type shown at right, with the coarse ricer insert. Allow potatoes to cool a bit before proceeding.
3. Add the eggs to the potatoes and mix gently. This can be done in a large bowl, but I prefer a flat surface.
4. Add about 3/4 cup flour and mix together to form a dough, which should be moist but not sticky. Add a bit more flour if necessary.
5. Divide the dough into eight pieces and, one at a time, roll each piece into a rope about a half inch thick. Cut the rope into 1-inch pieces. Roll each piece across a gnocchi board (photo) to form the classic ridges. Alternatively, this can be done by gently rolling the pieces with the back of a fork.
6. Place the formed gnocchi in a single layer on a floured surface and allow to air dry for about an hour.
7. Meanwhile, prepare the pesto. Begin by toasting lightly toasting the pignoli nuts over low heat in a pan with about 1 t olive oil. Remove and allow to cool.
8. Coarsely chop garlic and pignoli nuts together and set aside.
9. Chop basil, then add to the pignoli/garlic mixture and continue to chop together until all components are finely chopped. Add 3 T olive oil, mix, and set aside.
10. Return the pot of water to a boil, and carefully drop in the gnocchi. After several minutes, the cooked gnocchi will float to the top.
11. Remove them to a bowl, toss with the pesto and serve immediately with extra parmigiano and a drizzle of olive oil.

Clockwise from top:
Gnocchi al pesto; gnocchi rolling board, toasting pignoli, pesto sauce, ricing potatoes, gnocchi ready for the pot
Opposite: Fresh basil in my garden

Pasta con le Sarde

Pasta with Sardines

Pasta con le sarde is often referred to as the national dish of Sicily. However, you'll find that the recipe varies across different parts of Sicily; some include tomatoes while others do not. Among the towns on the Sicilian Mediterranean coast, like Noto - the birthplace of my father-in-law, - pasta con le sarde is always made with the day's fresh catch of sardines, but never a tomato!

Ingredients (Serves 4-6)

6 fresh sardines (approximately 2 lbs)

1/2 cup olive oil (plus more for drizzling)

Flour for dusting

1 onion, sliced thin

2 cloves garlic, chopped

1 fennel bulb sliced paper thin; reserve fronds and discard stalk

Pinch of saffron threads

1/4 cup dried currants

3 T cup pignoli nuts

3/4 cup dry white wine

4 slices ciabatta bread

Salt and coarse ground black pepper to taste

1 lb bucatini pasta

Directions

1. Clean and fillet the sardines as described below. Reserve intact fillets from two sardines and coarsely chop the remaining four.
2. Place the bread slices in the oven to toast, turning so that both sides are well toasted and the bread is hard. Remove from over and allow to cool. Once cooled, crumble the toast in a bowl or by briefly pulsing in a food processor. I prefer larger breadcrumbs for this recipe, so don't over do it.
3. Bring a large pot of salted water to a boil in preparation for cooking the pasta.
4. Heat oil in a large skillet. Salt and pepper the intact fillets, dredge in flour and brown in the oil. Allow to drain on a paper towel and set aside.
5. Add the fennel bulb and onion to the pan and cook over medium low heat until caramelized; this will be the start of the sauce for the pasta.
6. Add the pasta to the boiling water and cook until just barely *al dente*; about 9 minutes. The pasta will finish cooking in the sauce.
7. Lightly toast the pignoli nuts in a small frying pan and then add them to the sauce, along with the garlic and currants.
8. Add the chopped sardines to the sauce and cook until they have broken down.
9. Add about 1/4 cup chopped fennel fronds.
10. Crush the saffron threads between your fingers and into the white wine. Add to the sauce.
11. Reserve 1 cup of the pasta water and then drain the pasta. Add the pasta to the sauce along with the reserved pasta water. Continue to cook for a couple of minutes, tossing well to coat the pasta in the sauce.
12. Adjust seasonings, add the breadcrumbs and toss. Plate immediately, topping each plate with one of the sardine fillets, a drizzle of olive oil, and garnish with a fennel frond.

Note: Filleting sardines is pretty easy after a little practice. The scales can be easily removed just by rubbing them off under running water. Slice the belly from under the head to the anal opening and remove the innards. Use your finger to separate the fish from the anal opening to the tail, exposing the backbone. Remove the head. Grabbing the backbone at the head, run your fingers behind the rib cage and separate it from the meat. Continue to pull out the backbone all the way to the tail. The ribs, backbone and tail should come off in one piece. A quick rinse in water and you're done!

Above left: Laying out some of the ingredients; fennel fronds, pignoli nuts, currants, garlic and saffron

Above right: Floured and fried sardine fillets

Below: Pasta con le sarde

Pasta cui Cavuli

Cavatelli Pasta with Kohlrabi

This is going to sound a bit confusing, but try to follow along....*cavolo* (plural *cavoli* or *cavuli*) is kohlrabi in Sicily, but *cavolo* (or *cavolfiore*) is cauliflower in mainland Italy. *Cavolo verza* is used to mean cabbage, and "*che cavolo!*" – well – that basically translates to "what the hell!" OK, now that we're past that, this dish is typically made with a type of homemade pasta known by various names across Sicily (*causuneddi, gnocculi, gnucchiteddi, caviateddi*) but is basically a hand-shaped pasta that more or less resembles cavatelli. You can be adventurous and make your own homemade ricotta cavatelli (as shown here), or simply purchase some fresh or frozen cavetelli from your local market.

I typically grow the purple kohlrabi just because it's more attractive, but there is really no difference in the flavor of the bulb, and since you have to peel it anyway, any variety of kohlrabi would work with this recipe. Either way, if you're buying kohlrabi from the market, look for those with the leaves still attached, because that's an indicator of freshness; kohlrabi leaves will wilt after a few days.

This dish is another one of those simple, rustic concoctions made from just a few fresh ingredients that come together perfectly. Some recipes use quite a bit of the kohlrabi/pasta water so that the final presentation is almost like a soup. I prefer a less soupy dish; there's still plenty of the kohlrabi broth available to be able to dip your bread in when you're done.

Ingredients (Serves 4-6)

3 kohlrabi, bulbs and greens

1 medium onion, sliced

2 cloves garlic, chopped

1/2 t fresh thyme leaves

1/2 t crushed red pepper flakes

4 T olive oil, plus more for drizzling

Salt and ground black pepper

1/2 lb cavatelli pasta

Grated Parmigiano Reggiano

Directions

1. Remove leaves from kohlrabi and set aside. Peel the bulbs and cut into quarter moons no more than about 1/4" thick (see photo).
2. Slice a few leaves into thin strips to end up with about 2 cups, loosely packed.
3. Bring about 3 quarts of water, plus 2 t salt to a boil and cook the kohlrabi until just tender, about 15 minutes.
4. In a large sauce pan, sauté the kohlrabi greens, onion, garlic, red pepper and thyme in olive oil.
5. Remove the kohlrabi with a slotted spoon, plus 2 cups of water from the pot and add to the pan with the onion.
6. Add the pasta to the kohlrabi water and cook to *al dente*.
7. Transfer the cooked pasta to the pan with the kohlrabi, tossing together. You can add more of the kohlrabi/pasta water, if desired. Adjust seasoning with salt and pepper.
8. Transfer to serving plate and top with grated Parmigiano Reggiano cheese and an extra drizzle of olive oil.

Above: Pasta cui cavuli
Right: Purple kohlrabi
Below right: Kohlrabi greens cut into strips
Below left: Kohlrabi peeled and pieced
Opposite: Kohlrabi in my garden, ready for harvest

Breads and the Like

• Friselle •

Italian Pepper Biscuits

• Schiacciata Siciliana •

Sicilian Style Stuffed Flatbread

• Pizza a la Griglia •

Grilled Pizza

• Zeppole con le Acciughe •

Fried Dough Balls with Anchovies

• Focaccia •

Italian Flatbread

• Pane Italiano •

Classic Italian Bread

• Panini di Semola •

Semolina Rolls

• Pizza Chiena •

Naples Style Savory Pie

Friselle

Italian Pepper Biscuits

These simple, savory biscuits are nothing short of addicting! They can be eaten plain or with soups or stews. Have them with a glass of wine…awesome! Crumbled, they make great salad croutons. By far, my favorite use is as a base, or "sponge," for a dish like scungilli fra diavolo (page 193).

Ingredients (makes about 24 biscuits)

1 c whole grain flour

3 c bread flour

1 t salt

2 T coarse black pepper

2 T baking powder

2 T whole fennel seed

½ c olive oil

1½ c dry white wine

Directions

1. Preheat oven to 350°F.
2. Mix dry ingredients together in a mixing bowl.
3. In a separate bowl, or a 2-cup measuring cup, mix together wine and olive oil and whisk to produce a homogeneous emulsion.
4. Add the oil/wine emulsion to the dry ingredients and mix. A stand mixer with a dough attachment works well here. The dough should be moist enough to hold together, but not sticky.
5. Divide the dough in half and hand shape into two logs, each approximately 15" long and about 2" thick. This should be done on a shallow baking tray large enough to accommodate the loaves.
6. Place the tray on the middle rack of the pre-heated oven and bake uncovered for 30 minutes.
7. Remove from the oven; at this point the friselle won't be cooked all the way through. Carefully slice the loaves into biscuits approximately 1" thick. Lay the biscuits on their side (see photo) and return to the oven to bake for another 30 minutes. After 30 minutes, turn he biscuits over and return to the oven to bake for a final 15 minutes.
8. Remove from oven and allow cool completely to room temperature, uncovered. The biscuits should be hard and crunchy. If you wish to store them in a covered container, make sure they reach room temperature first, or they will "steam" themselves and lose some of their crunchiness.

Above: Friselle ready to eat

Below: Shaped loaves ready for the oven

Right: First baking completed; friselle cut to size for second baking

Schiacciata alla Siciliana

Sicilian Style Stuffed Flatbread

I learned to make schiacciata from my mother-in-law, Coradina, who is from Palazzolo, Sicily. *Schiacciata* means "squashed" or "flattened" in Italian. The name refers to any of a wide variety of different flatbreads popular across all of Italy. In Rome, schiacciata is typically just a flattened version of Italian bread, sometimes topped with roasted tomatoes, herbs or just sea salt. In Florence, schiacciata is more like a sweet, sponge cake. In Sicily, however, schiacciata (or "scacciata" in the Sicilian dialect) is a thin crust, stuffed flatbread. Think of a pizza with your favorite toppings folded in half on top of itself and then baked.

The various types of stuffing for schiacciata can be endless, but the typical ones – and my family's favorites – are shown below. Other stuffing ingredients, like sun-dried tomatoes, broccoli rabe, olives, artichoke hearts and anchovies, have also made appearances in my schiacciata at one time or another. Feel free to experiment with some of your own favorites.

Ingredients (makes 2 schiacciata loaves)

2 balls fresh pizza dough (see page 267), approximately 1 lb each, at room temperature

Olive oil for drizzling

For sausage schiacciata:

About 1 1/2 lbs uncooked Italian sausage meat (from about 6 links), hot or sweet, preferably homemade (see page 265) or substitute high-quality, store-bought sausage

1 medium potato, peel and sliced into thin half-moons (see photo)

1 medium onion. sliced thin

Salt and coarse ground black pepper to taste

For parsley schiacciata:

1 large bunch of fresh Italian parsley, chopped

Approximately 4 oz piece of Pecorino Romano, broken into 1/2 in pieces (i.e., not grated)

1 T capers in vinegar

Directions

1. Lightly oil a 12 x 17-inch , shallow baking tray (see photo). Stretch and shape 1 ball of dough to fit inside the tray. Use 1 ball of dough for each schiacciata.
2. Arrange the ingredients for each type of schiacciata down the center of the dough (see photo).
3. Drizzle with olive oil and then fold the sides of the dough over the contents, pinching the dough together to seal, leaving a few small openings for steam to escape.
4. Brush the top with olive oil, scatter some sesame seeds (optional) and bake for about 45 minutes in a pre-heated 425°F oven until nicely browned.
5. Allow to cool slightly and then slice, as shown, for serving.

Above: Sausage, potato and onion schiacciata

Right: Pecorino, parsley and capers schiacciata

Bottom right: Schiacciata fresh from the oven

Below: Filling a schiacciata in preparation for baking

Opposite: Coradina rolling out schiacciata dough

Pizza alla Griglia

Grilled Pizza

There's nothing quite like an authentic, wood-fired pizza oven to produce the perfect pizza - a thin crust that's both crispy and chewy, with just the right amount of char from the oven. If you don't own a pizza oven, you can come pretty close to the real thin with a hot grill and a pizza stone.

Below are some of my favorite toppings for grilled pizza. Feel free to use some of your own, or be creative - just don't go off the reservation, like "Hawaiian pizza." Putting pineapple on a pizza is like putting peanut butter on a good steak - some things just shouldn't be.

Ingredients:

1 lb prepared pizza dough (see page 267), for each pizza; room temperature

Corn meal for dusting

For the pizza sauce (makes 4 large pizzas):

1 qt jarred tomatoes (see page 275) or substitute canned San Marzano tomatoes

3 T olive oil

1 clove garlic, chopped

1 t dried oregano

Salt to taste

For pizza margherita:

1 cup pizza sauce

8 oz fresh mozzerella, sliced

Several leaves fresh basil, torn

Coarse ground black pepper

For sausage pizza:

1 cup pizza sauce

8 oz whole milk mozzerella, shredded

Meat from 4 links of fresh sausage (see page 265)

1 T Pecorino Romano cheese

1 t dried oregano

Directions:

1. Prepare pizza sauce by frying garlic in oil for 30 seconds. Add tomatoes and puree with an immersion blender. Add oregano and salt and heat to a simmer.
2. Place pizza stone on a cold grill and heat to highest setting, for at least 30 minutes prior to cooking pizza.
3. Since the pizzas cook so quickly on the grill, I typically stretch out and shape several balls of pizza dough at once and keep them on individual pizza trays, awaiting to be topped - that is, if you plan to make more than one pizza.
4. Scatter some cornmeal on a pizza peel, and transfer the stretched out dough onto the peel. Working quickly, spread the sauce (if called for in the recipe) onto the dough and to within about an inch of the edge.
5. Top with cheese and then the remaining ingredients for your particular pizza (note: for pizza margherita, top with the basil AFTER the pizza is removed from the grill).
6. Transfer the pizza from the peel to the pizza stone and grill until the edge of the pizza begins to char.
7. Slice and serve hot.

For white clam pizza:

4 oz Fontina cheese, shredded

2 T Pecorino Romano cheese

2 T olive oil

About 12 oz of fresh clam meat, coarsely chopped

2 cloves garlic, chopped

Several sprigs of fresh parsley, chopped

Crushed red pepper, to taste

For pepperoni pizza:

1 cup pizza sauce

8 oz whole milk mozzerella, shredded

1 T Pecorino Romano cheese

Several fried Palazzolo peppers (see page 3), or substitute similar (optional)

Above: White clam pizza

Right: Pizza Margherita

Below right: Pizza with homemade sausage

Below left: Pizza with pepperoni and Palazzolo peppers

Zeppole con le Acciughe
Fried Dough Balls with Anchovies

Zeppole (singular; *zeppola*) are deep-fried dough balls that are enjoyed in many parts of Italy, but most notable in Southern Italy. Zeppole can be sweet or savory. The classic savory variety - my personal favorite - is made with anchovies. In some recipes, a whole anchovy fillet is placed in the middle of each zeppola prior to frying. In my family's recipe, smaller pieces of anchovies are incorporated into the dough. The addition of semolina flour to the mix gives the savory zeppole a slightly sweet, rich flavor and a more cake-like texture than if only bread flour were used.

Sadly, my daughters are skeeved* by the thought of eating anchovies, and so I usually end up making the sweet variety, *zeppole dolce* (page 247). That said, there's nothing like loading up on empty carbs with a few ice-cold beers and a platter of zeppole con le acciughe!

Ingredients (makes about 16-20)

2 cups all-purpose flour

1 cup Caputo Semola Rimacinata flour (page 107)

2 t instant yeast

1 t salt

1/2 t black pepper

Approximately 1 1/2 cups water

1 tin (2 oz) flat filet of anchovies in oil

Canola oil for frying

Directions

1. Mix dry ingredients in a large bowl.
2. Add water and mix with a paddle mixer until a dough forms. The dough should be a bit sticky.
3. Coarsely chop the anchovies and add them, along with the oil from the tin, to the dough. Continue mixing until the anchovies are dispersed in the dough.
4. Cover doiugh and set aside in a warm room to rise; approximately 2 hrs.
5. Fill a pot with about 2-3 inches of canola oil and bring to 325ºF.
6. Working in small batches, scoop out balls of dough about the size of ping-pong balls and drop them in the oil. The dough will be sticky, so there is no need to form perfect balls.
7. Deep fry for 1-2 minutes until the zeppole are golden brown. Remove with a slotted spoon to paper towels to absorb excess oil.
8. Transfer to a platter and serve warm or at room temperature.

* The phrase, "to be skeeved" or "skeeved out" is a popular American slang that means to be utterly disgusted by something. Its root is in the Italian word *schifo* (or *schifío*; Sicilian), which, appropriately enough, means "disgust." Actual use in conversation would go something like this.... I would incite my daughter into offering her grandfather a bite of her PB&J sandwich. The immediate (and expected) response from my father-in-law would be "*Schifío!!!*" Never failed to amuse me.

Above: Zeppole con le acciughe
Below: Dough ready for the deep fryer

Focaccia

Italian Flatbread

Focaccia is an ancient Italian flatbread and probably the predecessor of pizza. The main dough components are pretty much the same as most breads - flour, water and yeast. Focaccia, however, is stretched into a sheet prior to the final rise and trip to the oven. The stretched dough is also topped with olive oil (a "must") and various herbs, spices and/or vegetables prior to baking. Typical toppings include rosemary, onion, olives, sun-dried tomatoes and cheese. I'm rather conservative when it comes to topping my focaccia; it should be more like a modestly seasoned bread than a pizza.

Enjoy focaccia as an accompaniment to any meal or just by itself with a piece of cheese and a glass of hearty red wine. Sliced, focaccia makes a great bread for panini.

Ingredients (for 1 focaccia)

Approximately 4 1/2 cups all-purpose flour

2 t non-iodized salt

2 cups warm water

1 packet instant-rise yeast

2 T olive oil, plus more for topping

Chopped fresh rosemary (about 2 T)

Optional toppings:

Chopped fresh sage

Whole fennel seed

Chopped oil-cured black olives

Chopped sun-dried tomatoes in oil,

Caramelized onions

Sliced red onion

Parmesan cheese

Coarse sea salt

Directions

1. Dissolve the yeast in the warm water (see note).
2. Mix salt into flour in a large mixing bowl.
3. Add the dissolved yeast and 2 T olive oil. Mix well and knead for approximately 10 minutes. This can be done by hand or with the aid of a stand mixer and dough hook. The dough should be only slightly sticky at this point. If necessary, add small amounts of flour to get the right consistency.
4. Place dough into a lightly-oiled bowl, cover and allow to rise for 1 1/2 hrs. Punch down dough and allow to rise for another hr.
5. Lightly oil a large (15 x 17 inches) baking tray and stretch dough into a rectangular shape onto the pan.
6. Cover dough with plastic wrap and allow to rise for a final 30 minutes.
7. Preheat oven to 475°F. With your fingers, press into the dough to produce dimples over the surface (see photo).
8. Drizzle olive oil over the dough. Top with fresh rosemary and any additional toppings of your choice, without "over-loading" the focaccia.
9. Bake until just browned. Remove from oven and allow to cool slightly. A little extra drizzle of olive oil at this point is always welcomed. Serve warm.

Note: I do realize that instant yeast does not need to be dissolved in water before use, but that's the way I've always done it. You can substitute active dry yeast if you prefer, but you will probably need to add a bit of time to the initial rise.

Above: Focaccia with rosemary, caramelized onions and sprinkle of Parmesan
Below left: Focaccia with fresh rosemary and a light sprinkle of sea salt
Below right: Fresh rosemary in my herb garden

Pane Italiano

Classic Italian Bread

Making homemade Italian bread is easy, requiring only a few simple ingredients common to most breads - flour, water and yeast - what could be simpler? Yet the one complaint that I hear all too often is "Why doesn't my bread come out like the bread from the Italian bakery down the block?" The answer lies in the key aspects of bread baking - quality of ingredients, technique and PATIENCE!

I always use a *biga* (pronounced BEE-gah) when making Italian bread. Biga is a starter culture that allows for a degree of pre-fermentation of the dough. It's what gives the best Italian bread that crunchy crust, airy center and distinctive "tanginess." The biga should be prepared at least the day before you plan to bake the bread, but can be stored in the refrigerator for up to a week before use.

I prefer Caputo Tipo "00" flour from Naples, Italy (photo). This flour is very finely milled by a process that preserves the gluten protein structure. Because this flour is so fine, you will use a bit less water to make the dough than if you were using all-purpose "0" flour. Finally, sufficient moisture during the baking process ensures a great exterior crust.

Ingredients (makes 1 large loaf)

For the biga:

2 cups Caputo Tipo "00" flour

1 cup bottled water, warmed in the microwave

1/2 t active dry yeast

For the bread:

3 1/2 cups Caputo Tipo "00" flour, plus additional for dusting

1 1/2 cups bottled water, warmed in the microwave

1 t active dry yeast

2 t non-iodized salt

1 T olive oil

Directions

1. Prepare the biga: Dissolve the yeast in the warm water and allow to stand 10 minutes until the yeast starts to foam.
2. Add the water containing the yeast to the flour and mix well by hand. I typically do this in a bowl with a snap-on plastic lid. The bigs should be rather sticky. Cover bowl and let stand 3 hrs in a warm area, and then place the bowl in the refrigerator overnight.
3. Remove biga from refrigerator and allow to come to room temperature.
4. Dissolve the yeast in the warm water and allow to stand 10 minutes until the yeast starts to foam. Add the olive oil and stir.
5. Using a stand mixer fitted with a dough hook, combine flour and yeast suspension in water. Beat on low speed until combined.
6. Add the biga and salt and continue beating on low speed until a homogeneous dough is formed. The dough should be only slightly sticky at this point. If dough is too sticky add a small amount of flour to get the right consistency.
7. Transfer dough to a large, lightly oiled bowl. Cover and allow to rise for 1 1/2 hrs. Transfer dough to a lightly floured work surface and gently fold it onto itself several times, shaping it into a loaf. Place the bread on a lightly oiled, perforated metal pizza pan and allow to rise for 1 hr.
8. Place a an empty metal tray on a lower oven rack Pre-heat oven to 475. With a sharp knife, make a shallow cut down the center of the loaf. Transfer the bread to a middle rack in the oven and immediately add 2 cups of water into the metal pan; the water will steam. Quickly close the oven door and bake for about 45 minutes until bread is golden brown and sounds hollow when tapped Remove from oven and cool on a wire rack.

Above: Pane Italiano, sprinkled with sesame seeds prior to baking (optional)

Right: Imported Caputo Tipo "00" flour

Below: Biga starter, glistening and bubbly

Panini di Semola

Semolina Rolls

Bread made from semolina flour comes straight from Sicily and is probably my favorite bread. Various shapes and sizes of semolina bread are available, but I particularly like it in the form of individual rolls,

Semolina flour is the type of flour from which pasta is typically made. It is high in protein (gluten), and made from the center kernel of durum wheat, which gives the flour its characteristic yellow color. Semolina flour, as most know it, is more coarse than bread flour, which makes it great for pasta, but not so great for bread. That's where imported Italian semolina flour comes in. The type I use for semolina bread is Caputo Semola Rimacinata (photo). The term *rimacinata* (literally, "re-machined") refers to the extra milling process that transforms the coarse semolina into very fine flour, while maintaining the necessary gluten protein structure that is so important when it comes to great bread. I typically use half bread flour and half semolina flour for this recipe, starting with a *biga* (see page 105).

Ingredients (makes about12 rolls)

For the biga:

1 cup Caputo Tipo "00" flour

1 cup Caputo Semola Rimacinata flour

1 cup bottled water, warmed in the microwave

1/2 t active dry yeast

For the rolls:

1 1/2 cups Caputo Tipo "00" flour, plus additional for dusting

1 1/2 cups Caputo Semola Rimacinata flour

1 1/2 cups bottled water, warmed in the microwave

1 t active dry yeast

2 t non-iodized salt

1 T olive oil

Directions

1. Prepare the biga: Dissolve the yeast in the warm water and allow to stand 10 minutes until the yeast starts to foam.
2. Add the water containing the yeast to the flour and mix well by hand. I typically do this in a bowl with a snap-on plastic lid. The bigs should be rather sticky. Cover bowl and let stand 3 hrs in a warm area, and then place the bowl in the refrigerator overnight.
3. Remove biga from refrigerator and allow to come to room temperature.
4. Dissolve the yeast in the warm water and allow to stand 10 minutes until the yeast starts to foam. Add the olive oil and stir.
5. Using a stand mixer fitted with a dough hook, combine flour and yeast suspension in water. Beat on low speed until combined.
6. Add the biga and salt and continue beating on low speed until a homogeneous dough is formed. The dough should be only slightly sticky at this point. If dough is too sticky add a small amount of flour to get the right consistency.
7. Transfer dough to a large, lightly oiled bowl. Cover and allow to rise for 1 1/2 hrs.
8. Working with a small handful of dough at a time and a lightly floured work surface, gently fold the dough pieces it roll shapes. Place the shaped rolls bread on a lightly oiled, perforated metal pizza pan and allow to rise for 1 hr.
9. Place a an empty metal tray on a lower oven rack Pre-heat oven to 475. Transfer the rolls to a middle rack in the oven and immediately add 2 cups of water into the metal pan; the water will steam. Quickly close the oven door and bake for about 35 minutes until rolls are golden brown and sound hollow when tapped Remove from oven and cool on a wire rack.

Above: Panini di semola

Right: Caputo Semola Rimacinata flour

Below: comparison of finely milled rimacinata flour (top) and coarser semolina pasta flour (bottom)

Pizza Chiena

Naples Style Savory Pie

Pizza chiena, also sometimes referred to as *pizza chena* or *pizza rustica*, is not at all like pizza as most folks know it. It is typically a deep-dish, savory pie that's traditionally prepared on Easter Sunday across southern Italy, particularly in and around Naples. The recipes for pizza chiena are as varied as there are neighborhoods in Naples, but all contain a variety of meats and cheeses that are loaded into a pie crust and baked.

I've had versions of pizza chiena that contain various cubed meats floating in a predominant sea of the egg/cheese mixture, and I've had others that contain orderly, alternating layers of thinly sliced meats and cheeses. Similarly, some crusts are made with classic pizza dough, which I find too dense and chewy for this dish; others are too much like a butter-based flake pastry. The recipe that I have landed on has just the right ratio of meat-to-cheese for my liking. The crust, made from pastry dough, is the perfect compromise between a classic pizza dough and flake pastry.

Ingredients

For the dough:

1 1/2 cups pastry flour

1/2 cup 00 semolina flour

1 t salt

2 T olive oil

1 egg

water (approx 6 T)

For the filling:

1 lb whole milk ricotta cheese

1/2 lb whole milk, low moisture mozzerella

4 oz Fontina cheese

1/4 cup grated Parmigiano Reggiano

4 oz each of prosciutto, sopressata, capocolla and mortadella (all sliced)

2 oz roasted red peppers, sliced

2 eggs

Few sprigs of parsley, chopped

For the egg wash:

1 egg, beaten

2 T water

Directions

1. Prepare the dough by first mixing the dry ingredients in a large bowl. Work in the olive oil (pulsing in a stand mixer makes this step easier).
2. Add the egg and begin forming the dough. Add 1 T of water at a time until the dough comes together - not too dry and not too sticky. Wrap the dough in plastic wrap and set aside.
3. Beat the ricotta until creamy. Dice the mozzerella and Fontina and mix into the ricotta; add the Parmigiano Reggiano.
4. Add the eggs and mix well.
5. Roughly tear the various sliced meats and add to the cheese mixture along with the parsley.
6. Divide the dough in two pieces, with one a bit larger than the other. Roll out the larger piece and shape it to fit into a well-oiled 9-inch spring form pan (see photo).
7. Transfer the cheese and meat filling into the pan.
8. Roll out the second piece of dough and cover the filling, crimping the edges of the pie together.
9. Prepare the egg wash by beating the egg and water, and brush the dough.
10. Puncture the dough with a fork at several places to allow steam to escape.
11. Bake in a pre-heated 350°F oven for 50-60 minutes until golden brown. Remove from oven and allow pie to rest for 20-30 minutes before serving.

Above: Pizza chiena

Right: Placing the bottom dough in the spring form pan

Below: Adding the meat and cheese filling

Below right: Laying on the top dough.

MASI
FRESCARIPA

BEACH
EST 87

guanciale
5/27/17
1862g.

Beef and Veal

• Braciole •
Stuffed Beef rolls

• Polpette •
Meatballs

• Ossobuco di Vitello •
Braised Veal Shanks

• Osso con Midollo Arrosto •
Roasted Bone Marrow

• Stracotto •
Italian Pot Roast

• Fegato e Cipolle •
Liver and Onions

• Polpettone •
Meatloaf

• Saltimbocca alla Romana •
Veal Cutlets with Prosciutto and Sage

• Costolette di Vitello alla Griglia •
Grilled Veal Rib Chops

• Stufato di Manzo •
Italian Beef Stew

Braciole

Stuffed Beef Rolls

When I think of family feasts, particularly around the holidays, one of the first things that comes to mind is BRACIOLE! Basically, a *braciola* (*braciole*, plural) is a slice of meat, pounded very thin, covered with herbs, cheeses and other stuff, and then rolled up and simmered in tomato sauce for hours. The result is an incredibly flavorful, fork-tender, packet of goodness that can serve as a standalone meal or, my favorite, served over pasta. While braciole can be made with pork (or even chicken), beef is the choice for classic braciole. I've had braciole with all kinds of crazy stuffing ingredients, but this family recipe (straight from Naples) is the one that never fails to impress.

Ingredients (Serves 6)

3 lb beef bottom round (see note)

1 1/2 cups breadcrumbs

3 cloves garlic, minced

1 1/2 cups chopped fresh parsley

1/2 cup grated Pecorino Romano cheese

1/4 cup pignoli nuts

6 T olive oil

Salt and coarse ground black pepper to taste

Directions

1. Toast pignoli nuts is a small frying pan (no oil) over low heat until golden brown. Remove from heat to cool and then coarsely chop.
2. In a bowl, mix together parsley, garlic, toasted pignoli nuts, breadcrumbs, cheese, salt/pepper and 3 T of olive oil.
3. Pound each slice of meat with a meat tenderizer and then divide the stuffing to cover each piece (see photo).
4. Starting at the wide end of the meat, tuck the corners in a bit and then roll tightly to the pointed end so that, once rolled, the narrow point of the meat is in the middle of the braciole.
5. Tie the braciole tightly with butcher's twine. You can either use several separate pieces of twine, spacing them along the braciole, or use a "butcher's wrap" with a single piece of twine, whichever is easiest for you.
6. Heat the remaining 3 T of olive oil in a pan and brown the braciole.
7. Transfer the braciole to your favorite tomato sauce for slow simmering - the longer the better, but at least 3 hours.

Note: I prefer bottom round for my braciole over other cuts of beef. If you don't have a meat slicer, ask your butcher to slice it "for braciole." Slices should be about 1/4" thick, which you will pound even a bit thinner. Don't even think of trimming off the fat - it gives extra flavor to the sauce!

Clockwise from top:

- Braciole ready to serve
- Tied braciole
- Browning braciole in olive oil
- Braciole simmering in tomato sauce

Opposite:

- Left - slices of beef bottom round
- Right - stuffing spread across slices, ready to roll and tie

Polpette
Meatballs

Meatballs represent another one of those dishes for which it seems every family has their favorite recipe. While I'm certainly in favor of creativity in the kitchen, some things are so sacred that they shouldn't be messed with - like meatballs! I've eaten meatballs that have contained some really strange ingredients - all very creative indeed - but far from the perfect accompaniment to a first-course pasta dish that I've become so accustomed to for most Sunday dinners growing up. This family recipe provides the perfect ratio of meat, eggs and breadcrumbs to produce a meatball of just the right consistency following hours of simmering in your favorite tomato sauce. The flavors of the parsley, garlic and cheese are perfectly balanced to make these meatballs irresistible, especially when sitting on top of your favorite pasta.

Ingredients (Serves 6-8)

2 lbs ground beef 85% lean

2 eggs

4 cloves garlic, chopped

1 cup chopped parsley

1/2 cup grated Pecorino Romano cheese

1 cup breadcrumbs

2 t salt

1 t coarse ground black pepper

3 T olive oil

Directions

1. In a large bowl, mix together beef, eggs, parsley, garlic cheese, salt an pepper.
2. Add about half the breadcrumbs, mix, then the other half and mix again.
3. Form meatballs, about 2 inches across and set aside.
4. Heat olive oil in a frying pan and brown meatballs, a few at a time so as not to over-crowd pan. The meatballs should only be browned and still rare in the center.
5. Drop them into your favorite tomato sauce recipe and simmer away for at least a couple of hours.

Above: Meatballs simmering in tomato sauce
Below: Meatball browning in olive oil
Opposite: A serving of penne with meatballs

Ossobuco di Vitello

Braised Veal Shanks

Ossobuco, literally translated, means "mouth of the bone," referring to the marrow-containing opening that's revealed in a cross-sectional cut of the veal's hind shank bone, technically the tibia (see note below). Young, milk-fed veal calves produce the prime cuts for ossobuco. Prepared correctly, there's no need for a knife to enjoy ossobuco. The slow braising in a sauce of fresh tomatoes and wine results in meat that falls away from the bone with just a fork. The prized marrow in each piece is an extra little forkful of goodness that makes the dish so special.

Ossobuco is said to have originated in Milan, where the classic presentation is over saffron-infused risotto and topped with gremolata. That's definitely pretty yummy, but the southern Italian version is more to my liking - that is, hold the rice and give me a bit more tomato sauce to sop up with my crusty Italian bread.

This is my family's version of ossobuco, from the Campania region.

Ingredients (Serves 4)

4 pieces veal shank, cut for ossobuco, at least 1 1/2 inches thick and approximately 12 - 16 oz each.

3 T extra virgin olive oil

Flour for dusting

1 carrot, chopped,

1 stalk celery, chopped

1 medium onion, chopped,

2 cloves garlic, chopped

4 bay leaves

1 cup dry Marsala

1 cup beef stock

16 oz jarred San Marzano tomatoes

Salt and pepper to taste

Chopped parsley for garnish

Directions

1. Salt and pepper veal pieces and lightly dredge in flour.
2. Heat 2 T olive oil in a deep frying pan and brown veal (photo). Remove from pan and set aside.
3. Add 1 T olive oil to pan and sauté carrot, celery and onion until slightly browned (about 5 minutes), adding garlic during final minute.
4. Add Marsala, scraping up browned bits from the pan.
5. Add the beef stock, bay leaves and jarred tomatoes.
6. Return the veal to the pan, season with salt and pepper, cover, and simmer for about 2 hrs, until the sauce thickens and the sauce components break down. Turn veal once during the cooking period.
7. Serve with a garnish of chopped fresh parsley.

Note: Here's a little veterinary anatomy tip to help you choose the best cut of meat for ossobuco. The best cut comes from the HINDLIMB. Unlike other species (including humans), bovine species lack a fibula - the thinner bone that runs next to the tibia (i.e., your shin bone). A cross-sectional cut of the calf hindlimb, therefore, will only show one bone - the tibia (see photo at right). If your cut shows two bones, it's from the FORELIMB; the bones being the radius and ulna (see Chapter photo). Not that the forelimb isn't also pretty tasty, but the hindlimb makes for the absolute best ossobuco. That's the cut you need to look for.

Above: Ossobuco di vitello

Right: Sautéing vegetables

Below: The perfect piece of fresh veal shank cut for ossobuco

Below right: Browned veal

Osso con Midollo Arrosto

Roasted Bone Marrow

Roasted marrow bones are nothing short of pure decadence. Once relegated to the trash bin, or perhaps fertilizer processing plants, beef bones are making a comeback as a delicacy among a variety of cuisines. Because marrow is predominantly composed of mono-unsaturated fats, it has a delicate, soft, buttery consistency, which is why it is typically served with plenty of crusty Italian bread (and a good Italian red wine). The preparation of roasted marrow bone should be kept simple in order to highlight the subtle flavor of the marrow; just a bit of seasoning and a sufficient amount of salt is all that's needed.

Ingredients (Serves 2 as an appetizer)

8 pieces of beef marrow bones, cut crosswise, not larger than 2" in length (see note)

1 clove garlic

A few sprigs of parsley

Several capers in vinegar

Coarse sea salt

Coarse ground black pepper

Directions

1. Preheat oven to 450°F
2. Chop parsley, garlic and capers together
3. Arrange marrow bones in a shallow baking tray and scatter chopped ingredients over the top
4. Sprinkle with black pepper to taste, and a generous amount of sea salt
5. Roast for 15 minutes until the marrow begins to bubble and caramelize
6. Serve with crusty Italian bread, either plain or rubbed with garlic and oil and lightly grilled or oven-toasted

Note: The best marrow bones for roasting are from the femurs of beef cattle (see illustration), as they contain the greatest amount of marrow. Marrow bones can be cut crosswise, as shown here, or lengthwise so that the bone provides kind of a "trough" in which the marrow sits. Both versions work fine for this recipe. I think the crosscut bones are more readily available, but don't get them too big - it will be harder to scoop out the marrow. That, of course, is not an issue if you go with the lengthwise cut, but you might have get a butcher to cut them for you.

Bone marrow - a primal source of nutrition:

There's a reason why dogs love bones so much - pure instinct handed down from their Paleolithic ancestors. It's not the bone, per say, but the prized marrow that helped sustain carnivores near the top of the food chain, particularly when prey was hard to come by. Fat provides about twice the calories per unit weight than does protein. Predators feasting on prey target the high-fat organs first, in order to maximize their caloric intake and help preserve precious metabolic resources that would otherwise be spent on chewing and digesting protein-dense material. Even vultures have figured out that dropping bones from great heights will crack them open to reveal the cherished contents.

While high-fat diets might be great for predators in the wild, it's not necessarily the best thing for us modern-day humans. A 4-oz serving of beef bone marrow packs about 500 calories - almost all from fat - so, enjoy in moderation. Oh, and the hollowed out bones make great treats for your dog.

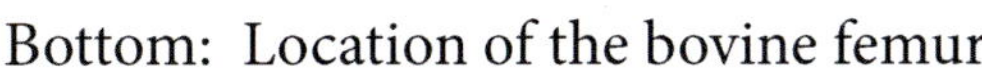

Right: Osso con midollo arrosto
Below: Fresh bone segments with marrow
Bottom: Location of the bovine femur

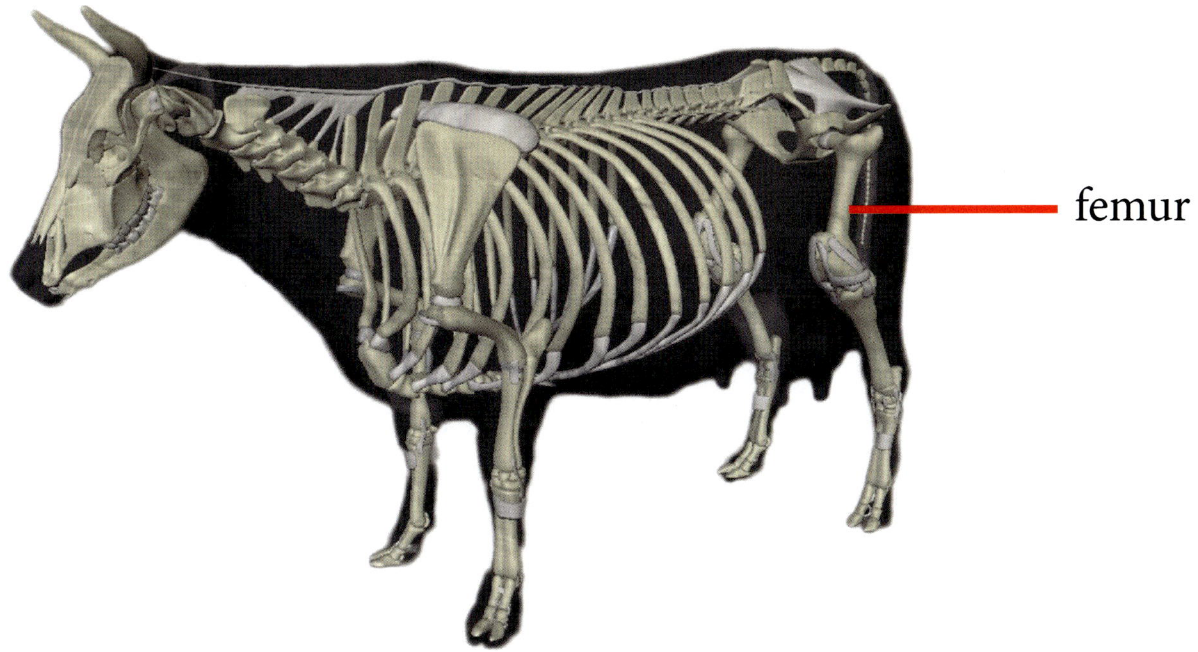

Stracotto

Italian Pot Roast

Stracotto, literally translated, means "overcooked" but in general use, it's "pot roast." As with so many Italian dishes, there are regional variations of stracotto, each more or less reflecting the subtle differences in local cuisine and availability of fresh, local ingredients. Stracotto is not very different from American-style pot roast; the key difference being that stracotto incorporates a red wine and tomato-based sauce instead of a brown beef gravy.

Ingredients (Serves 6)

1 (4-pound) boneless chuck roast

3 T olive oil

12 or so cipolline onions, peeled and left whole

2 cloves garlic, chopped

3 carrots, cut into 1-2" pieces

1 cup hearty red wine (like Nero d'Avola)

2 cups fresh, ripe plum tomatoes, chopped, or 16 oz jarred San Marzano tomatoes

6 fresh basil leaves, chopped

1/2 t dried oregano

Coarse ground black pepper and sea salt to taste

Directions

1. Preheat oven to 325°F.
2. In a covered roasting pan large enough to hold the meat and vegetables, salt and pepper the chuck roast and brown in 2 T of the olive oil. Remove the browned meat from the pan and set aside.
3. Add the remaining 1 T of olive oil to the pan and brown the onion and carrots.
4. Add the garlic and sauté for 30 seconds.
5. Add the wine to deglaze pan; remove vegetables and set aside.
6. Return the meat to the pan and arrange the vegetables around the meat.
7. Add the chopped tomatoes on top of the vegetables.
8. Scatter the oregano and basil over the meat and vegetables.
9. Cover and roast for about 3 hrs.
10. Remove the meat to a serving platter and surround with the vegetables.
11. Using an immersion blender, puree the tomatoes in the pan juices to make a sauce.
12. Slice the roast in the serving platter and top with the sauce.

Note: My kids like potatoes with pot roast, so I sometimes also add quartered, peeled potatoes along with the vegetables.

Opposite:

Top: Stracotto ready to serve

Middle left: Cipolline onions from my garden

Middle right: Beef chuck roast ready for browning

Bottom left: Browned beef chuck roast

Bottom right: Onions and carrots browning

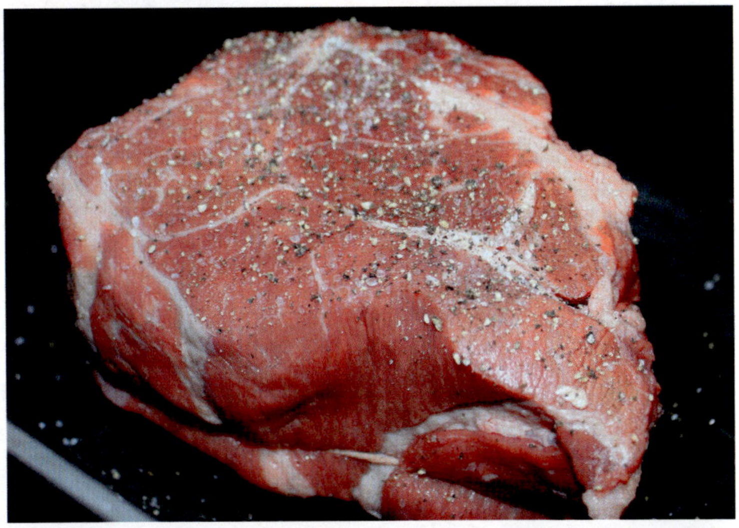

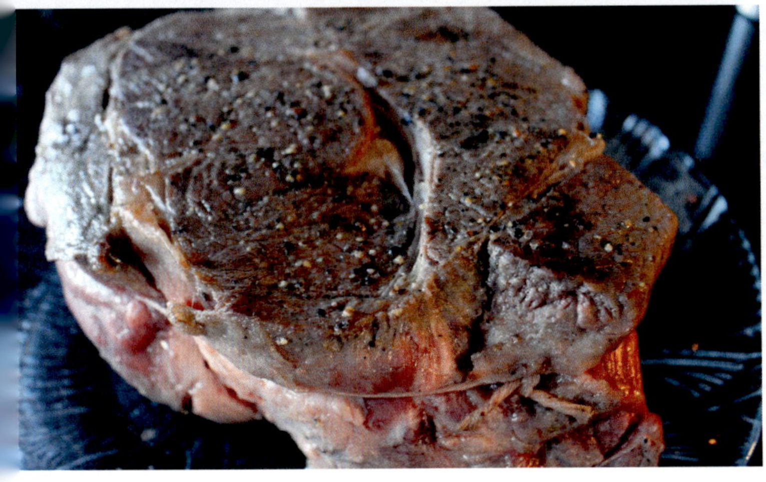

Fegato e Cipolle

Liver and Onions

Liver is one under-appreciated piece of meat. True, it contains a higher amount of cholesterol per serving than other cuts of beef, but it also packs impressive amounts of protein, vitamins and essential minerals (iron in particular); plus it is lower in total fat than most other cuts of beef. I find that there is no middle ground when it comes to liver - either you love it or hate it - and a good number in the latter camp (including my daughters) haven't even tried it!

This family recipe is my favorite way to prepare liver. You'll convert liver "haters" into "lovers" by keeping in mind a few key considerations. Firstly, choose calves' liver instead of "beef" liver. Calves' liver is much more pale in color (see photo) because of lower amounts of stored iron. This also gives calves' liver a much more delicate flavor than beef liver, without the heavy "mineral" taste that many find displeasing. Second, get a good outer "crust" on your liver. This is accomplished by a coating of flour and then frying at medium/high temperature in a non-stick pan, without moving the pieces in the pan until they are ready to be turned. Lastly...good balsamic vinegar - it totally makes the dish!

Ingredients (Serves 6)

- 6 pieces of calves liver, 1/4" - 1/2" thick
- 4-5 onions, sliced thin
- 1/2 lb pancetta, sliced thin and coarsely chopped
- Olive oil for frying
- 4 cups flour for dredging
- 1/2 cup dry white wine
- 1/3 cup balsamic vinegar
- Salt and coarse ground black pepper to taste

Directions

1. Place 2 T olive oil in a frying pan and brown pancetta. Remove pancetta from pan and set aside.
2. Add an additional 2 T olive oil to the pan along with the onions, salt and pepper and cook until the onions just start to caramelize. Remove onions from pan and set aside.
3. Place flour in a shallow tray and season with salt and pepper.
4. Add an additional 2 T olive oil to the pan and bring heat to medium high. Working with a few pieces of liver at a time, dredge the liver in the flour and place in pan, leaving undisturbed until well-browned on one side - about 2 minutes. Turn pieces over and brown other side. Remove from pan and repeat with remaining pieces.
5. With all the liver fried and removed from the pan, add back the onions and pancetta to the pan and the white wine; cook for 1 minute, scraping up browned bits from the pan.
6. Add the vinegar and cook for an additional minute.
7. Arrange the liver in a serving platter and top with the onion and pancetta mixture. Serve immediately. The liver should be cooked throughout but not dry.

Clockwise from top:

Fegato e cipolle

Raw calves' liver

Onions caramelizing

Liver browning in the frying pan on an outdoor propane burner

Opposite: Shaved pancetta

Polpettone

Meatloaf

When one thinks of Italian cuisine, meatloaf probably isn't the first thing that pops into mind. Italians do, however, make meatloaf, or *polpettone*. There are probably as many variations of polpettone as there are American meatloaf recipes, but most have the basics in common - some combination of ground meat, mixed with other "stuff" and then baked.

Truth is, I wasn't even going to include this recipe in this book, but so many people have asked me, "do you have a good recipe for meatloaf," that I felt compelled to include it. After decades of experimentation (see note), this is my "go to" meatloaf recipe. The key is the glaze and pancetta wrap, which impart a really nice flavor and textural element to the polpettone.

Ingredients (Serves 8)

2 lbs ground beef (75% lean)

1 lb ground pork

1 T olive oil

1 medium stalk celery, chopped

1 small onion, chopped

1 clove garlic, finely chopped

Several sprigs of parsley, chopped

3 eggs

1 cup bread crumbs

1/2 t dried oregano

1/2 t thyme

2 t salt

1 t coarse black pepper

Approximately 8 thin slices of pancetta

For the glaze:

3 T tomato paste

3 T balsamic vinegar

1 T Worcestershire sauce

1 T honey

1/2 t crushed red pepper

Directions

1. First, make the glaze and set aside.
2. Add oil to a frying pan and sauté celery and onion for 2 minutes.
3. Add garlic and sauté an additional 30 seconds; remove from heat and set aside to cool.
4. In a large bowl, mix together ground beef and pork.
5. Add the eggs, parsley, oregano, thyme, cooled onion and celery, half of the prepared glaze, salt and pepper, and mix well.
6. Sprinkle the breadcrumbs over the meat mixture and mix in.
7. Transfer to a shallow roasting pan (see photo) and shape into a loaf; it should be about a foot long and 4 or 5 inches wide.
8. Coat the loaf generously with the remaining glaze .
9. Cover the glazed loaf with pancetta slices, overlapping as necessary to completely cover the meat.
10. Preheat oven to 350°F and bake polpettone, uncovered, for 50 to 60 minutes, until the exterior is nicely browned and internal temperature reaches 165°F.
11. Remove from oven and let rest for 15 minutes before slicing and serving.

Note: You can serve the polpettone "as is" or prepare your favorite brown gravy from the pan drippings.

Above: Polpettone ready to serve
Right: Polpettone ready for the oven

Note: The favorite meal of my college house mate, Leo, was meatloaf and mashed potatoes. I have known Leo now for 40 years; he's still my best friend and still considers meatloaf his favorite meal - go figure. Anyway, I've been tinkering with this recipe for the entire 40 years, beginning with mom's recipe as a starting point. What I've learned is the following, (i) the beef-to-pork ratio should be 2:1, (ii) lean beef makes a dry meatloaf; 75-80% lean is the key, (iii) the addition of ketchup just doesn't cut it for me; might as well have a hamburger. The glaze that I've landed on gives just the right amount of tangy tomato flavor, with a faint background of heat and sweetness. Mixing some of the glaze into the meat mixture is a must, and (iv) the pancetta wrap is transformational; it bastes the polpettone as it cooks, keeping it nice and moist. Plus it adds great flavor and an outer "crust" that really makes the dish. You can wrap an old shoe in pancetta and it would taste good!

Saltimbocca alla Romana

Veal Cutlets with Prosciutto and Sage

The classic saltimbocca alla Romana is one of my favorite dishes. Unfortunately, my kids have a strange aversion to veal, so for them, I make chicken saltimbocca (page 157); for me, it's veal!

The classic preparation method for this dish is to attach a whole sage leaf to each cutlet with a toothpick, prior to frying. I've landed on a different approach, using chopped sage leaves instead - it's much easier and I think it better distributes the sage flavor throughout the dish. Plus, by pounding the prosciutto into the cutlet prior to flouring, the prosciutto stays firmly attached during the browning process, eliminating the need for a toothpick altogether.

Ingredients (Serves 6)

4 lbs veal top round cutlets

Extra virgin olive oil

Butter

Approximately 8 oz prosciutto

Approximately 3 T coarsely chopped fresh sage

All-purpose flour for dusting

1/2 t coarse ground black pepper

Grated Pecorino Romano cheese

1/2 cup white wine for deglazing

1/2 cup chicken stock

Directions

1. Pound veal cutlets to approximately 1/4 in thickness.
2. Cover each cutlet with a single layer of prosciutto and pound into veal using the coarse, textured surface of the meat mallet.
3. Heat 2 T olive oil,1 T butter and 1 T sage leaves in a large frying pan.
4. Lightly dredge the veal cutlets in flour and place, prosciutto side down, in the frying pan and brown for 1 minute. Turn over and cook several minutes until nicely browned. Remove to a warm platter. Repeat with the remaining cutlets, adding more oil, butter and sage, as needed.
5. Deglaze the pan with wine and reduce to half.
6. Add chicken stock and simmer 2 minutes.
7. Return the veal to the pan to heat throughout.
8. Serve veal, topped with pan sauce and a sprinkle of grated Pecorino Romano.

Above: Saltimbocca alla Romana
Right: Thinly pounded veal led cutlets

Costolette di Vitello alla Griglia

Grilled Veal Rib Chops

Veal chops are one of my favorite cuts of meat, and grilling is my preferred method for preparing them. Unfortunately, they are also among the most expensive cuts of meat, so I take great care in getting them just right. Veal has a much more delicate flavor than does beef, so the seasonings shouldn't be over-powering. Also, unlike beef, under-cooking veal to any temperature under medium results in a rather unappealing bite.

This family recipe is similar to the classic Tuscan-style grilled veal chops, which utilizes a variety of aromatic herbs to compliment the subtle flavor of veal. The addition of lemon - always a nice pairing with veal - really makes this dish.

Ingredients (Serves 4)

4 fresh veal rib chops, at least 1" thick (the chops shown at right are about 20 oz each)

1/2 cup extra virgin olive oil

Juice and zest of 1 lemon, saving a few slices for garnish

4 cloves garlic, chopped

Several sprigs of fresh thyme, chopped, about 1 T

Fresh oregano, chopped, about 1 t

1 cup dry white wine

Salt and coarse ground black pepper to taste

Directions

1. Whisk together olive oil, lemon, garlic, herbs and salt & pepper. Divide mixture in half, reserving one half for final basting. Add the other half to the wine to make the marinade.
2. Place veal chops in a shallow bowl and cover with marinade. Marinate for at least 2 hrs in the refrigerator.
3. Grill chops over high heat, turning once, until the internal temperature reaches bout 155ºC. Upon resting, the chops will reach an internal temperature of 160ºC, a perfect medium. You want the high heat to create a nice surface char on the meat (see photo).
4. While chops are resting, baste with the remaining oil/lemon mixture, and serve hot. Garnish with the grilled lemon slices.

Opposite top: Perfect cuts of fresh veal chops
Opposite bottom: Costolette di vitello alla griglia
Left: Marinating veal chops

Stufato di Manzo

Italian Beef Stew

I think every culture, with the possible exception of Chinese Buddhists, has a version of beef stew. Variations of this stew can be found across the regions Italy, primarily due to the preference for local ingredients. This family recipe originates from southern Italy, where the tomato reigns supreme. Consequently, the base has a lot more tomato than, say, a northern Italian beef stew might have. Of course, one must include a nice, southern Italian red wine; my preference is a Sicilian Nero d'Avola but other similar varieties would work.

There isn't a winter that goes by in my home that I don't make this hearty stew several times a month. It's my go-to, wintertime, comfort food.

Ingredients (Serves 6)

2 lbs beef chuck

1/4 cup plus 2 T Extra virgin olive oil

2 cups Nero d'Avola

1 qt jarred San Marzano tomatoes (or substitute 28 oz can of imported peeled tomatoes)

2 carrots, cut into 1" pieces

2 potatoes, peeled and cut into 1" pieces

2 or 3 cipollini onions, peeled and coarsely chopped

1 1/2 cups frozen peas

4 bay leaves

1 t dried oregano

1 clove garlic, chopped

Several sprigs of fresh thyme, chopped

1/2 t crushed red pepper flakes

Salt and coarse ground pepper to taste

Directions

1. Cube beef chuck into pieces of about 1 1/2".
2. Place beef in a bowl with 2 T olive oil, the red wine, chopped garlic, thyme, oregano, bay leaves and about 1/2 t each of salt and black pepper. Cover and marinate for at least 2 hrs in the refrigerator.
3. Place the 1/4 cup olive oil in a soup pot large enough to hold all ingredients and bring to medium heat. Working with a few pieces of beef at a time, remove from marinade, pat dry and brown in the oil. Remove with a slotted spoon to a separate bowl and repeat with the remaining beef, reserving the marinade.
4. Add the carrots and onions to the pot and brown, adding extra olive oil if necessary.
5. Transfer the browned beef back to the pot. Discard the bay leaves and add the remaining marinade to the pot.
6. Add the tomatoes, crushed red pepper, and salt and pepper to taste. Cover and cook on medium low heat for about 1 hr.
7. Add the potatoes and peas and continue cooking until the potatoes are fork tender, about another 20 minutes.
8. Adjust final seasonings and serve hot with crusty Italian bread and a drizzle of extra virgin olive oil (optional). I always top my bowl with a little extra red pepper, too!

Above: Stufato di manzo

Right: A row of cipollini onions in my garden; these onions are flavorful and versatile, and store well over winter

Below: Marinating beef chuck

Poultry

• Paella Italiana •
Italian Style Paella

• Pollo alla Stemperata •
Chicken Stemperata

• Pollo al Cacciatore •
Chicken "Hunter" Style

• Piccata di Pollo •
Chicken Piccata

• Tacchino al Marsala •
Turkey Marsala

• Pollo nel Forno alla Gremolata •
Oven-Roasted Chicken in Gremolata Sauce

• Saltimbocca di Pollo •
Chicken Saltimbocca

• Parmigiana di Pollo •
Chicken Parmesan

Paella all'Italiana

Italian Style Paella

Paella is so good that it SHOULD be Italian! I love a great Spanish paella, especially the authentic version from Valencia. This family recipe, however, substitutes some traditional Italian ingredients in place of the typical Spanish elements to produce an Italian version of the Spanish classic.

Homemade sweet and hot Italian sausage combine with Palazzolo peppers, Trionfo Violetto beans, and carnaroli rice to produce *paella all'Italiana*, my family's version of Spanish paella.

Ingredients (Serves 8)

3 lbs of chicken (bone in), cut up*

3 links Italian sweet sausage (approx 1 lb)

3 links Italian hot sausage (approx 1 lb)

4 cups carnaroli rice

8 cups good quality chicken stock

1 cup dry white wine

A generous pinch of Spanish saffron

4 Palazzolo peppers (or substitute 2 Italian frying peppers) cut into 1" pieces

1 cup coarsely chopped onion

2 cloves garlic, chopped

6 T olive oil

2 cups purple Italian beans, cut into 2" lengths

1 cup petite peas

Salt and pepper

*Breast halves should be cut in half again. Omit wings.

Directions

1. Heat 4 T olive in a large frying pan, sprinkle chicken with salt and pepper and brown, a few pieces at a time – don't over-crowd pan. Remove chicken and set aside. Note: chicken is not fully cooked at this point.
2. Add the sausage and brown. Remove from pan and set aside.
3. Add the onion, peppers and beans and lightly brown; the beans will turn green upon cooking. Add garlic and cook another 30 seconds.
4. Add the remaining 2T olive oil and the rice, stirring to coat the rice.
5. Add the wine to deglaze the pan.
6. When the wine has evaporated, reduce heat to medium low and add about 2 cups of stock and the saffron; stir well to distribute the saffron.
7. Arrange the chicken pieces and sliced sausage over the rice, pushing them into the rice, while keeping the rice at the bottom of the pan.
8. Scatter the peas over the pan.
9. Cover loosely with aluminum foil to allow the rice to absorb the stock, adding additional stock until all has been absorbed and the rice is cooked *al dente*, approximately 40 minutes.
10. Serve with lemon wedges, which should be squeezed over the dish upon serving.

Note: I use a 22" carbon steel paella pan for this recipe, and I typically cook the paella outdoors over a single propane burner on a sturdy stand large enough to hold the paella pan. If you have a grill that has a compartment for smoking wood chips, a nice touch is to expose the finished paella to some smoked hickory for 5 minutes or so before serving

Top: Paella all'Italiana
Above left: Homemade sweet and hot sausage (I always make extra for sandwiches)
Above middle: Home grown Trionfo Violetto beans
Above right: Imported carnaroli rice

Pollo alla Stemperata

Chicken Stemperata

Stemperata (or *stimpirata*; Sicilian) is a traditional, southern Italian dish. Though there are subtle regional variations in the preparation, the common theme is a sweet and sour (or *agrodolce*) undertone, which is typically achieved by combining good quality balsamic vinegar with a "sweet" component like honey, golden raisins, or even sugar (yuk – don't do that).

This recipe comes from my mother-in-law's family whose roots are in Palazzolo, Sicily. The agrodolce comes from the combination of balsamic vinegar and fresh mint leaves. Stemperata is traditionally done with rabbit (*cunigghiu a' stimpirata*, in the Sicilian dialect), which is my personal favorite. Unfortunately, that doesn't go over so well with my kids, so chicken it is. Frying, followed by low temperature braising is the ideal method for preparing this dish.

Ingredients (Serves 6)

4 lbs of chicken (bone in), cut up

4 T extra virgin olive oil

Sicilian green olives (16-20), cracked (or substitute pitted olives)

2 T capers in vinegar

2 carrots chopped

1 stalk celery chopped

1 medium onion, sliced

1 clove garlic, minced

1 cup fresh chopped mint leaves

3 T balsamic vinegar

1/2 c dry red wine

Salt and coarse ground black pepper to taste

Directions

1. Heat olive in a large frying pan and brown chicken pieces, a few at a time – don't over-crowd pan. Remove chicken and set aside. Note: chicken is not fully cooked at this point – merely browned (see photo).
2. Add carrots and celery to pan and sauté 1-2 minutes
3. Add onions and sauté an additional 2 minutes, until they begin to pick up some color.
4. Add garlic, olives and capers and sauté an additional minute.
5. Add wine to deglaze pan and cook until evaporated.
6. Reduce heat to low, return chicken to pan, add remaining ingredients, cover and simmer for 45 minutes to 1 hr.
7. Transfer chicken to a serving platter, top with pan ingredients, drizzle with additional olive oil (optional) and serve.

Above: Pollo alla Stemperata
Right: Fresh mint in my garden
Below: Browning chicken pieces

Pollo al Cacciatore

Chicken "Hunter" Style

Pollo alla cacciatore is another dish that calls for slow braising. This is my mother's recipe, which I much prefer over any other that I have tried. Note that the chicken isn't "swimming" in tomato sauce, which is too often the case in other recipes. Rather, the "sauce" comes primarily from the breakdown of the peppers and onions during the braising process, with just enough crushed San Marzano tomatoes to add flavor and color. The end result is chicken that falls right off the bone with that characteristic "peppers and onions" flavor that is the hallmark of this classic rustic dish.

Cacciatore is "hunter" in Italian. It is thought that the dish originally rose from the need for hunters to eat while out on a long hunt. They would prepare a stew with whatever small game they came across (probably rabbit) and other vegetables and herbs that are abundant in the forest (mushrooms, wild onions, etc). Most likely, tomatoes were not part of the original recipe, unless of course they thought to bring some along (not totally out of the question)!

Ingredients (Serves 6)

4 lbs of bone-in chicken breasts and thighs (breasts halves should be cut in half again), skin left on

4T olive oil

1 medium onion, chopped

1 large Italian frying pepper, chopped

2 cloves garlic, chopped

1/2 cup white wine

4 vine-ripened San Marzano tomatoes, crushed (or substitute 1 14-oz can of imported Italian tomatoes

1 t chopped fresh oregano

Salt and pepper to taste

Directions

1. Heat olive oil over medium heat in a large frying pan.
2. Sprinkle chicken pieces with salt and pepper and brown in oil, a few pieces at a time so as not to over-crowd pan. Remove browned chicken and set aside. Note that chicken is not fully cooked at this point, merely browned (see photo).
3. In the same pan, add peppers and onions, oregano, another sprinkle of salt and pepper, and cook until onions are softened. Add garlic and cook another 30 seconds.
4. Add wine to deglaze pan.
5. Add tomatoes.
6. Return chicken to the pan, toss to coat in the sauce, cover and simmer on low for 45 minutes to 1 hr, turning chicken occasionally. The dish is done when the vegetables have broken down, forming a sauce.

Above: Pollo alla Cacciatore
Right: Chicken browning
Below left: Fresh Italian oregano in my garden
Below right: Softening the peppers and onions

Piccata di Pollo

Chicken Piccata

Piccata di pollo is a "go to" dish in my house - it's quick, delicious and (almost) everyone loves chicken! This is another dish that, in Italy, is much more commonly prepared with veal (*piccata di vitello*, or *scaloppine al limone*), but - again - veal doesn't go over well with my kids, so "pollo" it is. You can't stray too far from the classic recipe and still call it "piccata." A kick of fresh thyme, however, really compliments the lemon and butter flavor combination.

Leftover chicken piccata can be chopped and transformed into a fantastic chicken salad with the addition of some chopped fennel bulb in place of celery, thinly sliced scallions and some mayo.

Ingredients (Serves 6)

3 lbs boneless, skinless chicken breast cutlets, sliced in half (see photo) and pounded to less than 1/2 inch thick

Flour for dredging

Sea salt and coarse ground pepper to taste

5 T butter

2 T olive oil

1 clove garlic, chopped

1/2 cup dry white wine

Juice and zest of 1 lemon, reserving a few lemon slices for garnish

1 t fresh thyme, chopped

2 T petite capers

Fresh parsley, chopped for garnish

Directions

1. Add 2 T butter and 1 T olive oil to a large frying pan. Lightly season flour with salt and pepper, dredge chicken in flour and shake off excess. Cook chicken over medium heat, a couple of pieces at a time, until browned on both sides - approximately 3 minutes per side. Remove from pan and set aside.
2. Add 1 more T butter and 1/2 T olive oil to pan. Repeat until the remaining chicken is cooked, reserving 1 T of butter.
3. Add the garlic to the pan and cook until aromatic, just a few seconds.
4. Add the wine, capers and thyme, scraping up any bits of browned chicken.
5. Add the lemon juice and zest to the pan, along with salt and pepper to taste.
6. Return the browned chicken to the pan, cover and simmer for 5 minutes.
7. Transfer the chicken to a platter, top with pan juices and garnish with lemon slices and fresh parsley.

Above: Piccata di Pollo

Right: Slicing chicken breasts

Below right: Pounding breasts to the proper thickness

Below left: Lemon and capers

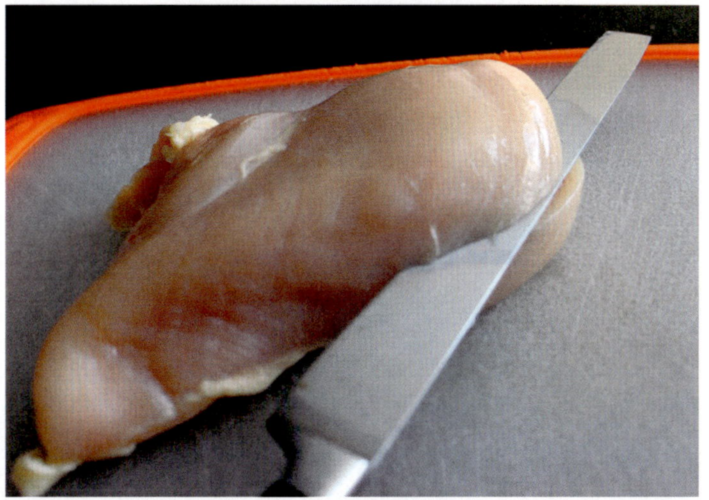

Tacchino al Marsala

Turkey Marsala

Tacchino al Marsala is the "feathered" version of the classic veal marsala. My youngest daughter can't bring herself to eat veal, because they're "too cute." Turkeys, on the other hand, are apparently ugly enough to make it to the dinner table - go figure. Anyway...though my personal preference is for veal, turkey actually pairs really well with the sweetness of marsala wine and the earthiness of cremini mushrooms.

I've actually prepared Tacchino al Marsala for Thanksgiving dinner on occasion, in place of the traditional roast turkey. It's much more flavorful, ready in minutes, no carving necessary, easily customizable to the number of dinner guests, no bickering over who gets which turkey parts, and best of all - easy clean up!

Ingredients (Serves 6)

3 lbs turkey breast cutlets, pounded to about 1/4 inch thick

Flour for dredging

Sea salt and coarse ground pepper to taste

16 oz cremini mushrooms, cleaned and sliced

4 -6 T butter

2-3 T olive oil

2 cloves garlic, chopped

1 cup sweet Marsala wine

1/2 t fresh rosemary, chopped

1/2 cup turkey stock (preferably homemade)

Directions

1. Heat 2 T butter and 1 T olive oil in a pan. Add the mushrooms and garlic. Lightly season with salt and pepper and cook, uncovered, over medium heat until the liquid from the mushrooms evaporates and mushrooms begin to brown. Remove from pan and set aside.
2. Add 2 more T butter and 1 T olive oil to the pan. Lightly season flour with salt and pepper, dredge turkey cutlets and cook them, a couple of pieces at a time until browned on both sides - approximately 2 minutes per side. Remove from pan and set aside.
3. Repeat with remaining cutlets, adding more butter and oil, as needed.
4. Add the Marsala wine, turkey stock and rosemary back to the pan, scraping browned bits off of the bottom of the pan. Bring to a boil and cook until liquid is reduced by about a third, approximately 5 minutes.
5. Return the turkey and mushrooms to the pan to reheat.
6. Transfer the turkey to a serving platter and top with mushrooms and pan sauce.

Above: Tacchino al Marsala

Right: Turkey cutlets pounded to the correct thickness

Below: Sautéing mushrooms

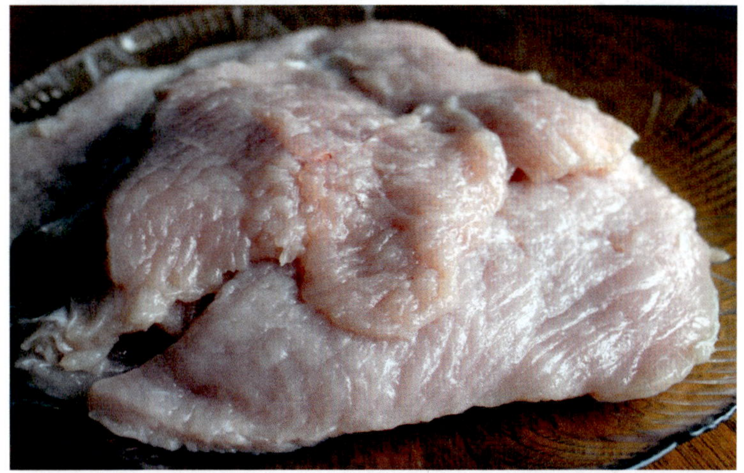

Pollo nel Forno alla Gremolata

Oven Roasted Chicken Gremolata

Gremolata has to be one of my favorite condiments - you can put it on just about anything, but there might be nothing better than combining it with oven roasted chicken. The aroma of this dish roasting in the oven brings me back to my childhood even to this day. I swear I could smell it halfway down the block as a kid! In those days, back in NY, we had access to a local poultry farm where my mother was able to get freshly butchered poultry of all kinds. Unfortunately, I no longer live near a poultry farm, but I do grow my own parsley and garlic!

The dish is simple to prepare; relatively few ingredients and requires almost no attention during the cooking process. As always, be sure to use the freshest ingredients possible.

Ingredients (Serves 8)

Approximately 6 lb chicken cut up (thighs, legs and breast - breast halves should be cut in half again)

For the gremolata:

1 bunch fresh parsley

6 cloves garlic, chopped

2 lemons

1 cup extra virgin olive oil

1/2 t salt

1/2 t coarse ground black pepper

Directions

1. Chop parsley to produce 2 cups and place in a bowl
2. Add chopped garlic
3. Cut lemons in half and add the juice and zest from 1 1/2 (reserve 1/2 lemon for garnish.
4. Add salt, pepper and olive oil. Mix well and let stand at room temperature for 30 minutes for the flavors to meld.
5. Place cut up chicken in a large bowl and mix in about half of the gremolata, reserving the rest for serving. Place chicken in the refrigerator and marinate for at least 1 hr.
6. Preheat oven to 375ºF
7. Spread chicken on a shallow roasting pan large enough to accommodate all the pieces without crowding
8. Thinly slice the remaining 1/2 lemon and scatter on top of chicken (see photo)
9. Roast chicken, uncovered, until internal temperature of the largest piece reaches 165ºF, approximately 1 hr.
10. Serve with the remaining gremolata

Above: pollo nel forno alla gremolata
Right: chicken ready for oven roasting
Below: freshly prepared gremolata

Saltimbocca di Pollo

Chicken Saltimbocca

The classic saltimbocca alla Romana, of course, is made with veal - one of my favorite dishes. Unfortunately, my kids have a strange aversion to veal, so - on occasion - I substitute chicken for veal. The other change I made was to used chopped sage leaves instead of the classic method of attaching whole sage leaves to each piece of meat with toothpicks - it's easier and I think it better distributes the sage flavor throughout the dish.

Saltimbocca literally translates to "jump in the mouth," a reference to how incredibly tasty this dish is - even with chicken ;)

Ingredients (Serves 6)

4 lbs boneless chicken breast, sliced and pounded to approximately 1/4" thick

Extra virgin olive oil

Butter

Approximately 8 oz prosciutto

Approximately 2 T coarsely chopped fresh sage

All-purpose flour for dusting

1/2 t coarse ground black pepper

Grated Pecorino Romano cheese

1/2 cup white wine for deglazing

1/2 cup chicken stock

Directions

1. Cover each piece of chicken with a single layer of prosciutto and pound into the meat using the coarse, textured surface of the meat mallet.
2. Heat 2 T olive oil,1 T butter and 1 T sage leaves in a large frying pan.
3. Lightly dredge the chicken pieces in flour and place, prosciutto side down, in the frying pan and brown for 1 minute. Turn over and cook several minutes until nicely browned. Remove to a warm platter. Repeat with the remaining chicken, adding more oil, butter and sage, as needed.
4. Deglaze the pan with wine and reduce to half.
5. Add chicken stock and simmer 2 minutes.
6. Return the chicken to the pan to heat throughout.
7. Serve chicken, topped with pan sauce and a sprinkle of grated Pecorino Romano.

Above: Saltimbocca di pollo
Below left: Fresh sage starting out in the Spring
Below right: Prosciutto do Parma

Parmigiana di Pollo
Chicken Parmigiana

When Italians think of "parmigiana," it is assumed to be the classic eggplant dish from Southern Italy. *Chicken* parmigiana is more of an Italian-American creation, thought to have appeared following the immigration of Italians to the U.S. Whatever the origin, I'm eternally grateful to whoever invented what has come to be revered by many as the ultimate comfort food - lightly breaded chicken cutlets, smothered in marinara sauce and melted mozzerella cheese!

Most commonly, one would see this dish presented as individual chicken cutlets topped with sauce and cheese. That's OK (I guess), but this family recipe calls for layers of thinly sliced cutlets, fried and then baked in a casserole, more along the lines of an eggplant parmigiana. I think this method makes for a much more flavorful dish; the chicken ends up extremely moist and fork-tender.

Ingredients (Serves 8)

Approximately 6 lbs boneless, skinless chicken breast, sliced and gently pounded to approximately 1/4" thick.

4 cups flour, seasoned with salt and pepper

4 eggs, beaten

2-3 cups Italian-flavored breadcrumbs

Olive oil for frying

Approximately 4 cups good quality marinara sauce (preferably homemade)

1 lb whole milk, *low moisture* mozzerella cheese (not fresh mozzerella), sliced thinly.

Approximately 1/4 cup grated Parmesan Reggiano cheese

Directions

1. Prepare the "breading" station by laying out a shallow dish of the seasoned flour, a bowl of the beaten eggs, and another shallow dish of breadcrumbs.
2. Add about 1/4 cup olive oil to a large frying pan and bring to medium heat.
3. Working in batches, lightly dust the chicken in flour, then dip in egg, allowing the excess drip off. Place the chicken in the breadcrumbs, and lightly coat both sides.
4. Immediately place the breaded cutlet in the oil and lightly brown both sides. You may work with a few pieces at a time, depending on the size of your frying pan. Don't over-crowd the pan. Remove cutlets to a separate dish with a few layers of paper towel to drain excess oil. Repeat until all the cutlets are browned, adding more olive oil to the pan, as needed.
5. Add a little marinara sauce to coat the bottom of a 2" deep baking tray, and then arrange layers of the chicken, mozzerella cheese, marinara sauce and grated Parmesan. Use just enough sauce to coat the top of each cheese-covered cutlet (you don't want the chicken to "swim" in sauce). I've used as few as 2 layers and as many as 4, depending on the size of the baking tray; end with sauce-coated mozzerella cheese on top.
6. Preheat oven to 400ºF, cover tray loosely with aluminum foil and bake until the top layer of cheese is melted, about 30 minutes. Remove the foil and bake an additional 5-10 minutes to lightly brown the cheese.
7. Remove from oven and allow to "set" for about 15 minutes. You can serve the individual cutlets or, as I prefer, cut into the casserole and serve a portion containing all the layers.

Above: Bubbling hot parmigiana di pollo fresh from the oven
Right: Jenna enjoying some
Below: Breaded and fried chicken cutlets

Pork

• Porchetta •
Stuffed Boneless Pork Roast

• Cotolette di Maiale Ripieni •
Stuffed Pork Chops

• Salsicce con Peperoni e Cipolle •
Sausage with Peppers and Onions

• Cotolette alla Pizzaiola •
Pizza-Style Pork Chops

• Cotolette Impanata •
Breaded Pork Cutlets

• Cotenne •
Pork Skin Braciole

Porchetta

Stuffed Boneless Pork Roast

Porchetta is a very special dish for Italians; the translation to "boneless pork roast" just doesn't do it proper justice. Traditionally, porchetta refers to a whole suckling pig, stuffed with garlic and herbs, and slow roasted on a spit for many hours. The meat ends up insanely flavorful and tender and juicy due to the basting by the fat content of the pig; the skin turns into this crunchy, crackling goodness that's just indescribable. Nowadays, porchetta is more commonly prepared using a rolled whole pork belly instead of the entire pig. For my taste, however, the fat-to-meat ratio of a pork belly by itself is just a bit too high. This family recipe makes use of a pork belly wrapped around a butterflied pork loin. The result is a perfect marriage of meat, fat and skin that will make you think you've died and gone to heaven!

This is a roast that one would make for a special occasion, and for at least 12 people.

Ingredients (Serves 12)

1 whole pork belly, skin on (approximately 10-12 lbs)

1 boneless pork loin (approximately 3-4 lbs), trimmed to a length approximately equal to the width of the pork belly

1 large bunch of fresh parsley, chopped

8 cloves garlic, chopped

Several sprigs of fresh thyme, chopped

2 springs fresh rosemary, chopped

6 fresh sage leaves, chopped

2 sprigs fresh regano, chopped

Zest of 1 lemon

1/4 cup fennel seed

1 T whole black peppercorns

Sea salt to taste

2 T olive oil

Opposite top: Porchetta

Middle: Cuts in pork skin and butterflied pork loin on pork belly

Bottom: Coating with herb mixture and tied porchetta awaiting the oven

Directions

1. Lay the pork belly on a flat surface, skin side up. With a sharp knife, make a series of shallow cuts into the skin to form a diamond pattern (photo).
2. Turn the pork belly over and make another series of diamond-shaped cuts across the belly meat.
3. Butterfly the pork loin so that it lies flat (photo).
4. Toast the fennel seed and peppercorns in a skillet until they are aromatic. Coarsely grind them in a spice grinder.
5. Mix together the parsley, garlic, thyme, sage, rosemary, oregano and lemon zest in a large bowl. Add the fennel/peppercorn mix and season with sea salt.
6. Take about 2/3 of the herb mixture and spread it evenly on the meat side of the pork belly.
7. Lay the butterflied pork loin on the pork belly and cover with the remaining herb mixture.
8. Roll the pork loin onto itself and then roll the pork belly around the pork loin. Secure the porchetta with butcher's string, either by using a butcher's knot or with individual pieces of string placed about an inch apart, whichever is easier for you.
9. Refrigerate the porchetta, uncovered, for several hours or overnight. Allow to come to room temperature before roasting.
10. Preheat oven to 325ºF. Place the porchetta on a roasting rack inside a roasting pan and rub the skin with olive oil.
11. Roast the porchetta to an internal temperature of 145ºF, about 4 hrs, removing the foil in the final 30 minutes to further crisp the skin.
12. Allow porchetta to rest for 20 minutes before carving.

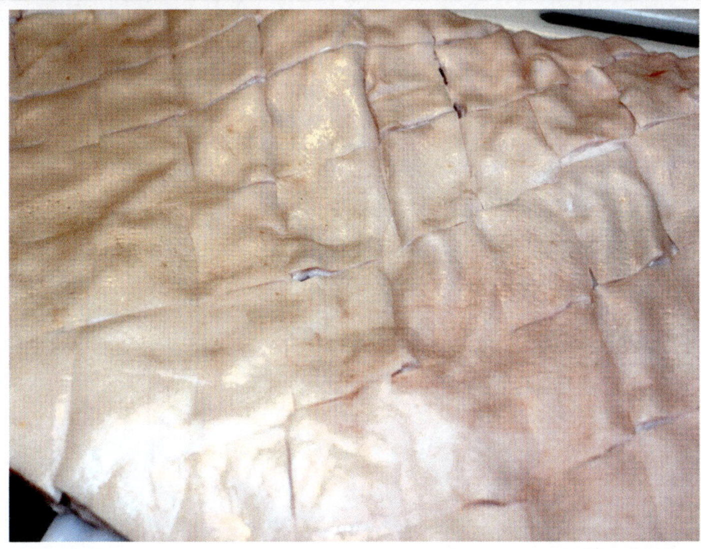

Cotolette di Maiale Ripieni

Stuffed Pork Chops

What could be better than pork stuffed with more pork? Wrap a few pieces of prosciutto around a chunk of mozzerella cheese and stuff it into a double-thickness pork chop for a meal that will satisfy even the hungriest of your family members.

These pork chops are first pan-fried in oil to produce a nice golden brown exterior and then finished in the oven.

Ingredients (Serves 4)

- 4 double thickness, bone-in, center cut pork chops
- 4 slices 1/4 inch thick, low-moisture, whole milk mozzerella cheese
- 8 slices Prosciutto di Parma
- Freshly ground nutmeg
- Salt and coarse ground black pepper to taste
- 4 t grated Pecorino Romano cheese
- 2 cups flour
- 3 large eggs, beaten
- 3 cups breadcrumbs
- Olive oil for frying

Directions

1. Prepare the stuffing contents for each pork chop by laying out 2 pieces of prosciutto and placing a piece of mozzerella cheese in the middle. Sprinkle each with 1 t Pecorino Romano and salt and pepper to taste. With a micro plane, grate a little nutmeg over each piece (see photo).
2. Wrap the prosciutto over the cheese to form a little bundle, which will be used to stuff the pork chops (one bundle for each pork chop).
3. With a sharp paring knife, make a deep pocket in each pork chop by cutting through the side, all the way to the bone. Make the cut only wide enough to accommodate the prosciutto and mozzerella bundle.
4. Stuff each pork chop with the prosciutto and mozzerella bundle, securing the opening closed with toothpicks.
5. Place the flour, eggs and breadcrumbs in three separate bowls.
6. Dredge the stuffed pork chops in the flour, then the eggs and then the breadcrumbs to coat evenly all around.
7. Preheat oven to 400ºF.
8. Fry the breaded and stuffed pork chops in olive oil to produce a golden brown exterior.
9. Transfer the browned pork chops to a baking dish and bake for about 30-40 minutes until the internal temperature of the thickest piece of meat near the bone reaches 145ºF.
10. Remove chops from oven and allow to rest for 10 minutes before serving.

Above: Cotolette di maiale ripieni

Right: Seasoned mozzerella and prosciutto before rolling up to form the stuffing bundle

Below: Center-cut pork chops with pocket for stuffing

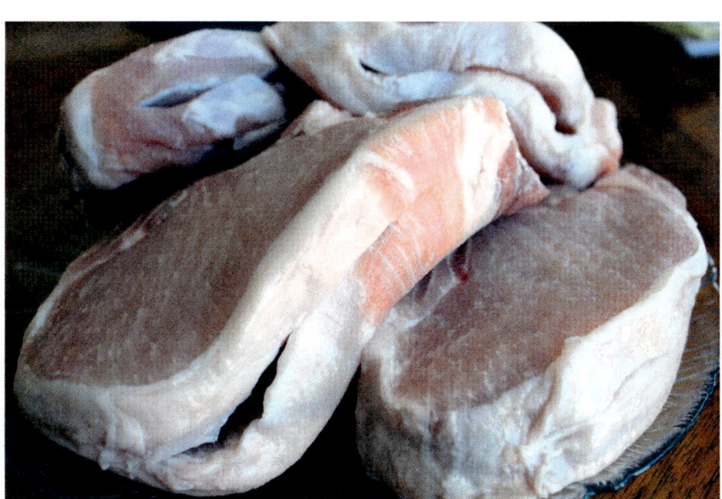

Salsicce con Peperoni e Cipolle

Sausage with Peppers and Onions

Sausage, peppers and onions - the Holy Trinity! Whether it be on an Italian sub roll or just on a big platter, the combination of sausage with peppers and onions is hard to beat for overall gastronomic gratification. Paired with an ice cold beer on a hot summer's day, this combo is nothing short of nirvana, and yet - it's astonishing how a dish with only three ingredients could have such a wide range of flavor and texture. It all comes down to quality of ingredients (as always). For me, the only way to go is homemade sausage (page 265), Palazzolo peppers (page 3) and large yellow onions - believe me, it's worth the extra effort. If you're not quite up to that task, at least seek out a good Italian butcher for your sausage, and instead of that green bell pepper, pick an Italian variety like Giant Marconi or Corno di Toro. I trust that finding a large yellow onion won't pose a problem!

Ingredients (Serves 4-6)

12 homemade sausage links; about 3 lbs

About 3 cups of prepared Palazzolo peppers (page 3) or substitute Italian-style frying peppers

About 3 cups of yellow onion, sliced

3 T olive oil

Directions

1. Grill sausage on a hot grill to get a bit of char,
2. Heat olive oil in a pan and fry onions until browned. If you don't have prepared Palazzolo peppers readily available (like that would ever happen n my house), you will have to slice and fry your peppers along with the onions.
3. In a large platter, mix together the sausage and however much of the pepper/onion mixture you'd like. You can add it all, or keep some on the side for folks to take as much as they'd like. If I'm serving the dish on a platter, I sometimes cut the sausage into 1-inch pieces. Otherwise, just leave them whole for ease of transfer to an Italian sub roll. Top with peppers and onions.

Opposite top: Salsicce con peperoni e cipolle

Opposite bottom: A bowl of fried Palazzolo peppers, just in case someone wants extra on their sub roll

Cotolette alla Pizzaiola

Pizza-Style Pork Chops

Pork chops alla pizzaiola is a quick and simple dish to prepare and a great way to make use of that leftover tomato sauce. Just about any type of meat can be prepared "*alla pizzaiola,*" which basically just means topping with tomato sauce and cheese - like a pizza - as the name would imply. I like to use pork and, in particular, bone-in, thick-cut pork chops, but feel free to use boneless chops, cutlets or even stuffed and rolled pork.

As mentioned above, I would typically use some of the leftover sauce from pasta to make pizzaiola, but a good quality jarred sauce can be used in a pinch (if you MUST). I go with the standard pizza topping of mozzerella cheese, a little provolone, a sprinkle of Pecorino Romano and dried oregano.

Ingredients (Serves 4)

4 bone-in, center cut pork chops, about 1 inch thick

2 T olive oil

1 clove garlic, chopped

About 2 cups prepared tomato sauce

4 oz of whole milk, low-moisture mozzerella, grated

1 oz provolone, grated

1 T Pecorino Romano, grated

1/2 t dried oregano

Salt and coarse ground black pepper to taste

Directions

1. Rub pork chops with 1 T olive oil and sprinkle with salt, pepper and oregano.
2. In a frying pan, sufficiently large to accommodate the 4 chops, heat 1 T olive oil over medium high heat.
3. Add the garlic to the pan and cook for 15 seconds.
4. Add the pork chops to the pan and brown, approximately 3 minutes on each side.
5. Add the sauce to the pan, and turn the pork chops to completely coat both sides.
6. Adjust the heat to low, cover pan and cook for 40 minutes, occasionally spooning the tomato sauce over the pork chops.
7. Meanwhile, mix together the three cheeses in a bowl.
8. Divide the cheese mixture in fourths and, in the final 5 minutes of cooking, top each pork chop with the cheese mixture.
9. Sprinkle with additional dried oregano and cover pan until the cheese mixture melts.
10. Serve immediately, topping each pork chop with a little of the pan sauce.

Above: Cotolette alla pizzaiola
Below left: Pork chops ready for browning
Below right: Browned pork chops

Cotolette Impanata

Breaded Pork Cutlets

Breaded pork cutlets make a quick, simple and delicious meal. Spruce up some plain breadcrumbs with some garlic, oregano and Parmesan cheese for a really flavorful cutlet.

Serve the cutlets with lemon wedges and - my all-time favorite pairing with this dish- roasted peppers (page 15).

Ingredients (Serves 6 to 8)

4 lbs pork loin cutlets pounded to about 3/8 inch thick

2 cups flour

4 large eggs, beaten

4 cups breadcrumbs

Few sprigs of parsley, chopped fine

1 t garlic powder

1 t dried oregano

2 T Parmigiano Reggiano cheese

1/2 t coarse ground black pepper

Olive oil for frying

Directions

1. Place eggs in a shallow bowl large enough to hold a pork cutlet.
2. Place flour in a second bowl.
3. In a third bowl, mix together the breadcrumbs, cheese, parsley, garlic powder and pepper.
4. Place an amount of olive oil in a large frying pan sufficient to cover the bottom. Heat to medium.
5. Working with one cutlet at a time, dredge in flour coating the cutlet completely; shake off excess flour. Dip cutlet in the egg to coat the flour, and then in the breadcrumb mixture to coat the cutlet evenly.
6. Fry in oil about 2 minutes per side until golden brown. Remove from pan and place on paper towel to pat off excess oil.
7. Transfer cutlets to a platter and serve.

Note: I usually get a center cut pork loin and slice my own cutlets, starting with about 1/2 inch slices and then pounding them to between 1/4 and 3/8 inch thick.

Cotenne

Pork Skin Braciole

Cotenne (singular, *cotenna*) are hard to come by in restaurants nowadays, unless you visit one of the authentic, Old-World restaurants in New York's Little Italy. Cotenne, however, are popular in southern Italy - particularly in and around Naples - where chances are good that you will find them simmering in a rich tomato sauce alongside the meatballs, sausage, and beef braciole on any given Sunday.

Cotenne, also referred to as *cotica* in some dialects, are made from pork skin, rolled around some sort of stuffing and then slow-braised until they are literally melt-in-your mouth tender, The flavor and velvety texture that cotenne impart to the tomato sauce is something to experience.

As a standalone dish, cotenne are sometimes stuffed with various meats and then sliced for serving. Also popular is to prepare the cotenne in a sort of pork stew with cannellini beans, onions and tomatoes, but by far, my favorite way to enjoy cotenne is with a simple stuffing of parsley and garlic, and then slow-braised for several hours in tomato sauce; great over some pasta, too!

Ingredients (Serves 4)

Approximately 1 lb of fresh pork skin, cleaned of excess fat

1 bunch of fresh parsley, chopped

2 cloves garlic, chopped

1/3 cup Parmigiano Reggiano cheese, grated

salt and coarse ground black pepper, to taste

A pinch of crushed red pepper

4 T olive oil

2 quarts of your favorite tomato sauce (see note)

Directions

1. Lay pork skin flat on a cutting board, skin side down.
2. Sprinkle the skin with salt and pepper.
3. Mix together the parsley, garlic, cheese and red pepper and then spread the mixture evenly over the skin.
4. Roll the skin tightly and tie it closed with pieces of butcher's twine, spaced about an inch apart, including as close to each end as possible (see photo).
5. Either add the cotenne as you are preparing tomato sauce (page 277) or place in prepared tomato sauce and simmer at least 3 hrs.
6. Transfer the cotenne from the sauce to a serving platter, remove the string and cut into rounds approximately 1 1/2 inches thick
7. Serve as is, or over pasta, with some crusty Italian bread.

Note: The preferred approach to making cotenne in tomato sauce is to braise the cotenne in the sauce as it is cooking. Typically, when I make cotenne it is alongside other meats (e.g., meatballs, sausage, etc) as part of a meat sauce for pasta (see page 277). Alternatively, you can used prepared sauce, but you will still have to simmer the cotenne for at least 3 hrs to get the proper result.

Above: Cotenne

Left: Pork skin removed from a section of pork belly

Below: Filling the cotenne

Below left: Cotenne, rolled and tied

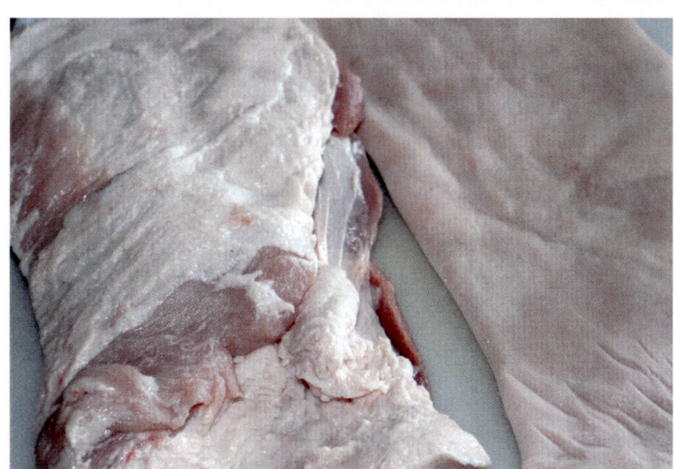

Lamb and Goat

Capretto al Forno

Slow-Roasted Weanling Goat

For the longest time, lamb was my favorite meat. That was until I had capretto one Easter Sunday at my in-laws' home. As I'm writing this, however, I'm struck by the sudden realization that I probably had capretto many times as a child, and was told that it was "lamb," just like the times I was told that rabbit was chicken, or that tripe was "a kind of fish!" I still wonder what the thinking was behind that smokescreen……but I digress.

Capretto made in this manner is a longstanding, traditional, Southern Italian dish, typically served on Easter Sunday. Slow-roasting is the key to super-tender meat. The aroma that permeates the house while the capretto is in the oven is unmistakable and incredibly tantalizing, in the same way that a turkey roasting on Thanksgiving Day might be.

If you're fortunate enough to live close to an Italian butcher (or a farm), you can usually place your order for a fresh, whole weanling kid – it's the only way to go. A good Italian butcher will know exactly how to piece the kid for this classic dish.

Ingredients (Serves 8-10)

7-8 lbs weanling goat meat, cut up, bone-in (see photo)

Extra virgin olive oil

4 cloves of garlic, chopped

4 sprigs of fresh rosemary

4 oz white anchovies in oil, finely minced

8-10 cipollini onions, peeled and left whole

2 lbs baking potatoes, peeled and cut into wedges

1 cup dry white wine

Salt and coarse-ground black pepper, to taste

Directions

1. Preheat oven to 300°F.
2. Chop the anchovies very fine.
3. In a bowl, mix together the anchovies, garlic, wine and 1/2 cup olive oil; pour the mixture over the capretto in a separate bowl and toss well to coat.
4. Transfer the capretto to a baking dish large enough to hold the pieces without over-crowding .
5. Toss the onions and potatoes with a drizzle of olive oil to coat, then distribute among the pieces of capretto in the baking dish.
6. Tear the leaves from the rosemary and scatter on top of the baking dish.
7. Sprinkle on a little salt and pepper; not too much salt - the anchovies provide some salt to the dish.
8. Cover with foil and bake for approximately 60-75 minutes. Remove foil during the last 15 minutes to brown a bit more.

A little bit about goats and goat meat:

The nutritional value of goat meat is unsurpassed among the more common meat choices. On a per weight basis, goat meat is substantially lower in calories, cholesterol and fat (particularly saturated fat) than beef, lamb, pork or chicken (even prepared without the skin), yet provides among the highest amounts of protein, B vitamins and essential elements (copper, zinc, phosphorous, iron and potassium).

On average, a goat kid weighs about 8 lbs at birth and can gain about 8 -12 lbs per month. Typically goats are weaned when they reach about 30 lbs. A 30-lb live weight kid will yield approximate 16 lb dressed. That's the size you want. The meat will have a very delicate flavor, not as "gamey" as meat from mature goats. I typically purchase a whole kid and use about half for this recipe, and then freeze the other half for another meal.

Clockwise from top:

Capretto al Forno ready to serve for Easter Sunday dinner

Garlic and white anchovies

Capretto ready for the oven

My butcher, Frankie "Chops," with a freshly dressed capretto

Fresh capretto, properly pieced

Cosciotto di Agnello al Forno

Roast Leg of Lamb

I prefer a roast leg of lamb to just about any other type of roast meat. Embellished with the classic combination of rosemary, thyme and garlic, a leg of lamb would almost always be served as part of an Easter or Christmas dinner in my family.

A boneless leg of lamb makes for easy carving, but you can certainly use a bone-in or semi-boneless roast. Just be sure you select a roast with the fat cap intact. Besides imparting lots of flavor, the fat provides a "holder" for the garlic cloves (see below) and serves to self-baste the meat during roasting.

The lamb can be served with pan drippings and/or my favorite, gremolata sauce (see chapter photo).

Ingredients (Serves 8)

1 whole boneless leg of lamb (5-7 lbs)

Several sprigs of fresh rosemary, chopped

Several sprigs of fresh thyme, chopped

6 cloves garlic, sliced lengthwise into thirds

3 T olive oil

Salt and coarse ground pepper to taste

Directions

1. Preheat oven to 375°F.
2. With a sharp paring knife, make several slits under the fat cap of the lamb creating small "pockets." Slide a sliver of garlic into each pocket.
3. In a small bowl, mix together the rosemary, thyme and olive oil. Spread the mixture over the lamb.
4. Season with salt and pepper.
5. Roast lamb, uncovered, approximately 20 minutes per lb to an internal temperature of 140°F. (medium) Remove from oven, tent loosely with foil, and allow to rest 15 minutes before carving.

To prepare pan drippings:

While lamb is resting, place roasting pan on a stove burner and add 1 cup of dry, red wine like Chianti.* With the burner on low, scrape up any brown bits from the pan. Strain pan contents through food-grade cheesecloth into a fat separator cup and allow to rest for several minutes to strain away most (not all) of the fat. Transfer to a sauce pan and simmer to reduce slightly. Adjust seasonings (salt/pepper) and serve with lamb.

To prepare gremolata:

Finely chop 1 small bunch of Italian, flat-leaf parsley and 2 cloves garlic. Transfer to a bowl and add the juice and zest of 1 lemon. Add 1/2 cup extra virgin olive oil and a pinch of salt. Mix and serve with lamb.

*Chianti is the best choice here. Chianti is made from Sangiovese grapes, which are low in tannins. High tannin wine can turn a bit bitter as wine is reduced for sauces.

Above: Cosciotto d'agnello, sliced for serving
Right: Fresh rosemary and thyme from my garden
Below right: Garlic spouting in the early spring
Below left: Seasoned lamb ready for the oven

Scottadito di Agnello
Grilled Lamb Chops

The word *scottadito* literally translates to "burned fingers" in Italian. It refers to the fact that lamb chops prepared in this manner are so delicious that one is willing to pick the scorching hot chops right off the grill to consume them. It's not uncommon to eat lamb chops in that manner, particularly rib chops, which have a convenient rib bone to grasp on to. Personally, I prefer loin lamb chops because I think they are a more tender cut of lamb. Further, I like buying a bone-in lamb loin roast, with the "cap" on, and cutting the individual chops myself.

I do tend to use a knife and fork on these delicious little nuggets but, admittedly, end up picking them up to get every last bit of tender, juicy meat from around the bone.

Ingredients (Serves 4)

1 bone-in lamb loin roast approx. 3 to 4 lbs.

About 1 cup of fresh mint leaves, chopped

2 sprigs of fresh rosemary, chopped

4 cloves garlic, chopped

1/4 cup dry white wine

6 T extra virgin olive oil

Sea salt and coarse-ground black pepper, to taste

Directions

1. Divide lamb loin roast into individual chops.
2. Add the remaining ingredients and marinate for at least 2 hrs or, preferably, overnight.
3. Grill chops over medium high heat to an internal temperature of 135°F, basting with the marinade.
4. Serve immediately.

Opposite top: Scottadito di agnello
Opposite bottom: Lamb loin chops marinating
Right: Bone-in lamb loin roast

Stinco di Agnello Brasato

Braised Lamb Shank

Slow-braising meat is a great way to develop flavor and to reduce tougher cuts of meat into fall-of-the-bone meaty goodness. Lamb shanks lend themselves exceptionally well to braising.

There are many choices for braising liquid. This particular family recipe is one that is typical of southern Italy, where tomatoes and red wine are the principal components for braising., along with some aromatics (garlic, rosemary and fennel). I use my home-grown and jarred San Marzano tomatoes in their juice for this recipe because of the exceptional flavor and consistency. If you must use store-bought tomatoes, look for the highest quality product available, preferably imported (DOP), whole, peeled San Marzano tomatoes.

Ingredients (Serves 4)

4 lamb shanks, approximately 1 1/2 lbs each

2 carrots, diced

6 oz fennel bulb, thinly sliced

8 oz small cippolini onions, peeled and left whole

4 cloves garlic, chopped

3 T olive oil

1 sprig fresh rosemary

1 qt jarred San Marzano tomatoes (or substitute high quality canned Italian tomatoes)

2 cups hearty red wine

Salt and coarse ground pepper to taste

Directions

1. Preheat oven to 350°F.
2. Heat olive oil in a Dutch oven. Salt and pepper the lamb shanks and brown them in the oil over medium-high heat. Remove shanks and set aside.
3. Add the carrots, fennel and onions to the pot and lightly brown. Add garlic and fresh rosemary and cook for 1 minute.
4. Add the red wine and cook for 2 minutes.
5. Add the tomatoes in their juice, stir and adjust seasoning with salt and pepper.
6. Return the lamb shanks to the pot, submersing them in the braising liquid.
7. Cover pot and place in oven for 2 hrs, turning shanks every 30 minutes.
8. Remove the shanks to a serving platter and top with braised vegetables.

Above: Stinco di agnello brasato served over polenta
Right: Browning vegetables and herbs
Below: Fresh lamb shanks

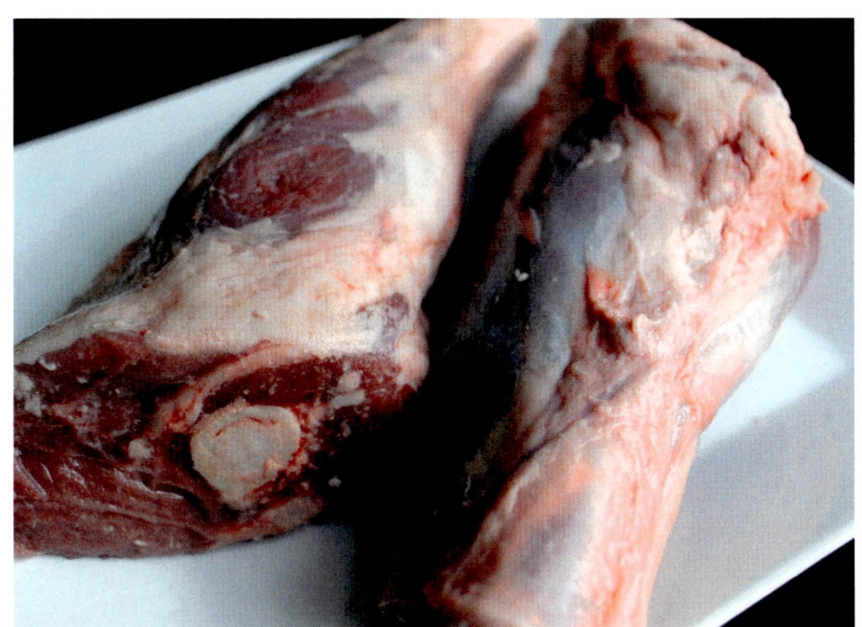

Spezzetino di Agnello alla Napoletana

Naples Style Lamb Stew

Piselli e patate (peas and potatoes) are what come to mind when I think of a classic southern Italian stew. Of course, there's all the other stuff but those can vary widely across regions. This family recipe incorporates cippolini (small Italian onions), Romano beans (home grown), which hold up very well to long cooking times, and the ever-versatile home-jarred San Marzano tomatoes.

Lamb is much more common than beef in southern Italian cuisine, so it's no surprise that it's the star of the show here. Garlic, rosemary and thyme are prefect compliments to lamb in just about any dish. Feel free to drizzle a little extra virgin olive oil on your plate, along with crushed red pepper. Oh, and don't forget the crusty Italian bread.

Ingredients (Serves 6-8)

2 lbs lamb shoulder cut into 1-inch cubes

About 6 T olive oil

1 large sprig fresh rosemary

Few sprigs of fresh lemon thyme

4 cloves garlic

2 cups hearty Italian red wine (like a Barbaresco or Nero d'Avola)

2 Marconi peppers (or substitute green bell pepper), roasted

A dozen or so small, cipollini onions, peeled and left whole

1 stalk celery, chopped

2 cups fresh Italian green beans (e.g., Romano variety), cut into 2-inch pieces

1 cup frozen petite peas

2 baking potatoes, peeled and cut into 1-inch cubes

1 quart jarred tomatoes (or substitute canned San Marzano tomatoes), in their juice

1 T tomato paste

1/2 t oregano

Coarse black pepper

Sea salt

Directions

1. Place lamb in a bowl and prepare a marinade of 2 T olive oil, 1/2 cup wine, 3 cloves garlic (crushed), 1 t coarse ground black pepper, 1/2 t sea salt and about half of the rosemary and thyme. Allow to marinate at least 2 hr or, preferably, overnight.
2. While lamb is marinating, roast peppers over an open flame, or on a grill until skin is charred. Remove, allow to cool, peel and seed, and coarsely chop. Set aside.
3. Remove lamb from marinade and pat dry with a paper towel. Heat 2 T olive oil in an 8-quart pot and brown the lamb, working in small batches at a time so as not to overcrowd. Remove lamb pieces as they brown and set aside.
4. Add another 1 T of olive oil to the pot and sauté the onions, carrots and celery until they pick up some color, about 2 minutes.
5. Add the garlic and sauté 30 seconds
6. Add the remaining 1 1/2 cups wine to deglaze the pan
7. Add the lamb back to the pot, along with the tomatoes, tomato paste, oregano and salt and pepper
8. Cover pot and simmer on low heat for about 1 hr
9. Add the potatoes, Romano beans, peas and roasted pepper.
10. Cover pot and simmer on low for another hr
11. Serve with crusty Italian bread

Note: The consistency of the sauce in the finished dish should be thicker than a soup, but liquid enough to be able to dip the Italian bread. Don't panic if the stew appears too watery in the early cooking stages - it will thicken as it cooks, following addition of the potatoes.

Above: Spezzetino di agnello alla Napoletana
Below: Marinating lamb

Ossobuco di Agnello

Lamb Ossobuco

The classic ossobuco is, of course, made with veal shanks (page 127), but can also be prepared with lamb. Whole lamb shanks, such as those used for the recipe on page 183, are relatively easy to come in meat markets. The cross-cut lamb shanks for ossobuco, however, can be more difficult to find and might require a special order from your butcher. If you love lamb as I do, and can get hold of these cross-cut shanks, this family recipe is a "must" to try.

There are some commonalities in the preparation of veal and lamb ossobuco. However, this family recipe doesn't rely on the rich, tomato-based braising liquid that is the hallmark of veal ossobuco. Instead, the lamb shanks are braised in wine and a little vegetable stock with only a hint of tomato in the background. I think this really lets the rich lamb flavor come through. The addition of yellow turnips - a very popular vegetable, particularly in northern Italy - brings even more "earthiness" to further compliment the flavor of the lamb.

Ingredients (Serves 4)

3 lbs lamb shanks for ossobuco

1 large carrot, diced

1 medium yellow turnip, diced

8 oz small cipollini onions, peeled and left whole

2 cloves garlic, chopped

3 T olive oil

Leaves from several sprigs of fresh thyme

2 t tomato paste

1 1/2 cups hearty red wine

1 1/2 cups vegetable stock

Salt and coarse ground pepper to taste

Directions

1. Place 2 T oil in a large, deep frying pan. Salt and pepper the lamb pieces and brown them in the oil, in batches to avoid over-crowding. Remove lamb and set aside.
2. Add the remaining oil to the pan and add the turnips, carrots and onions. When the vegetables are browned, add the garlic and cook for 30 more seconds.
3. Mix in the tomato paste to coat the vegetables, cooking for another minute or so.
4. Add the wine to deglaze and simmer for 3 minutes.
5. Add the vegetable stock and thyme.
6. Place the lamb pieces in a single layer at the bottom of the pan and arrange so that they are surrounded by the vegetables and sitting in the braising liquid.
7. Cover pan, turn heat to low, and simmer for about 90 minutes, carefully turning the lamb pieces once, halfway through.
8. Adjust seasonings with salt and pepper and transfer to a serving platter. Serve with crusty Italian bread.

Above: Ossobuco di agnello
Below left: Browning root vegetables
Below right: Lamb shank, cut for ossobuco

Seafood

• Sardine alla Griglia •
Grilled Sardines

• Scungilli fra Diavolo •
Ocean Conch in Spicy Tomato Sauce

• Pulpo alla Brace •
Grilled Octopus

• Calamari alla Marinara •
Squid in Marinara Sauce

• Stufato di Baccalá •
Salt Cod Stew

• Paella Sarda con Fregalo •
Sardinian Style Seafood Paella

• Branzino in Padella •
Pan-Seared Mediterranean Sea Bass

• Cacciucco alla Livornese •
Livorno Style Fish Stew

• Anguilla Affumicata •
Smoked Eel

Sardine alla Griglia

Grilled Sardines

Mention "sardines" to most people and they think of small oily fish jambed into a can. While canned sardines can be pretty tasty, they don't compare to fresh sardines right from the ocean. Sardines are enjoyed in many different ways in southern Italy; one of my favorites uses a classic Sicilian marinade of lemon, garlic and mint, prior to grilling over an open flame. Sardines prepared in this way are so flavorful that it's hard to stopping eating them once you start. Though this recipe is listed as serving 6-8 people, my father-in-law and I have easily polished off 24 sardines just between the two of us, so - word of caution - judge your dinner guests and plan accordingly!

Ingredients (Serves 6-8)

24 whole fresh sardines

3 lemons (plus additional for serving)

1 large bunch of fresh mint, coarsely chopped

6 cloves garlic, chopped

2 cups dry white wine

1 cup olive oil

Sea salt and coarse ground black pepper to taste

Directions

1. Clean sardines as described below and place in a large tray for marinating. I typically use one of those disposable aluminum lasagna pans.
2. Quarter 3 lemons and squeeze the juice into a bowl, reserving the rind. Add the remaining ingredients to the lemon juice, whisk together and pour all but about a half cup over the sardines, along with the lemon rinds. The reserved marinade will be used for basting the grilled sardines.
3. Marinate for at least 2 hrs in the refrigerator.
4. Heat a grill to medium/high. Place the marinated sardines in a fish basket (photo) and grill for about 3 minutes per side, turning once and basting both side with the reserved marinade.
5. Transfer to a serving platter and serve with extra lemon wedges.

Note: the fish basket makes things a lot easier, especially given the number of sardines and how quickly they cook. The grilled sardines should have a nice char on them. The flesh will be moist and will pull away from the bone very easily. With some practice, you will be able to remove an entire fillet without so much as a single bone.

Fresh sardines should be rather firm to the touch and have bright, clear eyes. Cleaning fresh sardines for grilling is rather easy, since you don't need to fillet them. Here's how:

(i) Using a fish scaler or the back of a paring knife, scrape the fish from the tail toward the head to remove scales. Rinse scales from the fish in cold water.

(ii) With a paring knife, slit the belly from the anal opening up to the base of the gills. Spread the abdominal cavity open and remove the guts with your finger. Rinse cavity well in cold water. You're done!

Above: A platter of sardine alla griglia
Right: Sardines cooking on the grill
Below left: Fresh sardines
Below right: Cleaned sardines marinating

Scungilli fra Diavolo

Ocean Conch in Spicy Tomato Sauce

The word *scungilli* is a southern Italian dialect word for ocean conch, or *conchiglia* in formal Italian. Scungilli is enjoyed in several ways in southern Italy, but my favorite is in a spicy tomato sauce, *scungilli fra diavolo*, which is usually served over pasta or - my personal favorite - over friselle (see page 95). All of the cleaned conch meat is edible. The "foot" muscle itself is very dense and, therefore, requires a long and slow cooking process to tenderize. Cooked correctly, scungilli has a great "ocean seafood" type flavor that's almost sweet - like a lobster tail might be if it were more dense. The heat from the red pepper pairs perfectly with the sweetness of the scungilli to make this one of my all-time favorite seafood dishes.

Fresh channel whelk are easy to process into scungilli, but some space is required; I typically do this outdoors.

Ingredients (Serves 6)

Approximately 2 lbs (6 cups) coarsely chopped scungilli

2 quarts jarred San Marzano tomatoes (or substitute canned)

1 6-oz can imported tomato paste

1/3 cup olive oil

3 cloves garlic, chopped

1 t crushed red pepper flakes

4 leaves fresh basil, torn

Salt to taste

Directions

1. Bring a large pot of water to a simmer. Place whelk in the pot, cover, and steam until they protrude from their shell.
2. Discard the hard foot plate and, with a fork, remove the whelk from the shell. The guts are at the trailing end of the shell contents and easily separated from the muscle. The muscle is what will be transformed into scungilli fra diavolo.
3. Coarsely chop the scungilli and set aside.
4. Heat olive oil in a pan and sauté garlic for a few seconds, until fragrant.
5. Add the tomatoes, paste, basil, red pepper and salt to taste.
6. Add the scungilli and cook on low heat for about 2 hrs, stirring occasionally, until the meat is fork tender.
7. Serve over pasta, friselle, or just with a side of crusty Italian bread and some nice Chianti.

About scungilli: There are many different species within the family that includes ocean conch. Included is the Channel Whelk, which is found along the North Atlantic coast from Massachusetts to the Carolinas. There was a time, when I was much younger, that you could go to one of the fishing villages on Long Island and get whelk for next to nothing. I remember paying $0.50/lb for fresh whelk right off the boat in Greenport, NY. Lobster fisherman considered them a nuisance and just threw them back in the ocean or sold them for bait. In recent years, however, the international demand for conch and whelk has skyrocketed, along with their price, as one might expect.

Scungilli can be purchased year-round, sold in cans or partially cooked and frozen - neither of which would I consider! I much prefer to wait for whelk season in the Northeast, which is from May to September. I load up my truck with a few coolers half filled with ice and head down to one of the coastal towns to pick up my supply of fresh whelk. I would take the weekend to process them and then vacuum seal and freeze the meat for use in various recipes throughout the year, being sure to save enough for l*a Festa dei Sette Pesci* (the Feast of the Seven Fishes), on Christmas Eve.

Clockwise from above:

Scungilli fra diavolo over friselle biscuits

Scungilli in a large pot of simmering water

Cleaned scungilli meat

Chopped scungilli

Freshly harvested channel whelk

Pulpo alla Brace
Grilled Octopus

Pulpo alla brace (literally, octopus over embers) is one of my favorite ways to enjoy octopus. Improperly prepared, octopus can be very rubbery - like biting into an old tire! This family recipe mimics one of the age-old techniques employed by Italian fisherman, who would tenderize freshly-caught octopus by repeatedly thrashing them against the rocks that line the southern Italian coast. The process would help break down the tough protein structure, tenderizing the octopus prior to cooking. Thankfully, a meat mallet substitutes nicely for the Amalfi shoreline rocks. That, combined with parboiling the octopus prior to charring over white-hot embers, produces incredibly tender meat.

Finishing the grilled mollusk with a lemon and olive oil mix makes a simple yet elegant first course.

Ingredients (Serves 4)

1 whole octopus, approximately 3-4 lbs

2 T baking soda

1/2 cup extra virgin olive oil

1 lemon, juice and zest

1 T fresh parsley, chopped

1 clove garlic, chopped

Salt and coarse ground black pepper, to taste

Directions

1. Bring a large pot of water to a low boil. Add baking soda.
2. Place the octopus on a solid cutting board and pound the tentacles for several minutes with the meat mallet and then place the octopus it into the pot. Cook for 20 minutes.
3. In the meanwhile, prepare the marinade/dressing by whisking together the oil, lemon juice, zest, parsley, garlic, salt and pepper.
4. Remove octopus from pot to a bowl and allow to cool.
5. Piece the octopus by separating each of the eight tentacles where they join at the mouth. Remove and discard the hard "beak" at the center. Remove the head sac and slice it open to clean out any of the internal structures. Note - the entire octopus is edible with the exception of the beak and head contents.
6. Now for round 2 with your mallet...give the tentacles another minute or so of a sound pounding to further tenderize.
7. Pour HALF of the marinade over the octopus and allow to marinate while you start your charcoal.
8. When the coals are white hot, place the octopus on the grill, which should be as close as possible to the coals.
9. Give the octopus a nice char on the entire surface, which should only take a couple of minutes.
10. Transfer the grilled octopus to a serving platter, and top with the reserved lemon and oil dressing.
11. Serve hot with a slice of lemon (optional).

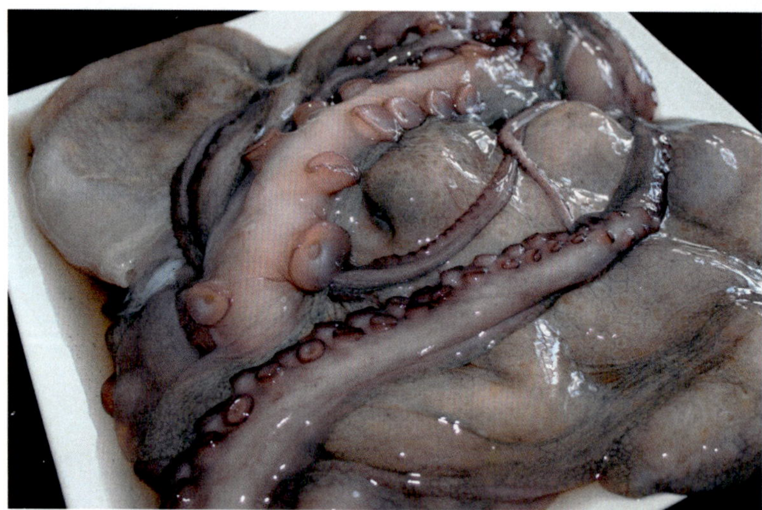

Above: Charring the octopus over hot coals

Below: Pulpo alla brace

Opposite: Fresh octopus

Calamari alla Marinara

Squid in Marinara Sauce

Spicy Calamari alla Marinara is one of my favorite seafood dishes. I look forward to summertime, when fresh calamari and vine-ripened San Marzano tomatoes join forces to produce a spectacular dish. Of course, there's always frozen calamari and canned tomatoes, if need be, to get you through the winter.

Calamari alla Marinara is fabulous served over linguine or, my personal preference, over friselle (page 95). Slow cooking in tomato sauce produces exceptionally tender calamari.

Ingredients (Serves 8)

2 lbs cleaned calamari; tubes and tentacles

1 qt jar San Marzano tomatoes (or substitute 1 28-oz can of high-quality, whole, peeled, Italian plum tomatoes)

4 cloves garlic, finely chopped

A few sprigs of Italian parsley, chopped

4 T olive oil

4 basil leaves, coarsely torn

1/2 t crushed red pepper flakes (optional)

Salt to taste

Directions

1. Slice the calamari into rings about an inch wide; leave tentacles whole; set aside in a bowl
2. Heat olive oil over medium-low heat in a pot large enough to accommodate all ingredients
3. Add garlic and red pepper flake and cook for 30 seconds until garlic is aromatic; don't allow the garlic to brown
4. Add the tomatoes in their juice and break them up into large pieces with a fork
5. Add the parsley, basil and salt
6. Add the calamari and bring to a simmer over medium heat
7. Cover pot, and simmer for 30-40 minutes until calamari are tender.
8. Adjust seasonings (salt and red pepper) to taste; serve hot

About squid:

Squid are actually mollusks, related to clams, oysters and other bivalves. However, unlike their relatives, squid have an internal "shell," or endoskeleton called a quill or "pen" rather than an external shell. There are more than 300 species of squid in the Earth's waters, ranging in size from just a few inches to giants weighing in at more than a half ton!

The Long Island Sound is a squid fisherman's paradise. Beginning around May through August of each year, the long-finned squid (*Loligo pealei*) migrate into the Sound from the North Atlantic continental shelf to feed and spawn. Trawlers haul in thousands of pounds of squid during this period.

The Italian word for squid, *calamari*, is derived from the Latin term, *calamarium*, a vessel for holding a pen, or an ink pot, which probably refers to the squid's ink sac and the "pen" that makes up its endoskeleton.

Above: Calamari alla Marinara, served over friselle

Right: Amanda on one of Long Island's south shore beaches (great spot for surf casting for bluefish, by the way)

Below: Dried Sicilian hot chili peppers (*peperoncini secco*), grown in my garden

Stufato di Baccalá

Salt Cod Stew

Of the dozens of ways to prepare baccalá, this one has to be my favorite. A staple as a Christmas Eve course, baccalá can be enjoyed any time of the year because of the year-round availability of preserved, salt-cured cod.

So as to avoid any confusion, fresh cod in Italy is known as *merluzzo*; when it is air-dried, it's known as *stoccafisso*,and when salt-cured, it's *baccalá*. This particular family recipe is one that is typical of the region in and around Naples.

Ingredients (Serves 6)

About 3 lbs of hydrated baccalá, cut into serving-sized pieces (see note)

3 C dry white wine

Healthy pinch of saffron threads

3 T olive oil plus more for drizzling

2 cloves garlic, chopped

1 medium onion, sliced

16 oz crushed Italian tomatoes

A handful of Kalamati olives

2 t capers in vinegar

A few sprigs of parsley, chopped

Pinch of crushed red pepper flakes

Coarse ground black pepper and seat salt, to taste

Directions

1. Add the olive oil to a large sauté pan, and cook the onions until just translucent; add the garlic and cook for an additional 30 seconds.
2. Add the tomatoes, olives, capers, red pepper and parsley. Cover pan and cook on low while the baccalá is prepared.
3. In another sauté pan, bring the wine to a low simmer; crush the saffron threads and add to the wine.
4. Poach the pieces of baccalá in the wine for 2-3 minutes, covered. You may need to do this in batches, depending on the size of your pan.
5. Transfer the poached baccalá to the pan with the tomato sauce. When all the baccalá has been poached, add the remaining poaching liquid to the tomato sauce mixture.
6. Spoon the sauce over the baccalá, cover, and simmer for about 30 minutes.
7. Transfer to a serving vessel and drizzle with extra olive oil. The dish can be served hot or at room temperature with lots of crusty Italian bread.

Note: Make sure to plan 3 or 4 days in advance of using baccalá in any recipe - that's the time necessary to properly rehydrated the salt-cured fish. First, however, you need to purchase a good quality baccalá for this recipe, preferably from an Italian fish market. Select a single large piece of fish that is at least 3/4" thick at the wide end of the fillet. Avoid baccalá sold in those small wooden boxes for this recipe - those are fine for recipes calling for small pieces of baccalá - not this one.

Fill a large container with cold water; the container should be large enough to accommodate the fish lying flat. I use a food-grade plastic lug (see photo). Place the fish in the water, making sure that it's completely submerged. Change the water twice daily until it is no longer salty. Depending on the thickness of the fish, this can take anywhere from 2 to 4 days. The baccalá will expand considerably over this time at it rehydrates. When the baccalá has been desalted and rehydrated, carefully remove it from the container, pat dry and cut into serving-sized pieces, about 3-4" wide. The baccalá is now ready for use in this recipe.

Above: Stufato di baccalá

Right: A piece of baccalá fresh from the market

Below right: Hydrating a piece of baccalá in a food-grade plastic tub of water

Below: Fully hydrated baccalá

Paella Sarda con Fregola

Sardinian Style Seafood Paella

A great variation of seafood paella comes from the island of Sardinia, where *fregola* takes the place of rice to produce an incredibly flavorful seafood and pasta paella. Fregola is a rustic pasta similar to couscous but larger in size and with a texture (in the uncooked state) like that of dried peppercorns. Fregola is typically made with semolina flour and water, sometimes flavored with saffron, shaped and then toasted, giving the pasta a nutty flavor. I like to use the plain, unflavored, fregola for this recipe and add the saffron during preparation.

Ingredients (Serves 6)

1 1/2 lbs (approximately 16) Littleneck clams

1 lb (approximately 24) mussels

6 oz fresh shrimp, shelled and deveined

6 oz fresh squid bodies, cleaned and cut into 1/2" rounds

1 lb dried, plain fregola

3 T olive oil

Generous pinch of saffron threads

1 medium onion, chopped

1 clove garlic, chopped

Several sprigs of parsley, chopped

Zest of 1 lemon

2 cups Vermentino wine

1 qt of fish stock, preferably homemade or substitute high-quality alternative

Coarse ground black pepper to taste

Directions

1. Scrub clams and cover with cold water for 30 minutes. Drain and inspect clams, discarding any that feel underweight or sound hollow when tapped with a spoon. Rinse mussels and remove any "beards" that may be present.
2. Heat about 2 cups of the fish stock in a sauce pan. Crush the saffron threads and add to the hot stock along with the lemon zest Remove from heat and set aside.
3. Heat the olive oil in a large, covered pan (I use a 13" pan with 4" sides), and cook onion for 2 minute until softened. Add garlic and cook for 30 seconds more.
4. Add the dried fregola to the pan, stirring to coat the pasta in the oil. Add the wine and cook for 1 minute over moderately high with stirring.
5. Add the stock with the saffron and then the clams and mussels. Cover pot and cook for about 4 to 5 minutes until the shellfish have opened, discarding any that have not started to open.
6. Add the shrimp, squid and parsley along with the rest of the fish stock. Turn heat to medium low, cover pot and cook for 10 minutes or so. The fregola should be cooked *al dente* at this point, and most of the broth should be absorbed (see photo). If necessary, you can add a small amount of water to get the right pasta consistency.
7. Season with pepper; salt will probably be unnecessary as the fish stock and shellfish have sufficient amounts.
8. Serve hot with crusty Italian bread and a nice glass of Vermentino.

Above: Paella Sarda con fregola
Right: Dried fregola pasta

Branzino in Padella

Pan-Seared Mediterranean Sea Bass

Branzino, or *spigola* as it's known in Southern Italy, is a Mediterranean sea bass and a close relative of the well-known striped bass of the North Atlantic coast. Branzino is prepared in countless different ways in Italy, but one of my favorites is to pan-fry the whole, dressed branzino and serve it in a tomato-olive-caper-garlic sauce...out of this world!

Branzino has a mild, almost sweet, flavor that's appealing even to those who aren't big fans of seafood. While *branzini* (plural) can be as large as 15 pounds, a typical branzino that one might find in a fish market is about 1 1/2 pounds and just about right for two people

I particularly like to prepare this dish outdoors in the summertime; it gives me that "campsite" feel like cooking a fish that was caught only minutes earlier.

Ingredients (Serves 4)

2 branzini, dressed (see opposite), about 1 1/2 lbs each

3 T olive oil

2 cups jarred San Marzano tomatoes (page 275) or substitute high-quality, whole, peeled, Italian plum tomatoes)

2 cloves garlic, chopped

1 T capers in vinegar

4 oz pitted oil-cured olives

1 cup dry white wine

1/2 t crushed red pepper

A few sprigs of Italian parsley, chopped

Mediterranean sea salt

Directions

1. Rub 1 T of the olive oil over the dressed branzini and sprinkle lightly with the sea salt, skin and body cavity.
2. Heat the remaining olive oil to medium-high in a skillet large enough to accommodate the fish. Place fish in pan and fry about 5 minutes per side until the skin is nicely browned. Remove fish from pan and set aside.
3. Add the chopped garlic and red pepper to the pan and cook for 30 seconds.
4. Add the tomatoes, capers and olives and cook for about 2 minutes.
5. Add the wine and continue cooking for another 2 minutes, until the sauce is reduced.
6. Add the branzini back to the pan with the chopped parsley. Spoon the sauce over the fish until it is reheated and cooked throughout (about another 2 minutes).
7. Serve with crusty Italian bread to sop up the sauce.

Above: Branzino in padella

Below: Dressed branzini (gutted, scaled and fins removed) ready for the pan

Cacciucco alla Livornese

Livorno Style Fish Stew

Livorno is a port city on the Ligurian Sea in the Tuscany region of Italy, about 55 miles west of Florence. The city is known for its fabulous seafood, represented by the classic dish, "cacciucco," a seafood stew whose origin in Livorno dates back to the early 16th century. As the story goes, fishermen would prepare a stew at the end of each day made from the various fish and shellfish leftover from the day's catch. That's probably why there are so many variations of this recipe, even to this day. Although cacciucco was traditionally made with the "bottom of the barrel" fish, some very "high end" varieties of fish are sometimes found in modern day recipes. One requirement, however, that most agree with is that cacciucco livornese has to incorporate five different types of seafood, one for each "c" in the name. Also a requirement is that it is served in a bowl over a thick slice of crispy, oven-toasted Tuscan bread.

The rich, deep flavor of cacciucco is worth the time it takes to prepare. I typically prepare a quick fish stock for use in this recipe, or use some from the freezer that I previously prepared. Alternatively, you can substitute a good quality store-bought fish stock in a pinch.

This family recipe uses clams, calamari, octopus and two types of firm-fleshed fish that stand up well in a stew. Two of my favorites are Mediterranean sea bass (*branzino*) and black grouper (*cernia*), although other types of fish can be used; sea bream (*orata*), monkfish (*coda di rospo*) or mahi-mahi (*lampughe*).

Ingredients (Serves 6-8)

1 whole branzino about 1 1/4 lb
1 lb grouper filet
1 lb calamari, cut into 1" pieces
1 octopus, approximately 2 lbs
18 littleneck clams in the shell
5 cloves garlic, chopped
1 bulb fennel with fronds
1 medium onion, chopped
1 leek, green and white parts
Italian flat-leaf parsley
1 cup dry white wine
4 T olive oil, plus more for drizzling
1/2 t crushed red pepper flakes
28 oz canned San Marzano tomatoes
1 carrot
1 stalk celery
Salt and coarse black pepper to taste
Crusty Italian bread, oven-toasted

Directions

1. Gut, fillet and skin the branzino. Set aside the fillets and prepare a stock as follows: place branzino bones, carrot, celery, the green part of the leek, fennel fronds, salt and black pepper in a stock pot, cover with water, bring to a boil and then lower to simmer for at least 1 hr. Strain stock through cheesecloth and reserve.
2. Tenderize octopus with a meat mallet and then poach whole for 10 minutes in a pot of boiling water containing 1 T of baking soda. Remove and set aside to cool and then cut tentacles into 1 inch pieces; discard the head.
3. Heat oil in a large sauce pan and add the onion, garlic, 1/2 cup chopped fennel bulb, the white part of the leek, chopped, and red pepper flakes. Sauté until vegetables are softened.
4. Add the octopus and calamari and sauté for 2 minutes.
5. Add the wine and cook until reduced by half.
6. Add tomatoes, and then 2 cups of the reserved fish stock. Stir, adjust seasonings, cover and simmer for 30 minutes.
7. Cut the grouper and branzino fillets into 2 inch pieces, add to the stew long with the clams and several sprigs of chopped parsley.
8. Simmer until clams are opened and fish are cooked throughout. Serve over crusty Italian bread, with an extra drizzle of olive oil.

Above: Cacciucco alla Livornese
Right: Whole, fresh branzino
Bottom right: Filleted branzino
Bottom left: Black grouper fillet

Anguilla Affumicata

Smoked Eel

Eels, of course, are fish. That is, they are cold-blooded vertebrates with gills, fins and scales. Despite their snake-like appearance, eels should not be confused with their distant relatives, the reptiles (like sea snakes). In Italy, eels are enjoyed in a variety of ways – fried, grilled, marinated and braised in stews. By far, however, smoked eel is my favorite. The fat content of the fish lends itself exceptionally well to smoking; the meat doesn't dry out during the process like other, less oily fish might. The flavor of eel is milder than mackerel or sardines.

I used to smoke eels in a grill-type smoker with a separate fire box, but I have since used an electric vertical smoker (pictured) mostly because I have better control of the smoke temperature and the eels seem to smoke more uniformly when hung vertically as opposed to lying on a grill.

Ingredients (Serves 6-8)

4 fresh Atlantic eel, approx. 2 lbs each

Salt for brining

Directions

1. Clean and brine eels as described below.
2. Place the eels in a smoker so they are not touching each other. Smoke eels for about 90 minutes at 185°F. At this point, the skin will have a lightly crisped appearance and will begin to pull away from the meat. Note: A temperature-controlled smoker is the best way to go to ensure even smoking.
3. Remove eels from smoker and cut into pieces to serve. Peel away skin to reveal the moist and flaky meat. I prefer to enjoy my eel "as is," but I wouldn't be averse to an optional squeeze of lemon.

The American eel, the only freshwater eel of North America, has a rather complex life cycle. Eels are categorized as catadromous fish, meaning that they migrate from fresh water into the ocean to spawn. That's opposite of the migration pattern of anadromous fish, like salmon, which migrate from the ocean into freshwater rivers and streams to spawn.

Eels have tiny scales that give the fish an appearance of a smooth "skin." Their scales are covered with a relatively thick slime layer that is thought to give them some protection as they migrate between fresh and salt water.

Cleaning eels is rather straightforward and basically involves removing the slime/scales and gutting the fish, as one would do with other types of fish. Rubbing the eel with coarse sea salt, followed by a quick rinse in water, is the most efficient way to remove the slime layer and scales. To gut an eel, insert the tip of a sharp knife into the anal opening and slice just through the skin up to the gills. Dislodge the guts with your fingers; they will come out cleanly in one piece. Give the cavity a quick rinse and you're done.

I like to brine the eels prior to smoking. A fisherman friend of mine in Southold, NY did this on a large scale (55 gallon drums) using a little trick. He would fill the drum 3/4 full with fresh water and then add salt until a peeled, whole potato would be suspended in the water (i.e. neither sink nor float). The final salt content would be exactly correct for brining. The eels would then be placed in the brine for an hour or so, then given a quick rinse prior to smoking.

Above: Anguilla affumicata
Right: Vertical style electric smoker
Below: Freshly caught Atlantic eels

Vegetables and Side Dishes

• Melanzane alla Parmigiana •
Eggplant Parmesan

• Carciofi •
Artichokes

• Funghi Anneriti •
Blackened Mushrooms

• Senape •
Mustard Greens

• Rapini con Salsiccia •
Broccoli Rabe with Sausage

• Crocchette di Patate •
Potato Croquettes

• Arancini •
Stuffed Rice Balls

• Cavalfiore alle Acciughe •
Cauliflower with Anchovies

• Patate al Sugo •
Potatoes in Sauce

• Zucchini alla Scapece •
Zucchini with Mint and Vinegar

Melanzane alla Parmigiana

Eggplant Parmesan

Eggplant Parmesan is one of my all-time favorite dishes. Of course, I prefer my garden-grown eggplant for this dish (see recipe for melanzane sott' olio), but if you must rely on supermarket eggplant, be sure to follow the tips in the note below.

I know there are different opinions on how to prepare eggplant for Parmesan. In this family recipe, there is no pre-salting step to remove bitterness - homegrown eggplant aren't bitter if you know when to harvest them, and neither are store-bought eggplant if you select them properly. I use a light coating of breadcrumbs for the eggplant and low-moisture, whole milk mozzerella rather than fresh mozzerella - makes for a much less "soupier" dish. Finally - the sauce - I prefer my homemade, meatless pasta sauce for this recipe. Overall, this dish is hearty, filling and has an incredible depth of flavor, and it is one that can be enjoyed by even the vegetarians in your family (say it ain't so). This is definitely one of those dishes that gets better in the days after it's baked. In fact, one of my favorite sandwiches is sliced, cold eggplant "parm" between two slices of *pane rustica* -yum!

Ingredients (Serves 8-12)

3 medium eggplant, about 4-5 lbs in total

2 quarts good quality, meatless tomato sauce

Olive oil for frying, about 2 cups

6 large eggs

About 6 cups seasoned breadcrumbs

1/2 cup chopped fresh parsley

2 lbs low-moisture, whole milk mozzerella, sliced thin

1 cup grated Parmesan Reggiano

Salt and coarse ground black pepper

Directions

1. Prepare bowls for breading before slicing eggplant; in one bowl, beat eggs with about 2 T water and set aside. In a second bowl (or shallow platter), mix breadcrumbs with chopped parsley.
2. Working with one eggplant at a time, partially peel from top to bottom so that the eggplant looks striped (see photo). Slice eggplant into rounds about 3/8" thick.
3. Place 1/4" olive oil in a large frying pan and heat oil to medium/ high (not smoking).
4. Dip eggplant into egg wash and then into breadcrumbs to lightly coat. Fry eggplant in batches, turning once until both sides are golden brown (see photo). Remove eggplant to a platter , lightly sprinkle with salt and pepper and repeat, peeling and slicing the remaining eggplant as you go. Replenish olive oil as needed, until all the eggplant are fried.
5. Get a baking tray. I use a ceramic tray about 11 x 17" and 2 1/2" deep. First, coat the bottom with a few spoonfuls of tomato sauce, then place a layer of fried eggplant, fitting them together to cover as much of the bottom as possible. Cover with about a third of the mozzerella, spoon on tomato sauce to lightly cover, then sprinkle with Parmesan. Repeat until the tray is filled; you should have at least 3 layers. Make sure you save enough mozzerella to top the dish. End with a coating of tomato sauce and a sprinkle of Parmesan
6. Preheat oven to 400ºF and bake for about 45 minutes until the cheese on top is melted and just starting to brown.
7. Remove from oven and let rest for 20 minutes before serving.

Above: Melanzane alla Parmigiana

Right: Platter of fried eggplant ready for assembly

Below: Sliced eggplant ready to be breaded and fried (note creamy white color and absence of mature seeds)

Note: To choose the freshest eggplant, look for smooth, shiny "skins." The eggplant should be firm (not hard) and have some weight to them; lighter eggplants are probably past their prime. The skin should be uniform and free from scars and blemishes. The stem should be green, not brown.

Carciofi
Artichokes

For most of my adolescent life, I thought there was only one way to prepare artichokes. That's because whenever my mother would say, "I think I'll make artichokes on Sunday," this is the way they would come out. Now that I've made it to adulthood (ostensibly), I realize that there are, in fact, MANY ways to prepare artichokes. Despite having come to that realization, I still think there isn't a better recipe for artichokes than mom's. It's pure and simple - nothing fancy - just fresh ingredients and a LOT of patience while the artichokes simmer slowly through Sunday afternoon until dinner time when the platter of artichokes would be brought to the table - a side dish of one of the most flavorful vegetables on the planet. The key is the long and slow cooking process that yields the most tender leaves, each one infused with that incredible parsley-and-garlic flavor combination.

Ingredients (Serves 6)

6 artichokes (see note)

1 large bunch of Italian flat leaf parsley

8 cloves of garlic

1/2 cup extra virgin olive oil, plus more for drizzling

1 lemon, halved

Coarse ground black pepper to taste, and plenty of salt

Directions

1. Prepare the parsley and garlic "stuffing" by finely chopping both together. Alternatively, several pulses in a food processor will do the trick. Transfer to a bowl, add 1 t salt, pepper to taste, the juice and zest of 1/2 lemon and the olive oil. Mix well and set aside.
2. Prepare the artichokes as follows: (i) remove the stems with a sharp knife, flush with the base of the artichoke, (ii) slice about a half inch from the top of the artichoke, (iii) with a sharp pair of scissors, go around the artichoke and trim off the tips of the exposed outer leaves to remove the prickly ends (see photo), (iv) rub the top of the artichoke with the remaining half lemon to prevent browning.
3. Turn the artichoke upside down on a flat surface and press hard on the base with the palm of you hand. This will act to spread apart the closely packed leaves to facilitate stuffing the artichoke. Turn the artichoke upright again and, with your fingers, gently pry apart the layers of leaves to make room for the stuffing.
4. This is the time-consuming (and slightly messy) part.... place a bit of the parsley/garlic mixture in between the leaves, pushing it toward the base of the artichoke. Try to fill in as many spaces as you can so that each leaf holds a bit of the mixture. Now you can appreciate why you made so much in the first place!
5. Choose a 6- or 8-quart sauce pan that's deep enough to hold the artichokes. They should be arranged such that they are not tightly packed, yet close enough to each other to keep them from falling over. You want them to remain upright during the cooking process.
6. Using a quart container, fill the pan with water such that about 2/3 of the artichoke is submerged. Make note of the amount of water needed, because you will add 1 1/2 t of salt for each quart of water. This may seem like a lot, but it's necessary for the artichokes to cook properly.
7. Drizzle olive oil over the top of each artichoke, bring the water to a simmer, and cover the pan. Simmer artichokes for about 4 hrs undisturbed, periodically replacing water, as needed, to maintain water level. The artichokes are done when they've darkened slightly in color and the outer leave fall away easily. Remove artichokes and serve in individual bowls.

Above: Carciofi simmering

Below left: Trimming an artichoke for stuffing

Below right: Parsley/garlic stuffing mixture

Note: Choosing fresh artichokes is absolutely essential for this dish. A fresh artichoke will have tightly packed, bright green leaves. Some varieties may have a tinge of purple, but avoid any with brown leaves. Artichokes with widely splayed leaves are past their prime and too dry. The artichoke should have some weight to it, and the leaves should "squeak" when the artichoke is squeezed - a sure sign of freshness!

To eat an artichoke cooked as described here, pull off one leaf at a time, place it in your mouth, and drag it across your teeth, removing the tender pulp on the inner side of the leaf. Work your way to the center where you will eventually find the heart - a total flavor explosion of melt-in-your-mouth goodness.

Funghi Anneriti
Blackened Mushrooms

The term "blackened mushrooms" (*funghi anneriti*) is one that I came up with to describe the method of preparing this fantastic side dish. The mushrooms aren't actually "blackened," per say, but cooked for a long time over low heat to the point where they lose most of their water content. As a consequence, the mushrooms substantially reduce in mass, intensely concentrating that earthy mushroom flavor. The complementary garlic and oregano flavors bring the mushrooms to a whole new level.

Blackened mushrooms are always a side dish for Thanksgiving dinner in my family. Since the turkey takes several hours to cook anyway, it's no extra effort to prepare the mushrooms concurrently. However, it's not the kind of side dish one would consider if you're planning a quick dinner fix.

Don't let the required amount of fresh mushrooms scare you; they will shrink down considerably during the cooking process.

Ingredients (Serves 6-8)

6 lbs (8 12-oz packages) of small to medium whole white button mushrooms

3/4 cup olive oil

6 cloves garlic, peeled and left whole

Dried oregano

Salt and coarse ground black pepper to taste

Directions

1. Clean mushrooms with a brief rinse in a colander (see note).
2. Cut medium-sized mushrooms in quarters (see photo); smaller mushrooms can be cut in half.
3. You will be cooking in phases to get to the final product. Divide the batch of mushrooms in thirds. Add 1/4 cup of olive to a large frying pan (or wok). Add one batch of mushrooms, 1/2 t salt and black pepper to taste. Cook uncovered until the mushrooms soften and reduce in volume (see photo).
4. Transfer the mushrooms and any liquid from the pan to a bowl. Repeat with the remaining two batches of mushrooms, cooking each in 1/4 cup olive oil, salt and pepper.
5. For the second phase of cooking, return all mushrooms and liquid to the pan, add the oregano, and simmer on low, uncovered, with occasional stirring, until most of the liquid is evaporated. This phase could take about an hour.
6. In the final phase of cooking, there should be very little liquid in the pan, other than the olive oil, Add the garlic cloves, cover the pan, and continue simmering until the mushrooms darken and further reduce in volume, about another 30-45 minutes. Adjust seasoning and serve.

Note: There's considerable debate on how to clean mushrooms. Some say washing in water is a no-no, as the mushrooms would absorb too much water. Of course, being a scientist, I actually ran a controlled experiment to see if that claim is true. Turns out that the amount of retained water, following rinsing mushrooms clean in a colander, is minuscule and represents only a tiny, barely measurable, fraction of the total weight of the mushrooms. So go ahead and given them a rinse; or, if you have no trust in science, feel free to use a damp kitchen towel or a mushroom brush (yes, that's a real thing).

Above: Funghi anneriti

Right: Washed and pieced mushrooms

Below right: Mushrooms during the initial cooking phase

Below: Mushrooms near the end of the cooking process

Senape
Mustard Greens

Mustards greens are prepared and enjoyed in so many different ways, in so many different cultures. There are almost 50 varieties of mustard plant known, but only a handful are used for cooking. The plant species best known around the Mediterranean, and particularly in southern Italy, is *Sinapsis alba*, or the white mustard plant. This variety is, in fact, the source of the standard yellow mustard that you might put on your hot dog. The plant itself, however, is a favorite across southern Italy. Quickly sautéed in olive oil, garlic, with a touch of crushed red pepper, senape (pronounced *sin-á-pee*) makes for a great side dish. The flavor is peppery and a bit bitter - really delicious!

Senape plants are annuals and very easy to grow. My original seeds came from relatives in Italy, but they're also commercially available (see photo). I have since propogated my own plants by letting a few go to seed and then collecting the seeds for planting the subsequent year. Alternatively, you can let the plants themselves re-seed, but I would rather control where the plants grow. The young plants can be cut multiple times to harvest senape throughout the Spring.

The senape that I grow and harvest takes only a few minutes of cooking time, unlike the more common mustard greens that you might pick up in the supermarket that typically take an hour or more of cooking until they are tender.

Ingredients (Serves 4)

1 large bunch of fresh white mustard plants; leaves and stems

2-3 cloves garlic, chopped

1/2 cup olive oil

Sea salt to taste

Crushed red pepper flakes to taste

Directions

1. Wash senape well under cold water and pat dry.
2. Heat olive oil in pan large enough to accommodate the senape (they will shrink down almost immediately during cooking).
3. Sauté garlic for just a few seconds and then add senape, salt and crushed red pepper.
4. Cook until all the leaves are wilted and the largest stems are fork tender. This should only take a couple of minutes.
5. Serve immediately as a side dish, or as a standalone lunch with some crusty Italian bread and a glass of red wine.

Note: Mustard greens rank right up there with kale, as being among the healthiest foods. They are packed with anti-oxidant flavanoids and with glucosinolates, which your body converts to cancer-fighting isothiocyanates. In addition, mustard greens reign supreme for vitamins (particularly A, K and E), minerals and iron.

Above: Senape

Below right: Senape seed pack from Italy

Below: Senape growing in my garden; multiple cuttings can be made from each plant.

Opposite: Senape plant allowed to flower, for collection and propagation of the annual seed.

Rapini con Salsiccia

Broccoli Rabe with Sausage

Rapini, or alternatively, broccoli rabe or broccoli raab, is a favorite leafy vegetable across southern Italy and is enjoyed in many different ways. Among the most favored is simply sautéed in olive oil, garlic and red pepper flakes. That's the "vegetarian" option; for me, broccoli rabe and sausage are made for each other! Of course, I use my homemade sausage for this recipe, but high-quality, store-bought Italian sausage would do in a pinch. The sausage can be grilled or fried. I prefer the latter for this dish because the fat left behind in the pan after frying the sausage adds further flavor to the fried broccoli rabe.

Broccoli rabe is more closely related to mustard and turnip species than to conventional broccoli. It has a bitter and slightly pungent flavor that's really fantastic. The stems, leaves, buds, and even the tiny yellow flowers, if present, are all edible, though I always harvest my home-grown broccoli rabe well before they begin to flower. If you go with store-bought broccoli rabe, look for very fresh bunches with deep green leaves and firm stems; avoid bunches that appear wilted. You might have to trim the very thick bottom part of the stem, since these will take substantially longer to cook than the rest of the plant, and you don't want the leaves and buds to get mushy while waiting for the thick stems to fully cook.

Ingredients (Serves 6)

3 to 4 bunches of broccoli rabe

6 links good quality Italian sausage

2 cloves garlic, chopped

Extra virgin olive oil

Red pepper flakes to taste

Salt to taste

Opposite:

Top: Rapini con salsiccia

Bottom left: Frying sausage

Bottom right: Sautéing the blanched broccoli rabe

Directions

1. In a large frying pan, add 2T olive oil and fry sausage links until browned and cooked throughout. Remove from pan and set aside. Reserve pan with residual oil.
2. Trim broccoli rabe, discarding only the tough bottom portions of each stem. Rinse the trimmed broccoli rabe in cold water.
3. Bring a large pot of salted water to a boil and blanch broccoli rabe for 5 minutes. Remove from water to a separate bowl. You might have to work in batches depending on how much broccoli rabe you have and the size of the pot.
4. Add 2 more tablespoons of olive oil, garlic and crushed red pepper to the pan in which you fried the sausage and sauté for 30 seconds.
5. Add broccoli rabe (in batches, if necessary) and sauté, tossing until the thickest part of the stem is tender. Remove to a serving bowl. If working in batches, add more olive oil with each batch.
6. When all of the broccoli rabe has been sautéed, slice sausage and return to pan to reheat. Add back all of the broccoli rabe and toss to reheat throughout.
7. Add salt to taste and serve with an extra drizzle of olive oil.

Crocchette di Patate

Potato Croquettes

Crocchette di patate (potato croquettes) are a great alternative to the more common potato side dishes of baked or mashed potatoes. Not that those aren't yummy also, but potato croquettes seem, to me at least, to be a bit more "elegant," maybe, than other potato options. I always remember potato croquettes as being associated with some special holiday dinner occasion, but given how easy they are to make, there's little reason not to prepare them more often.

This pretty simple recipe is the one my mom passed down and the one that I stick with - my kids absolutely love them!. The croquettes are crispy on the outside and wonderfully moist on the inside, with great flavor from Parmesan cheese and a hint of freshly grated nutmeg.

Ingredients (Serves 6)

For croquettes:

3 lbs russet potatoes

3 eggs

1/4 cup chopped fresh parsley

1/2 t freshly grated nutmeg

1/2 cup Parmesan cheese

1 t salt and coarsely ground black pepper to taste

For breading/frying:

2 cups flour

3 eggs

2 cups Italian flavored bread crumbs

Vegetable oil for frying

Directions

1. Peel potatoes and cut into approximately 2-inch pieces so that they cook evenly.
2. Boil potatoes in salted water until they are just fork tender. Drain in a colander.
3. Pass the potatoes through a ricer into a large bowl. Allow to cool.
4. Add the parsley, nutmeg, Parmesan, salt and pepper, and gently fold in.
5. Beat eggs and add to potatoes; gently fold in.
6. Shape potato mixture into croquettes and place on a sheet of parchment or waxed paper (see photo).
7. Fill a large frying pan with vegetable oil to about 1/2 inch deep and heat to 350°F. A deep fry thermometer is handy here to monitor temperature.
8. Place flour, beaten eggs and breadcrumbs into separate bowls. Working with a few croquettes at a time, roll in flour to lightly coat. Dip croquettes into egg wash and then into breadcrumbs.
9. Fry croquettes in oil until golden brown, turning to brown evenly.
10. Serve hot or at room temperature.

Note: The key to lighter croquettes is to use a potato ricer instead of a beater, as one might use when making mashed potatoes.

Above: Crocchete di patate
Right: Formed croquettes awaiting breading
Below: Riced potatoes

Arancini

Stuffed Rice Balls

Arancini are, of course, stuffed rice balls. According to most sources, arancini originated in Sicily centuries ago. Arancini were typically made as a way to use leftover risotto, but these little nuggets are so good that I often make risotto for the sole purpose of making arancini. For me, the only way to go is with the classic saffron-infused risotto alla Milanese.

The classic stuffing for arancini is either cheese or some sort of meat-based ragú, but other ingredients (mushrooms, spinach, pistachios, etc) have made it to the center of these tasty packages. After frying, the final product should be crisp on the outside and creamy on the inside.

Ingredients (Serves 6)

For the rice:

1 cup carnaroli rice

1 T olive oil

1/2 t crushed saffron threads

1/2 cup dry white wine

2 1/2 cups chicken stock

1 small yellow onion, chopped

1/4 cup Parmigiano Reggiano cheese

For the cheese filling:

3 oz mozzarella cheese

3 oz Fontina cheese

For the meat filling:

1 T olive oil

4 oz ground beef

4 oz prosciutto, chopped

1/4 cup chopped onion

1 clove garlic, chopped

1 cup canned, crushed tomatoes

1/2 cup peas

Salt and pepper to taste

For frying:

3 eggs, beaten

1 cup flour

2 cups fine breadcrumbs

Vegetable oil for deep frying

Directions

1. Prepare risotto. Add saffron to chicken stock and bring to a simmer. In a large frying pan, sauté onions in olive oil until soft. Add rice, stir to coat and cook until lightly toasted.
2. Add the wine and cook, with stirring, until evaporated.
3. Add hot stock, a ladle-full at a time, cook with stirring until absorbed by the rice. Continue adding until all the stock is added and absorbed, and the rice looks creamy.
4. Stir in Parmesan, remove from heat and allow to cool. The rice will become more "shape-able" when cooled.
5. Prepare the meat filling. Sauté onion and garlic in olive oil. Add ground beef and brown.
6. Add tomatoes and peas and cook uncovered until most of the moisture is evaporated.
7. Remove from heat and add prosciutto. Allow to cool.
8. Dice the cheese into small cubes.
9. Assemble the arancini. When the rice is cool enough to handle, pick up a palm-sized amount, make a depression in the middle, and add about a tablespoon of filling - either cheese or meat mixture. Shape the rice into a ball, entrapping the filling in the middle. Prepare all of the arancini before moving to the breading and frying step.
10. Fry the arancini. Heat vegetable oil to 350ºF in a deep fryer or a sauce pan large enough to submerge the arancini.
11. Working with one at a time, roll the arancini in flour to coat, then in the egg. Shake off excess and then roll in breadcrumbs.
12. Careful place the arancini, a few at a time, in the hot oil and fry until golden brown all around, approximately 4 to 5 minutes,
13. Remove from oil and allow to drain on paper towels.
14. Sprinkle with Parmesan and serve as is or with marinara sauce.

Above: Arancini

Right: Forming arancini around a piece of cheese

Below right: Cooking the meat filling

Below left: Preparing the risotto for arancini

Cavalfiore alle Acciughe

Cauliflower with Anchovies

Cauliflower varieties number in the scores - a multitude of shapes, sizes and colors. In southern Italy, cauliflower is prepared in many different ways - this one is among my favorites. Don't be taken aback by what might seem as an excess amount of anchovies. In the final, prepared dish, they really only provide an undertone of flavor that nicely compliments the very mild character of the cauliflower. The tanginess of the capers and lemon provide nice balance to the saltiness of the anchovies, and the crunch of the homemade breadcrumbs lends added texture.

Ingredients (Serves 4-6)

1 large head, or 2 smaller heads of cauliflower, about 2 lbs in total

1 can (2 oz) flat fillet of anchovies

2 slices of Italian bread

2 cloves garlic

Several sprigs of parsley, chopped

4 T olive oil plus more for drizzling

2 t capers in vinegar

Juice of 1/2 lemon

Crushed red pepper to taste

Sea salt and coarse ground black pepper to taste

Directions

1. Preheat oven to 425ºF.
2. Remove leaves from cauliflower and divide into flowerettes
3. In a large bowl, toss cauliflower with one clove of chopped garlic, 2 T olive oil and a sprinkle of salt and pepper. Spread cauliflower on a shallow roasting pan and roast until slightly golden and just tender; about 25 minutes.
4. While cauliflower is roasting, finely chop anchovies. Heat 2 T olive oil in a large frying pan (or wok) and add the anchovies, capers, and crushed red pepper. Cook for several minutes until the anchovies completely break down to form a sauce.
5. Toast Italian bread slices in a toaster, and then drizzle a little olive oil on each and rub with the remaining clove of garlic (halved). Chop toast into coarse breadcrumbs and set aside.
6. When the cauliflower is done, transfer to the frying pan and toss well with the anchovy mixture, cooking for several minutes until the cauliflower is coated in the sauce.
7. Transfer the cauliflower to a serving bowl and add the parsley, breadcrumbs and lemon juice. Toss well and adjust seasoning. Serve with a little extra drizzle of olive oil.

Above: Cavalfiore alle acciughe

Right: Italian bread slices, rubbed with olive oil and garlic

Below right: Anchovy mixture prior to cooking

Below left: Roasted cauliflower ready for tossing in the anchovy mixture

Patate al Sugo

Potatoes in Sauce

Patate al sugo couldn't be simpler to prepare - basically potatoes, onions and tomato sauce. The three meld together to form a great side dish for dinner.

Here's an interesting tid-bit…potatoes are among the few things that I have never grown in my garden! Potato plants take up a lot of room, and given that you can pick up a 10-lb bag for only a few bucks, I'd rather reserve precious garden space for "high value" and hard-to-find fruits and vegetables. The choice is between planting a garden row to yield a bushel of potatoes or three bushels of vine-ripened San Marzano tomatoes - I call that a no brainer!

Ingredients (Serves 6)

3 lbs of fresh Russet potatoes

2 cups prepared tomato sauce (preferably homemade)

2 T olive oil

1 medium onion, sliced

1 t dried oregano

Salt and coarse ground black pepper to taste

Directions

1. Preheat oven to 400°F.
2. Peel potatoes and cut them into pieces of about 1 to 1 1/2 inches.
3. Toss potatoes, onion, sauce and oregano in a bowl to coat the tomatoes in the sauce. Transfer to an oven-proof baking dish large enough to accommodate the potatoes.
4. Drizzle olive oil over the mixture and sprinkle with salt and pepper to taste.
5. Cover with foil and bake for approximately 30 to 40 minutes until the potatoes are just fork tender. Remove fol and bake an additional 10 minutes to just brown on top.
6. Serve while oven-hot.

Zucchini alla Scapece

Zucchini with Mint and Vinegar

Zucchini alla scapece is another one of those simple, rustic dishes common to Southern Italy. *Scapece* is typically used to denote something with a vinegar-based marinade. Though some recipes call for roasting the zucchini, frying is the more traditional method. The key is to let them air dry a bit before frying, and then fry briefly in medium hot oil. In this way, the zucchini will soak up less of the oil and retain some firmness. Other recipes call for salting the zucchini before frying to help extract moisture, but I don't particularly like doing that - makes them a bit soggy.

Zucchini alla scapece is typically served at room temperature as a side dish, or on some *crostini* as a snack. It's delicious the next day, chilled, as part of an antipasto.

Zucchini are extremely easy to grow, but you need quite a bit of garden space. When I first started growing them, I made the mistake of planting a half dozen or so plants. The amount of zucchini I harvested that year could fill the back of my pickup truck! I have long since learned that a single zucchini pant is more than sufficient to meet my culinary needs for the season.

Ingredients (Serves 6)

Approximately 3 lbs of fresh zucchini (about 8 small zucchini)

1 clove garlic, chopped

Olive oil for frying

A generous handful of fresh mint leave, coarsely chopped

1 t capers in vinegar

1/4 cup Prosecco vinegar

Sea salt and coarse ground black pepper to taste

Directions

1. Wash zucchini and trim off both ends. Cut into rounds about a half inch thick.
2. Line a large tray with paper towels and arrange the zucchini on the tray. Cover with another layer of paper towels and just let them rest at room temperature for about a half hour.
3. Place olive oil in a large skillet, enough to cover the bottom. Heat to medium-high.
4. Fry the zucchini and chopped garlic until the zucchini just start to pick up some color (see photo). You might have to do this in two batches, depending on how much zucchini you have and the size of your skillet. Remove zucchini from skillet and allow to drain on paper towels.
5. Toss the zucchini with the mint, capers and vinegar. Season to taste with salt and pepper. Serve at room temperature.

Above: Zucchini alla Scapece

Right: Zucchini seedlings starting out (I make extra and give them to friends and neighbors to plant)

Below right: Zucchini plant in my garden

Below left: Mint starting out in Spring

Desserts

• Cannoli di Estelle•
Mom's Cannoli

• Torta di Formaggio •
Mom's Cheesecake

• Tartelette alle Noci •
Walnut Tassies

• Struffoli Napoletani •
Naples Style Honey Balls

• Tiramisu •
Tiramisu

• Biscotti all'Anice •
Anise Cookies

• Biscotti Siciliani ai Pignoli •
Sicilian Pine Nut Cookies

• Zeppole Dolci •
Sweet Italian Fritters

Cannoli di Estella

Mom's Cannoli

I've had cannoli all over the U.S., and all over Italy. I can say, without reservation, that no one makes cannoli like my mom, Estelle, or "Peggy," as she was known by friends and family. Fortunately, this was one recipe that mom actually wrote down, for which I (and everyone I know) am eternally grateful.

Sicily is credited with inventing the *cannolo* (the Italian singular of *cannoli*), which translates to "little tube." Cannoli are rather simple in design - a tube-shaped pastry shell and some filling. The details, of course, are what make the cannoli. First off, the filling should be sweetened whole milk ricotta - no whipped cream, no cream cheese, and no artificial crap. The shell is deep-fried in fat, not baked. If you want a healthy dessert, have an apple! If you want the best dessert that Italy has to offer, read on.

As long as the two above-mentioned requirements are met, there are many different embellishments that one can make to cannoli. The addition of candied citrus peel to the filling is not uncommon. The ends of the filled cannoli can be dipped in chocolate chips, ground pistachio, ground espresso beans, or any of a multitude of options. The cannoli shells can be made with cinnamon, Marsala, cocoa and other ingredients. I sometimes experiment with some of these options, but always return to the base recipe that I knew growing up - mom's cannoli.

Ingredients (makes approx. 24)

For the filling:

- 3 lbs whole milk ricotta
- 2 cups whole milk
- 8 T cornstarch
- 1 T vanilla
- 2 1/2 cups sugar
- 1 cup mini semisweet chocolate chips

For the shells:

- 1 1/2 cups flour
- 1 T cocoa powder
- 1 T sugar
- 1/2 t baking soda
- 1/4 t salt
- 2 T vegetable shortening (Crisco)
- 1/2 cup red wine

48 oz Crisco for deep frying

Directions

1. Prepare filling: In a saucepan, mix milk, sugar and cornstarch. Heat gently to a low boil and then cook the mixture for 30 minutes, with stirring. Set aside to cool. It should look like a thick custard after cooling.
2. Beat ricotta until smooth, then beat in custard and vanilla. Mix in chocolate chips. Store refrigerated until shells are made.
3. Prepare shells: Mix together the dry ingredients and then work in the Crisco. Add wine to make the dough.
4. Melt the rest of the Crisco in a pot large. The melted shortening should be about 3 inches deep. Bring to 350ºF.
5. Take a piece of dough about the size of a quarter and roll it very thin in the shape of a circle or slight oval. Wrap the dough around a cannoli tube, overlapping ends. Seal with a little beaten egg.
6. Working with 6 tubes at a time, carefully drop them into the Crisco to fry until browned, typically less than 1 minute.
7. Remove the shells and allow to drain/cool. A cardboard egg carton works great here (see photo).
8. When shells are cool enough to handle, carefully side them off the tube. I typically keep the shells unfilled until the cannoli are ready to serve. This helps keep the shells crispy.
9. Fill shells with ricotta filling and dust with powdered sugar.

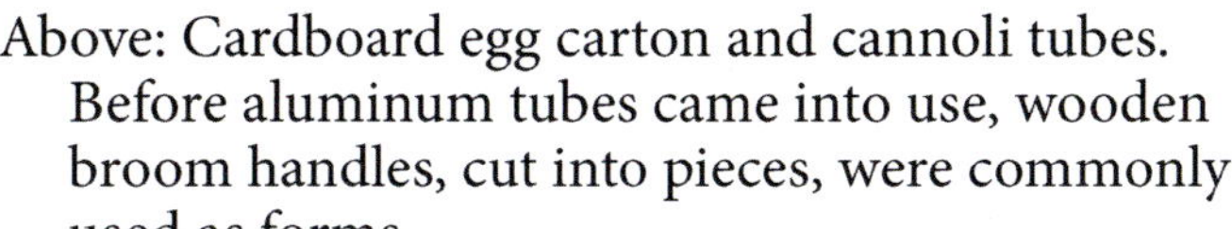

Above: Cardboard egg carton and cannoli tubes. Before aluminum tubes came into use, wooden broom handles, cut into pieces, were commonly used as forms

Above right: Fried cannoli shells cooling off

Right: Finished cannoli shells

Below: Mom's canoli

Opposite: Mom's hand-written recipe, still well-preserved after more than 50 years

"Leave the gun...take the cannoli"

- Peter Clemenza

Torta di Formaggio

Mom's Cheesecake

Traditional Italian cheesecake is made with ricotta cheese, and while the traditional version is certainly yummy, my family's favorite is Mom's "New York style" cheesecake. This cake has a homemade graham cracker crust and is finished with a thin layer of a sour cream topping. The cake is super-creamy and just dense enough. Classic New York cheesecake is served plain, and that's the way I prefer it, but feel free to add your favorite toppings - raspberry sauce, fresh strawberries, blueberries, etc.

People have literally begged me for this recipe but, up until now, it has remained a family secret. I'm sure Mom will forgive me.

Ingredients (Serves 6 to 12)

For the crust:

5 oz Honey Graham crackers

1/4 cup sugar

3 T butter, melted plus 1 T softened for coating pan

For the cheesecake filling:

3 8-oz packages Philadelphia Original cream cheese

5 large eggs

1 cup sugar

1 t vanilla

For the topping:

10 oz sour cream

1/2 cup sugar

1/2 t vanilla

Directions

1. Important: butter, eggs and cream cheese need to be at room temperature.
2. Butter the inside of a 9-inch spring form pan with 1 T softened butter.
3. In a food processor, mix together the graham crackers and sugar to form a fine grind. Add the melted butter and mix well.
4. Transfer the crust ingredients to the spring form pan and press evenly against the sides and bottom to form the crust (see photo); refrigerator while you prepare the cake.
5. With a stand mixer and wire whip, beat the softened cream cheese until smooth.
6. Add one egg at a time, beating for 3 minutes between each egg. Pause to scrap down the sides of the mixing bowl with a spatula, if necessary.
7. Add sugar and vanilla and mix well.
8. Place a container of water on the lower rack of an oven and preheat to 350ºF.
9. Transfer the batter to the spring form pan and place on the middle rack of the oven. Bake for 1 hr at 350ºF.
10. Remove from oven an allow to cool for 20 minutes. Don't worry if there are a few cracks on the surface (see photo), they will close up as the cake cools and contracts.
11. While the cake cools, prepare the topping. Beat together the sour cream sugar and vanilla. When the cake has cooled, pour the topping over the top, spreading with a spatula, if necessary.
12. Return the cake to the 350ºF oven for an additional 10 minutes to allow the topping to set up.
13. Remove and refrigerate overnight or for at least 2 hrs before serving; the cheesecake can be easily cut into 12 pieces after fully cooled.

Above: Torta di Formaggio della Mamma

Right: Spring form pan with graham cracker crust

Below right: Cheesecake after the initial bake, before cooling.

Below: Serving of Mom's cheesecake

Opposite: Jenna helping with the batter

Tartelette alle Noci

Walnut Tassies

Every cuisine probably has a version of nut tassies - basically little cups of baked goodness filled with sugar and nuts. In the U.S., pecans are the favored nuts for tassies. In Italy, however, walnuts are king. Walnut trees have been cultivated for centuries in Italy. Walnuts are probably among the nuts most widely used in Italian cuisine, along with pine nuts (*pignoli*), hazelnuts (*nocciole*) and chestnuts (*castange*).

Tartelette alla noci would be among the (huge) collection of sweets that my mother would prepare for holiday celebrations. I scaled back her recipe here to yield a more reasonable number - she would typically make way more for a family celebration! My kids love these things!

Ingredients (makes 24)

For the shells:

1 stick (8 oz) butter, room temperature

1 cup all-purpose flour

3 oz cream cheese

For the filling:

2 eggs

1 cup light brown sugar

Pinch of salt

3/4 cup unsalted walnuts, chopped

Directions

1. In a bowl, beat together the butter and cream cheese until blended and smooth.
2. Add the flour and mix until a dough forms. Cover the dough ball with plastic wrap and let rest in the refrigerator for 15 minutes.
3. Divide the dough into 24 pieces. I usually do this by dividing it in half and then rolling out each half into logs about 12 inches long. It's easy, then, to cut each into 12 1-inch pieces to end up with 24 pieces of approximately equal size.
4. Spray a 24-cup mini-muffin pan with cooking spray. Working with one piece of dough at a time on a floured worked surface, press each into a flat disc with the palm of your hand and then transfer to the muffin pan, pressing the dough into the shape of a cup. Repeat with the remaining pieces of dough.
5. In a separate bowl, beat eggs together with the brown sugar and pinch of salt, for several minutes.
6. Spoon the mixture equally into each of the 24 dough cups. Each should end up about 3/4 filled.
7. Top each cup with chopped walnuts, about a teaspoon on each.
8. Bake at 350ºF for 15-20 minutes.

Above: Tartelette alle noci

Right: Dough pieces cut to size for each mini-muffin cup

Struffoli Napoletani
Naples Style Honey Balls

Struffoli is an Italian dessert - most notably, from Naples - that's traditionally prepared for Christmas and Easter, however, I've always associated struffoli with the latter. It is composed of deep-fried dough balls - about the size of marbles - soaked in honey and mixed with *canditi*, candied fruit of various types. The large mass of struffoli would then be shaped into a dome or a ring - "glued" together by the generous amount of honey - and then topped with decorative accents like confetti, sprinkles, etc. One would then separate a small chunk of struffoli from the gigantic mass and enjoy it with a nice cup of espresso.

Struffoli is nothing short of addicting! The fried dough balls, which by themselves are not overly sweet, are crispy on the outside and softer in the middle - perfect for soaking up the sweet honey goodness. The *canditi* (orange peel, citron, cherries, etc) put it over the top.

Oh, and you have to eat struffoli with your fingers - there's just no other way.

Ingredients (makes 1 large ring or mound)

2 cups all-purpose flour

The zest of 1 lemon and 1 medium-sized orange

2 T sugar

1/2 t baking powder

1/2 stick of butter, room temperature

3 eggs

1 t vanilla extract

1 T brandy

1 cup honey

Approximately 3/4 cup candied, mixed fruit, chopped

Colored sprinkles

Canola oil for frying

Directions

1. In a bowl, mix together the flour, orange and lemon zest, sugar and baking powder.
2. Transfer the mix to a food processor and add the butter. Pulse several times to blend.
3. Add the vanilla, brandy and one egg at a time - pulsing in between - until a dough forms.
4. Wrap the dough ball in plastic wrap and refrigerate for 30 minutes.
5. Working with about a quarter of the dough at a time, roll it into a rope about 1/2 inch thick. You might need some additional flour for dusting here if the dough is too sticky. Cut the rope into 1/2 inch pieces and roll each one into a ball, about the size of a marble. Set the dough balls aside on a large tray, making sure they don't stick to each other.
6. Fill a pot with about 2 inches of oil and heat to 350°F. Fry the dough balls in batches until they are golden brown - about 3 minutes per batch - making sure that the oil temperature stays close to 350°F. Transfer the fried dough balls to a platter lined with paper towels to drain.
7. Transfer the fried dough balls to a large bowl and add the candied fruit.
8. Heat the honey briefly in a microwave until it is more fluid and then pour it over the fried dough balls. Toss them gently to coat evenly with the honey.
9. Arrange the struffoli in a mound or ring, top with a little extra honey and candied fruit (optional) and the colored sprinkles.

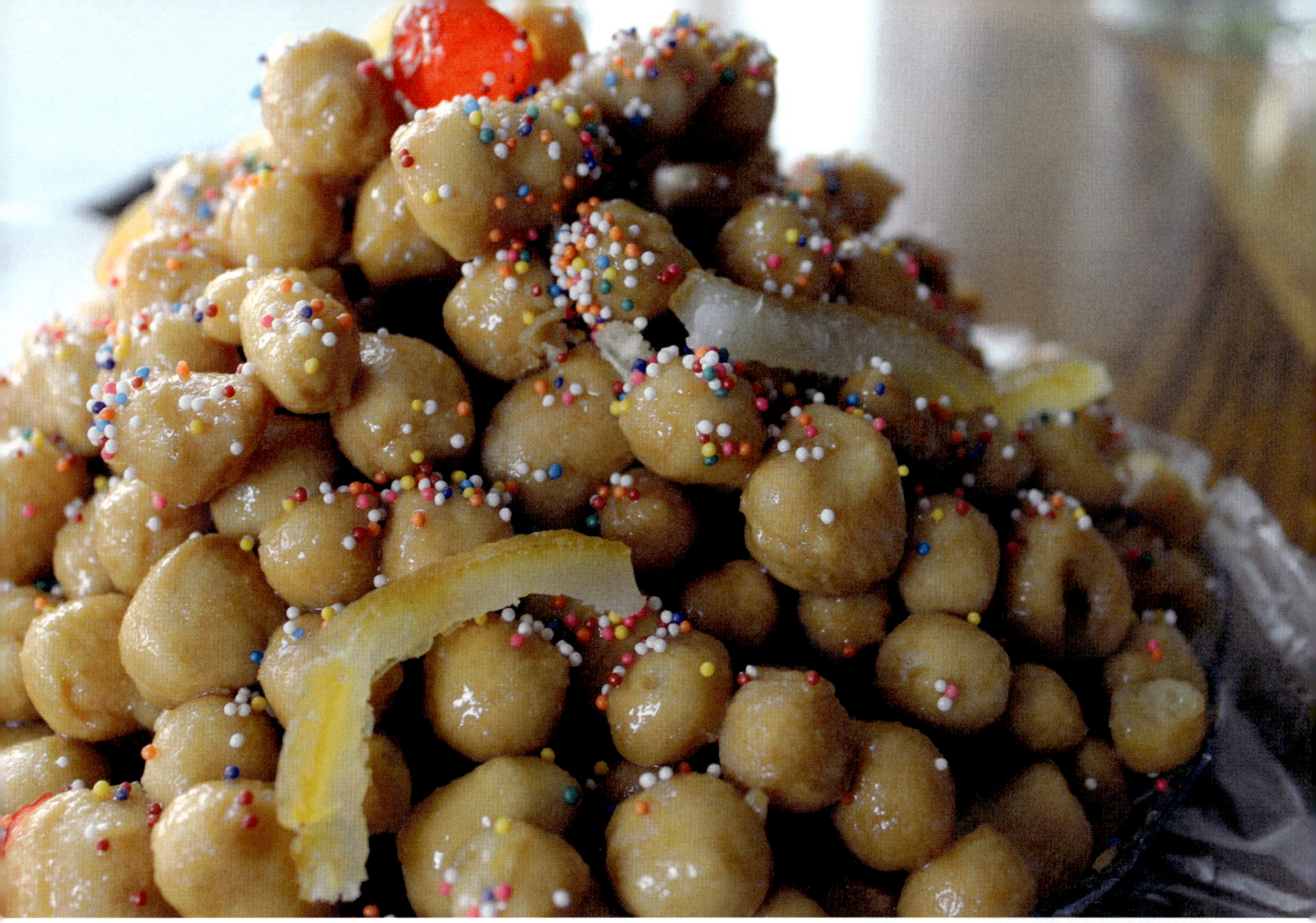

Above: Struffoli Napoletani
Right: Candied fruit

Buona Pasqua!

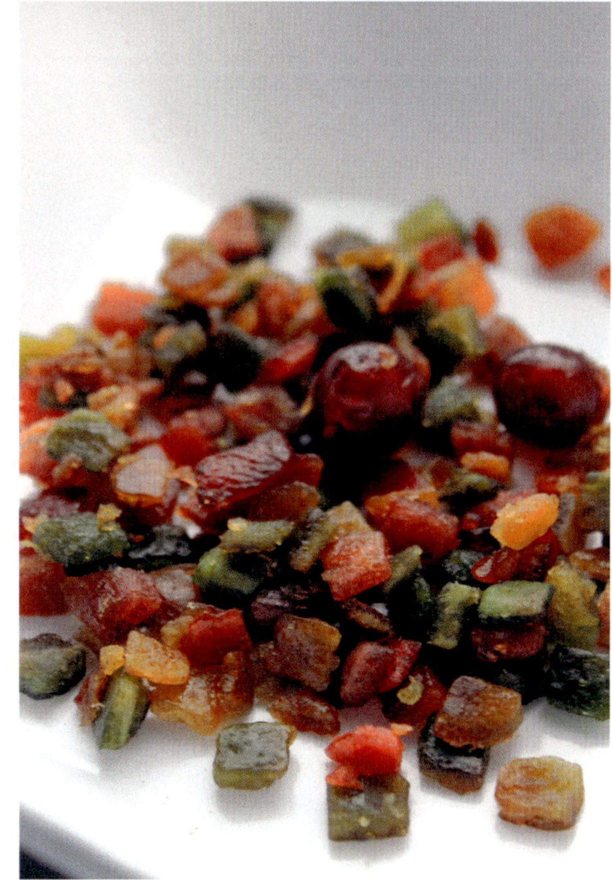

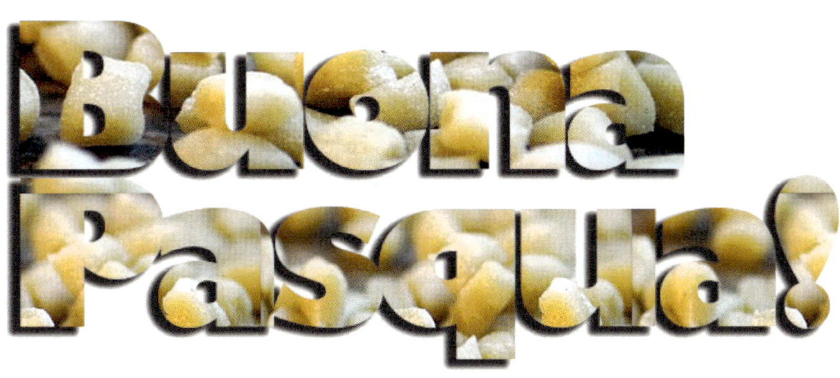

Tiramisú

Tiramisu

Tiramisu is probably my kids' favorite dessert, with strong competition from cannoli. It is an elegant concoction of alternating layers of espresso-soaked savoiardi ("lady fingers") and mascarpone-based zabaglione. Though traditional zabaglione is made with Marsala wine, this family recipe incorporates Frangelico into the custard instead - TOTALLY make the tiramisu!

As always, the quality of ingredients makes or breaks the dish, and this is particularly true for tiramisu. Avoid the spongy lady fingers typically found in supermarkets - *biscotti savoiardi* imported from Italy are a must. Secondly, the mascarpone cheese must be dense, like a block of Philadelphia cream cheese. Depending on the fat content and production method, some mascarpone cheeses are too "soft" for use in this recipe, resulting in a zabaglione that doesn't hold together well. Finally, since the zabaglione is made with raw eggs, it is important to use the freshest eggs possible. If you are concerned about the use of raw eggs, you can substitute pasteurized eggs (yes, that's a real thing).

Ingredients (Serves 8 to 10)

Savoiardi cookies, about 12 oz

2 cups freshly-brewed espresso, cooled to room temperature

3 eggs, whites and yolks separated

1 lb mascarpone cheese

2/3 cup sugar

1/3 cup Frangelico liqueur

Cocoa powder

Directions

1. In a medium-sized mixing bowl, beat egg yolks with sugar until thickened and very pale.
2. Mix in Frangelico.
3. Add mascarpone cheese and mix until incorporated.
4. In a separate bowl, beat egg whites to stiff peaks, and then gently fold whites into cheese mixture.
5. Pour espresso into a container to facilitate dipping the savoiardi (see photo). Dip savoiardi, one at a time, into the espresso and arrange side-by-side into the final dessert tray. This should be a brief dip - just a few seconds - just enough to allow the espresso to penetrate the surface of the savoiardi (see photo).
6. With the bottom of the dessert tray cover with espresso-dipped savoiardi, pour half of the mascarpone mixture on top and spread evenly.
7. Repeat process with a second layer of savoiardi on top of the mascarpone layer.
8. Finally, cover the savoiardi evenly with the remaining mascarpone mixture.
9. Dust the top with cocoa powder and refrigerate overnight, or at least 4 hrs before serving.

Above: Serving of tiramisu

Opposite top: Going slightly off the reservation with shaved semi-sweet chocolate and scattered chocolate chips instead of cocoa powder (at my daughters' suggestion)

Opposite bottom panels: Mixing in the mascarpone; imported savoiardi; first layer of espresso-dipped savoiardi; zabaglione mixture covering first layer of savoiardi and starting of the second layer

IMPORTATO
ALESSI®
PERFECT FOR
TIRAMISU
See recipe
on back
panel
BISCOTTI SAVOIARDI
Lady Fingers
NET WT. 7 OZ. (200g)

Biscotti all'Anice

Anise Cookies

Biscotti all'anice are popular dessert cookies in Italy. I have memories from my very early childhood of the aroma of these cookies baking in the oven. My mom made them in a few different varieties - sometimes with almonds, sometimes orange zest and sometimes just plain. They are typically enjoyed following a dip in espresso or in a sweet Italian desert wine, like Vin Santo.

Anice is anise seed from which anise extract is produced, which of course has a very intense, licorice-like flavor. It is the flavor on which the cordials anisette and Sambuca are based.

Ingredients (makes about 20 biscotti)

- 2 cups all-purpose flour
- 2 t baking powder
- 3/4 cup sugar
- 1 stick of butter at room temperature
- 2 large eggs plus the white from one additional egg
- 1 t anise seed
- 1 t anise extract
- 1 cup whole almonds, coarsely chopped

Directions

1. Preheat oven to 350ºF.
2. Sift together the flour and baking powder.
3. In a large bowl, beat together the sugar and butter until creamed.
4. Beat in 2 eggs, one at a time, and then beat in the anise seed and anise extract.
5. Add in the flour mixture and almonds. Mix with a spatula to form a dough.
6. Spray a cookie sheet or shallow baking pan with cooking spray and light dust with flour.
7. Place the dough on the pan and shape it into a slightly flattened log about 15" long.
8. In a small bowl, mix the remaining egg white with 1 T of water and brush the mixture over the surface of the dough log.
9. Bake the log for about 35 minutes until just slightly browned (see photo).
10. Remove from oven and allow to cool for 10 minutes.
11. Slice the log into diagonal slices about 3/4" to 1" thick. A serrated or bread knife works well.
12. Return the slices to the baking tray, lay them on their side and bake for an additional 10-15 minutes until they are nicely browned.
13. Remove from oven and allow to cool. The final biscotti should be crunchy and crumbly.

Above: Biscotti all' anice
Below: Dough log after the initial bake

Biscotti Siciliani ai Pignoli

Sicilian Pine Nut Cookies

Biscotti Siciliani ai pignoli (or just "pignoli cookies") is a favorite Southern Italian confection, typically part of an Italian Christmas cookie platter. Authentic pignoli cookies are made with almond paste and no flour. The quality of the almond paste is critical in order to get the proper consistency of the finished cookie (see note below). Properly prepared, pignoli cookies with have a similar texture and chewiness as, say, a macaroon, and not overly sweet. Perfect with a nice cup of freshly brewed espresso!

Ingredients

(makes about 16 cookies)

1 10-oz can of almond paste

3/4 cup granulated sugar

1 cup pine nuts

2 egg whites

1/2 t orange extract

Powdered sugar for dusting (optional)

Directions

1. Break up the almond paste and place it in a food processor. Add 1/4 cup granulated sugar and pulse several times to break up the almond paste.
2. Add the remaining 1/2 cup sugar and pulse again several times until the almond paste is uniformly ground.
3. Add the egg whites and orange extract. Process until a smooth dough is formed; about 30 seconds. The dough will be very sticky, so it helps to keep a bowl of water handy to moisten your hands to shape the cookie dough.
4. Place the pignoli nuts in a single layer in a flat dish.
5. Scoop out a piece of dough and roll it into a ball something smaller than a ping pong ball - about the diameter of a quarter.
6. Press the ball into the pignoli nuts, flattening it into a disc about 2 inches in diameter.
7. Place the cookie, pignoli side up, on a baking sheet lined with parchment paper.
8. Repeat with the remaining dough, dampening your hands between cookies.
9. Place cookies in a pre-heated 350°F oven and bake for 15 minutes.
10. Allow cookies to cool to room temperature.

Note: Almond paste is very different than marzipan, do not try to substitute the latter for almond paste. The best quality almond paste I've found is a product from Love 'n Bake (photo). You can purchase a 10-oz can for about $9 (not inexpensive, but worth it). I've tried other paste in tubes and haven't been happy with the quality.

Above: Biscotti Siciliani ai pignoli (pignoli cookies)

Below left: Raw pignoli nuts

Below right: Almond paste

Zeppole Dolci

Sweet Italian Fritters

Father's Day in Italy is celebrated on March 19 and coincides with *La Festa di San Giuseppe*, the Catholic feast day in honor of St. Joseph (as in Mary and Joseph), Jesus' father figure on earth.

So what does this have to do with zeppole, you might ask? Well, probably the most notable street food that has become synonymous with the Feast of St. Joseph is the *zeppola* (plural = *zeppole*). Depending on what region of Italy you're in, zeppole can take on a number of different variations, but the common element is a deep-fired pastry along the lines of a New Orleans beignet. Some versions are filled (or topped) with Italian *pasticciera* cream, others are dipped in chocolate or drizzled with honey. I've had zeppole that are way too dense for my liking - more like a deep-fried pizza dough consistency. The best zeppole are light and airy, and my preference for topping is a simple dusting with confectioners sugar. Absolutely addicting!

To be honest, I'm not a big "dessert guy." My favorite zeppole is the savory version with anchovies (page 101), which is popular in Calabria and Sicily. Having said that, this family recipe for *zeppole dolce* is pretty darn good, and my kids' favorite.

Ingredients (makes about 16)

1 cup all-purpose flour
1/4 cup super-fine Semolina flour
2 1/2 t baking powder
1/3 cup granulated sugar
1/4 cup whole milk
Pinch of salt
2 eggs
8 oz whole milk ricotta cheese
1 t vanilla extract
Confectioners sugar
Vegetable oil for frying

Directions

1. In a bowl, beat together the ricotta, sugar and vanilla until creamy. Set aside.
2. In a separate bowl, beat the eggs with the milk, and then add in the flours, baking powder and salt.
3. Fold in the ricotta mixture. The final product should be like a thick batter, or very wet dough (see photo).
4. Place about 2 inches of oil in a pot and heat to 350°F.
5. Scoop up about a tablespoon of batter at a time and carefully drop it into the oil, turning them to brown evenly. You can fry several zeppole at a time, but don't over-crowd the pot. Frying time should be about 1 minute.
6. When the zeppole are golden brown, remove them with a slotted spoon and drain on paper towels.
7. When all zeppole are fried and slightly cooled, transfer to a serving platter and dust with confectioners sugar.

Note: The zeppole will double in size during frying. Avoid dropping in too much batter; large zeppole will not fully cook in the center by the time they're properly browned.

Above: Zeppole dolce
Below left: Deep frying the zeppole
Below right: Fried zeppole draining on paper towels
Opposite: Consistency of prepared zeppole batter

Be Adventurous

• Meat Curing Cabinet •

• Guanciale •

• Lamb Prosciutto •

• Bresaola •

• Capocollo •

• Sopressata •

• Pancetta •

• Homemade Italian Sausage •

• Pizza Dough•

• Pasta Dough•

• Fresh Mozzerella •

• Fresh Ricotta •

• Jarred Tomatoes •

• Slow-Cooked Tomato Sauce •

• Marinara Sauce •

• "Sun Dried" Tomatoes •

• Pickling •

• Curing Olives •

Meat Curing Cabinet

Dry curing has been practiced for thousands of years for the long-term preservation of meat. The principle is simple - once a sufficient amount of water is removed from meat (typically by salt), bacteria are unable to thrive and your meat remains edible for long periods of time. Today, the need for long-term preservation of meat is not the main driving force behind meat curing, as it was centuries ago. Rather, curing has evolved into a culinary art form that can elevate a plain old piece of meat to new heights of flavor and texture.

I love curing my own meat products; not for lack of commercially available high quality cured meats. For me, it's part science experiment and part culinary creativity. It connects me in a strange sort of way to family generations before me in whose subterranean caves hung rows of perfectly aged delicacies – a true art form, indeed. Meat curing is not difficult, and can be very rewarding. The recipes in this chapter are ones that I have landed on after many years of experimentation. There are also many books available that provide detailed instruction and recipes for various types of cured meats; I would encourage you to do a little experimenting on your own.

Now, you can certainly just purchase a meat curing cabinet, but be prepared to pay several thousands of dollars. Alternatively, for a few hundred dollars and some basic skills, you can construct your own meat curing cabinet to start you on your way to preparing some great, home-cured meats.

Directions

1. The components of a meat curing cabinet are as follows: (i) a simple, basic refrigerator; "apartment" size, about 16 cubic feet. I bought one new from Sears for under $400, but a perfectly suitable used refrigerator can be bought for less - just make sure you clean the inside well, (ii) a temperature/humidity monitor, (iii) a standard ultrasonic humidifier, (iv) a small electric fan, and (v) a fan speed controller (optional).
2. Remove all of the interior racks from the refrigerator and drill a hole through one of the side walls, approximately in the middle of the wall. The hole must be large enough to allow an electrical plug to fit through. DO NOT drill through the back wall or bottom of the refrigerator - that's where the refrigeration and electrical components are typically positioned. The side walls are just insulation between two layers of plastic.
3. Re-position only the top rack in the refrigerator and place the electric fan on the rack. Run the fan' s cord out through the hole you just drilled.
4. Place the filled humidifier on the bottom of the refrigerator, and run it's cord out through the hole.
5. Place the temperature/humidity sensor on the rack, not directly in front of the fan. Run the sensor's cord out through the hole.
6. Mount the temperature/humidity controller on the exterior side wall of the refrigerator, close enough to the hole so that the cord plugs are in reach.
7. Connect the sensor cord to the controller. Plug the humidifier into the outlet on the controller that regulates HUMIDITY. Plug the refrigerator's power cord into the outlet on the controller that regulates TEMPERATURE. Plug the fan motor into any wall power outlet, or into the optional fan speed controller.
8. Program the desired temperature and humidity set points according to your controller and you're done! The refrigerator and humidifier will turn on and off to maintain the desired set points.

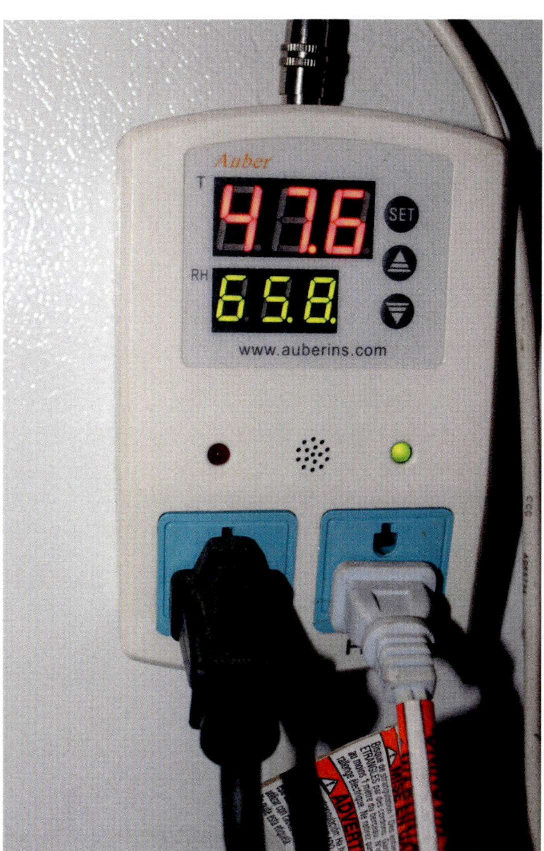

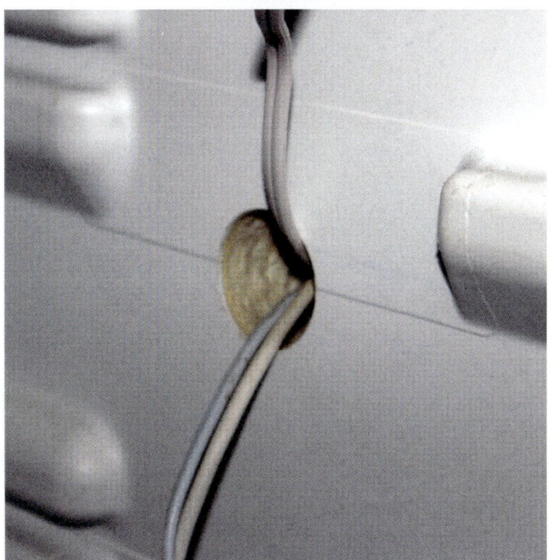

Clockwise from above:

Converted refrigerator interior showing electric fan, temperature and humidity monitor, ultrasonic humidifier, and freshly hung sopressata.

Temperature and humidity controller (Auber Instruments)

Equipment cords passing through a 1 1/4" hole drilled through the refrigerator side

Optional motor fan speed controller (Speed Bully)

Guanciale

Cured Pork Jowl

Guanciale is foreign to most Americans. It's similar to bacon in that both are cuts of pork with a high fat-to-lean ratio, but that's where the similarities end. Guanciale is made from pork jowls, or cheeks (*guancia* is the Italian word for cheek), while bacon is from pork bellies. Guanciale is not smoked, as is bacon, but rather cured with salt and other spices and then air dried. The flavor of guanciale is so amazing that, once you've tasted it, you may never go back to bacon again - and that's coming from someone who loves bacon!

Unfortunately, guanciale can be hard to find unless you have access to a good Italian meat market. It's also considerably more expensive than bacon. The solution, therefore, is simple - make your own guanciale! I sometimes come across fresh pork jowls in specialty meat markets. Alternatively, there are a number of internet sites from which you can buy fresh pork jowls. Transforming them to guanciale is pretty straightforward, but you will need some equipment (as described in the previous pages) and some patience. It's worth the effort!

Ingredients

4 to 5 lbs fresh pork jowl

For the cure (see table):

- Kosher salt 3% w/w
- Sugar 2% w/w
- InstaCure™ #2 0.3% w/w
- Black peppercorns, 1% w/w
- 10 bay leaves, crushed
- 1 T dried thyme
- 1 T dried rosemary
- 1 T dried minced garlic
- 1 t dried allspice berries, ground

2 T dried fennel seeds, ground

Opposite top: Finished guanciale

Opposite middle: Fresh, packaged pork jowl

Opposite bottom: Seasoned pork jowl ready for the initial curing

Directions

1. Prepare the fresh pork jowl for curing by removing any skin and extraneous tissue. Occasionally, you will find that salivary glands are attached to the jowl; these should be removed. You should be left with only fat and lean muscle. Important - record the weight of the meat.
2. Add the InstaCure to the salt and mix well. Coarsely grind the peppercorns and allspice berries in an electric spice grinder and add to the salt, along with the sugar, rosemary, thyme, bay leaves and garlic. Reserve the fennel for the drying stage.
3. Cover the jowls with the cure mixture, making sure that the meat is entirely covered.
4. Transfer the jowls and any remaining cure mix to sealable plastic bags or, preferably, vacuum sealer bags. Remove as much air as possible to maintain contact between the cure and the meat.
5. Refrigerate the sealed bags for 7-9 days, turning occasionally.
6. Remove the jowls from the bag and rinse off the cure under cold running water. The jowls should feel somewhat stiff and hard at this point.
7. Sprinkle the ground fennel over the jowls and prepare for hanging in your meat curing cabinet. I typically punch a whole through one end of the meat (not too close to the edge) and use butcher's twine to suspend it. I also attach a tag to the twine to indicate the date and weight of the meat.
8. Dry at 40-45ºF, 75% relative humidity until the meat loses 20% of its starting weight, approximately 3-4 weeks.

The amounts of key curing components are based upon the starting weight of the meat to be cured. In this example, the total weight of meat is 4.74 lbs or 2155 grams (g). The % by weight of each key curing ingredient, and final amount in grams, is shown in the table below. Example: the amount of Kosher salt in the cure is 2155 g x 0.03 = 64.7 g.

For the initial cure:		
Ingredient	**Weight (g)**	**% by Weight**
Pork jowl	2155	-
Kosher salt	64.7	3% w/w
Sugar	43.1	2% w/w
Instacure #2	6.5	0.3% w/w
Black peppercorns	21.6	1 % w/w
Other ingredients as listed		

Guanciale can basically be used in place of bacon for most recipes. It is traditionally used for dishes like bucatini all'amatriciana and spaghetti alla carbonara. Guanciale pairs great with hearty beans like cannellini or fave, whether in soups and stews or sautéed with greens.

Lamb Prosciutto

Classic prosciutto is, of course, made from the whole hind leg of a pig and can take a year or more of meticulous care to cure to pure ham perfection. "Prosciutto," however, can also be made with lamb, and because a lamb leg is so much smaller than a pig's, only a few months are required for the entire process. If you love lamb, as I do, you have to try lamb prosciutto. At the risk of sounding blasphemous, I might even like lamb prosciutto better than the classic! The end product, sliced paper thin, literally melts in your mouth, with an intense lamb flavor that can only be achieved by dry curing.. The undertones from rosemary, fennel and juniper berries elevate the lamb to astonishing heights.

I would typically start a lamb prosciutto sufficiently in advance of a special holiday or family get together, and serve it simply as part of a great antipasto. Try some in a semolina roll (page 107) topped with some melanzane sott'olio (page 7) - WOW!

Ingredients

3 to 4-lb fresh boneless leg of lamb

For the cure (see table):

Kosher salt 3% w/w

Sugar 2% w/w

InstaCure™ #2 0.3% w/w

Black peppercorns, 1% w/w

Juniper berries, 0.4% w/w

Fresh rosemary, 3 sprigs

Fresh garlic. 4 cloves, minced

2 T Fennel seeds, ground

Directions

1. Record the weight of the meat.
2. Add the InstaCure to the salt and mix well. Coarsely grind the peppercorns and juniper berries in an electric spice grinder and add to the salt, along with the sugar, rosemary, and garlic. Reserve the fennel for the drying stage.
3. Cover the lamb with the cure mixture, making sure that the meat is entirely covered.
4. Transfer the lamb and any remaining cure mix to seal-able plastic bags or, preferably, vacuum sealer bags. Remove as much air as possible to maintain contact between the cure and the meat.
5. Refrigerate the sealed bags for 7-10 days, turning occasionally.
6. Remove the lamb from the bag and rinse off the cure under cold running water.
7. Wrap the lamb in netting and coat with the ground fennel.
8. Dry at 40-45ºF, 75% relative humidity until the meat loses 30% of its starting weight, approximately 3-4 weeks.

For the initial cure:		
Ingredient	**Weight (g)**	**% by Weight**
Lamb leg	1800	-
Kosher salt	54	3% w/w
Sugar	36	2% w/w
InstaCure #2	5.4	0.3% w/w
Black peppercorns	18	1% w/w
Juniper berries	7.2	0.4%
Other ingredients as listed		

Above: Whole lamb prosciutto

Right: Thinly sliced and ready to enjoy

Below right: Fresh from the meat curing cabinet

Below: Fresh leg of lamb salted and seasoned for the initial curing step

Bresaola

Bresaola is a cured beef product originating from the province of Sondrio in the Lombardy region of Italy. The bresaola recipe from this region is so prized and protected that it holds IGP (*Indicazione Geografica Protetta*) certification by the Italian government. Sure, you can travel to the Italian Alps to pick up what is probably the best bresaola on the planet, or you can come pretty darn close with a meat curing cabinet (page 251) in your garage.

The preferred cut of beef for bresaola is the eye round, a single, lean muscle from the hind leg. Making your own bresaola is actually easier than most other cured meats. Just start with a high quality cut and you're halfway there. The hardest part is waiting for the beef to completely cure.

Ingredients

1 eye round of beef, 3 to 4 lbs

For the cure (see table)

2 T dried fennel seeds, ground

Note: Netting (below) can be purchased online. I made my own stuffing tube from 4" PVC pipe.

Directions

1. Trim eye round of exterior fat. Record the weight of the meat.
2. Mix cure ingredients in a bowl, making sure that the InstaCure is well-dispersed.
3. Completely coat the eye round in the curing mix and place it in a sealable plastic bag. I use vacuum sealer bags for this initial cure step. Note - you must use the entire cure. Any excess cure mix should be added to the plastic bag.
4. Seal the bag and refrigerate for about 10 days for the initial salt cure, massaging and turning the bag every couple of days.
5. After the initial cure, remove the meat from the bag and rinse well under cold water, then pat dry.
6. Tie the meat for hanging, either in butcher's netting (photo) or by string. I typically write the weight of the meat on a tag that I attach to the netting.
7. Sprinkle the meat with ground fennel seed and additional coarse ground black pepper.
8. Dry at 40-45°F, 75% relative humidity until the meat loses 30% of its starting weight, approximately 4 to 6 weeks.

For the initial cure:		
Ingredient	**Weight (g)**	**% by Weight**
Beef eye round	1453	-
Kosher salt	43.6	3% w/w
Sugar	29.1	2% w/w
InstaCure #2	4.4	0.3% w/w
Black pepper	14.5	1% w/w
Juniper berries	2.9	0.2% w/w
Dry sage	1.5	0.1% w/w

Above: Paper thin slices of bresaola ready to enjoy

Right: Trimmed eye round of beef

Below right: Fresh eye round salted and seasoned for the initial curing step

Below: Fresh from the curing cabinet

Opposite: Scale, netting and stuffing cylinder

Capocolla

Capocolla (also sometimes referred to as capicollo, capicola or coppa) is a type of Italian *salume* (plural, *salumi*) made from pork. Specifically, the *coppa* is part of the pork shoulder (or butt) that runs along the back of the neck, above the shoulder blade. The word *capocolla* is derived from *capo* (head) and *colla* (neck). If you plan on making your own capocolla (which I fully encourage), you'll have to pick up a whole boneless pork butt, sometimes called a Boston butt in the U.S. With a little practice, and some basic knowledge or porcine anatomy, you'll be able to separate the *coppa* from the rest of the shoulder; it is located at the opposite end from where the should blade itself would be attached. The rest of the pork but can be saved and used for making sausage or any number of other pork dishes.

I make both sweet and hot capocolla.The latter is my favorite, but both are fantastic. When properly cured and spiced, the paper thin slices melt in your mouth, almost like a fine prosciutto. The hardest part about making capocolla is waiting for it to fully cure!

Ingredients

3 to 4-lb *coppa*, separated from a whole pork butt (see photo)

For the cure (see table):

- 10 bay leaves, crushed
- 1/2 t fresh ground nutmeg
- 1 T dried thyme
- 1 T dried minced garlic

2 T dried fennel seeds, ground

For the initial cure:		
Ingredient	**Weight (g)**	**% by Weight**
Pork coppa muscle	1589	-
Kosher salt	47.7	3% w/w
Sugar	31.8	2% w/w
InstaCure #2	4.8	0.3% w/w
Black peppercorns	16.0	1% w/w
Juniper berries	5.6	0.4% w/w
Other ingredients as listed		

Directions

1. Record the weight of the meat.
2. Add the InstaCure to the salt and mix well. Coarsely grind the peppercorns and juniper berries in an electric spice grinder and add to the salt, along with the sugar, thyme, bay leaves, nutmeg and garlic. Reserve the fennel for the drying stage.
3. Cover the coppa with the cure mixture, making sure that the meat is entirely covered.
4. Transfer the coppa and any remaining cure mix to seal-able plastic bags or, preferably, vacuum sealer bags. Remove as much air as possible to maintain contact between the cure and the meat.
5. Refrigerate the sealed bags for 7-9 days, turning occasionally.
6. Remove the coppa from the bag and rinse off the cure under cold running water. The coppa should feel somewhat stiff and hard at this point.
7. Wrap the coppa in netting and coat with the ground fennel.
8. Sprinkle the ground fennel over the coppa and prepare for hanging in your meat curing cabinet.
9. Dry at 40-45ºF, 75% relative humidity until the meat loses 30% of its starting weight, approximately 3-4 weeks.

Note: For hot capocolla, sprinkle hot paprika over the coppa prior to hanging/drying.

Above: Sweet capocolla

Right: Hot capocolla curing

Below: Separating the *coppa* muscles (right) from the rest of the pork shoulder butt

Sopressata

Sopressata is a southern Italian,dry-cured, pork product similar to salami but different with respect to composition, method of preparation and taste. This family recipe combines traditional methods with some modern day "science" to produce an incredibly flavorful sopressata.

Pork butt (which is actually the shoulder) is the cut of choice for sopressata. The meat should be coarsely ground. I find that pork butt from pigs raised here in the States is just a bit too lean for sopressata, so I supplement the mix with hand-cut pieces of salt pork to give the sopressata the traditional appearance and texture (se photo).

Finally, there's the fermentation. The best sopressata has that slightly acidic and unmistakable tinge that's the result of slow fermentation at cool temperatures. This is achieved by the addition of a starter culture of "good" bacteria that slowly convert sugars to lactic acid.

Ingredients

Approximately 13 lbs fresh boneless pork butt (4 butts)

2 lbs salt pork

Kosher salt 3% w/w

InstaCure™ #2 0.3% w/w

1 T garlic powder

6 t ground white pepper

1 cup dry white wine

1/2 t starter culture (Bactoferm™ T-SPX) in 1/4 cup spring (or distilled) water

Directions

1. The ingredients and directions are for 15 lbs of pork (no sense of going through this for one sopressata!). The pork should be as cold as possible, but not frozen.
2. Trim and coarsely grind the pork butt (I use a stand mixer with a meat grinder attachment). Hand-cut the salt pork into 1/4 inch dice.
3. In a large container (like a food-grade plastic lug), mix the pork and dry ingredients, and then mix in the wine.
4. Add the water containing the starter culture and mix well.
5. Fill the mixture into individual 65 mm collagen casings, available from sausage supply stores.
6. Hang sopressata and dry at 40-45ºF, 75% relative humidity until the sopressata loses 30% of its starting weight, approximately 3-4 weeks.

Above: Sliced sopressata
Below right: Filled casings ready for controlled air-drying
Below left: Finished sopressata with collagen casings removed
Opposite left: Salt pork
Opposite right: Whole, boneless pork butt

Pancetta

Pancetta is made from pork belly, the same cut that is use to make bacon. Unlike bacon, however, pancetta is not smoked but cured. Here's where it gets a little confusing....most uses of pancetta call for cooking the meat as part of the recipe. This type of "semi-cured" pancetta requires only a relatively short curing time (about 3 weeks). If you plan to cook your pancetta, it's sufficient to use InstaCure™ #1 as part of the curing mix. This curing salt contains nitrites but no nitrates. If you plan to fully cure your pancetta, which can be consumed without cooking, you must use InstaCure™ #2, which contains both nitrites and nitrates, the latter being the slow-release form of nitrites. Also, fully cured pancetta will take longer to cure.

Pancetta can be cured as a flat slab, which is common throughout southern Italy. The rolled version (or *pancetta arrotolata*) is an alternative form and one that is most commonly seen in U.S. meat markets.

My preference is for the rolled version because I find it much easier to slice on my deli slicer if thin slices are needed. I also like to fully cure my pancetta because I think it's more versatile in that form, in that it can cooked for use in various recipes or thinly sliced for a salumi platter or as part of an Italian sub!

Ingredients

4 to 5-lb fresh pork belly*

For the cure (see table):

For the initial cure:		
Ingredient	Weight (g)	% By weight
Pork belly	2155	-
Kosher salt	64.7	3% w/w
Sugar	43.1	2% w/w
InstaCure #2	6.5	0.3% w/w
Black peppercorns	21.6	1% w/w
Juniper berries	8.6	0.4%
Garlic powder	4.3	0.2%

*Note: Pancetta is made with skinless pork belly. If you purchase a pork belly with skin on, simply remove it - and save it to make cotenne (page 173)

Directions

1. Record the weight of the meat.
2. Add the InstaCure to the salt and mix well. Coarsely grind the peppercorns and juniper berries in an electric spice grinder and add to the salt, along with the sugar and garlic powder.
3. Cover the pork belly with the cure mixture, making sure that the meat is entirely covered.
4. Transfer the pork and any remaining cure mix to sealable plastic bags or, preferably, vacuum sealer bags. Remove as much air as possible to maintain contact between the cure and the pork.
5. Refrigerate the sealed bags for 7-10 days, turning occasionally.
6. Remove the pork from the bag and rinse off the cure under cold running water.
7. Roll the pork and tie with a butcher's knot (see photo). Sprinkle the pork with coarsely ground black pepper.
8. Hang and dry at 40-45ºF, 75% relative humidity until the pork loses 20% of the post-cure starting weight, approximately 4-5 weeks.

Above: Fully-cured pancetta

Right: Rolled and tied pancetta after the initial cure step, ready for hanging and drying

Below: Vacuum-sealed pork belly in the initial cure step

Homemade Italian Sausage

I can't bring myself to buy store-bought Italian sausage, unless it's from an authentic Italian butcher. Even then, the price per pound is 4 or 5 times what it would cost me to make my own, equally good, sausage. With a relatively modest initial investment in some basic equipment - a meat grinder and a sausage stuffer - making your own sausage is really very easy, and there's a great deal of satisfaction in knowing that you've chosen the freshest of ingredients.

I typically make about 30 lbs of sausage at a time and freeze most of it in smaller (2-3 lb) packages for use as needed. The recipe below is for 5 lbs of sweet Italian sausage. You can scale the ingredients to accommodate as much sausage as you want to make. Add crushed red pepper to make hot sausage.

You can purchase a dedicated meat grinder, but I find that the meat grinding attachment on a KitchenAid™ stand mixer (photo) works just fine.

Ingredients (per 5 lbs of pork)

Whole boneless pork butts*

5 t salt

1 t course ground black pepper

2 T fennel seed

1/2 cup red wine

Natural hog casings

*Note: Take the total weight of pork butts and calculate the amount of ingredients for each 5 lbs.

Directions

1. Cut pork butts into manageable pieces for grinding. Trim excess connective tissue, but leave the fat. Refrigerate until very cold; a short time in the freezer prior to grinding helps keep the structure of the meat and fat in the grind.
2. Grind pork into a large container using the coarse grind setting or attachment. I typically use a food-grade plastic lug (photo).
3. Add the dry ingredients and wine. Mix well, but gently, by hand; the idea is to season throughout while maintaining the structure of the meat and fat in the grind.
4. Rinse casings well and allow to sit in cold water for 20 minutes. Load casing onto stuffing tube attached to sausage stuffer, tying off the end.
5. Fill sausage stuffer with sausage mix and dispense into casing. Tie off other end and twist the filled casing into sausage links of desired size.

Above: Homemade sausage
Right: Grinding pork butts
Below: Sausage stuffer
Opposite: Whole boneless pork butts and hog casings

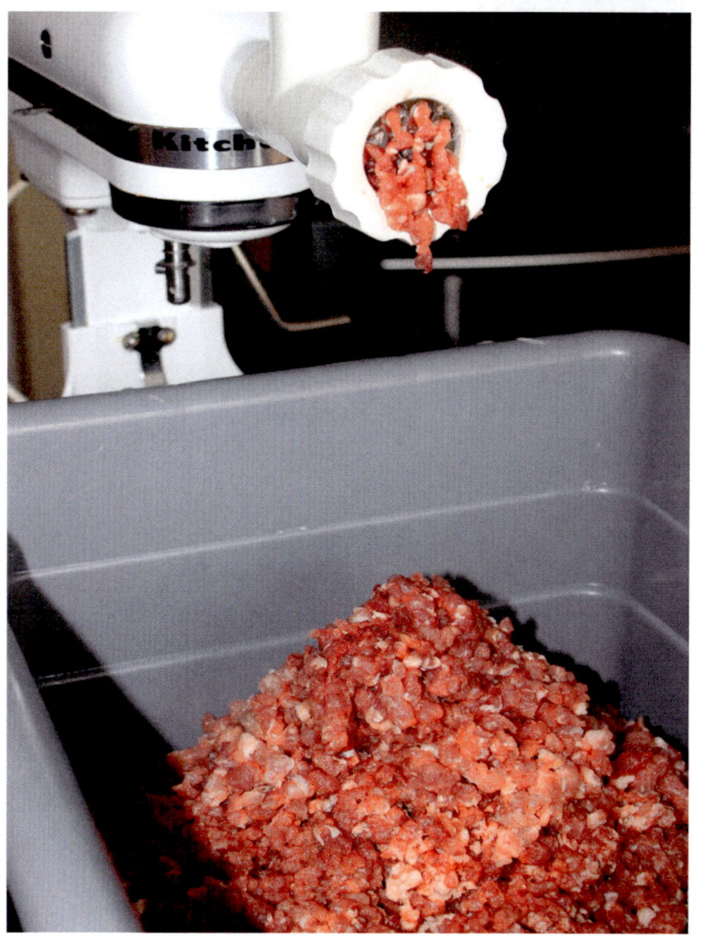

Pizza Dough

I judge a great pizza by its crust, which begins with the perfect dough. The ideal pizza crust should be crispy on the outside and soft and chewy in the center. Of course, the baking method contributes to that property, but it all starts with the dough!

Here are some essentials for producing the best pizza dough: (i) toss out the measuring cups and spoons and measure all dough ingredients by weight, not by volume. I use a digital scale religiously when I make pizza dough; (ii) get used to thinking like professional bakers, and measure out ingredients as a percentage of the amount of flour in the recipe. This makes it so much easier to scale the amount of dough according to how many pizzas you want to make; (iii) use a high quality flour. My favorite for pizza is "Caputo Antico Molino Tipo 00" pizzeria flour, a product of Naples, Italy. This flour is made from grain with the ideal amount and type of wheat gluten, and it is ground to a super-fine consistency by methods that preserve the gluten. The result is a soft dough with superior "extensibility," the property that allows the dough to be stretched without contracting back.

If you have a little extra time, making your own pizza dough is well-worth the effort. I like using a stand mixer fitted with a dough hook to make my pizza dough, but hand-kneading is fine if you're up to it.

Ingredients (makes 2 large pizzas)

500 g "Caputo Antico Molino Tipo 00" pizzeria flour

325 g bottled water (i.e., "65% hydration")

10 g non-iodized salt

3 g active dry yeast

Directions

1. Add the dry ingredients to the bowl of a stand mixer fitted with a dough hook. With the mixer at slow speed, slowly add the water.
2. When the dough ball has formed, turn the mixer off and allow the dough to rest for 10 minutes for the flour to absorb the water.
3. Turn the mixer back on at medium speed and knead the dough for about 5 minutes.
4. Transfer the dough into bowl that is lightly oiled with olive oil to prevent sticking. Cover the bowl with a damp towel, and let it rise until doubled in size, about 2 hours.
5. Punch down the dough to remove air bubbles and divide in half.
6. Shape each piece into a ball by gently stretching the top down and around the dough, tucking it underneath to form a smooth ball with a tight outer "skin."
7. Place each ball seam-side down on a flour-dusted tray. Dust the top of each ball with flour, cover with a clean, damp towel and allow to rest for about 1 hr.
8. At this point, the dough will be soft and extensible and can be easily stretched to form your crust.

Above: Two balls of dough, ready for stretching into two large pizzas

Below: Stretched dough

Below right: Caputo pizza flour

Pasta Dough

I don't always make fresh pasta dough for each pasta dish, but on special occasions it's worth the little extra effort (and mess). Pasta made from freshly prepared dough has a soft silkiness to it that isn't attainable with dried pasta out of the box. Plus, if you're interested in making something like homemade ravioli, you're going to have to make your own dough.

While fresh pasta dough might seem a bit intimidating, it's really very simple - only a few basic ingredients. A pasta-making machine, while not absolutely necessary, makes rolling and shaping pasta extremely easy - Jenna was doing it at 4 years old (photo).

Finally, the use of all-purpose flour makes perfectly good pasta, but I prefer an Italian flour like Caputo Antico Molino "00" pasta flour, from Naples. This type of flour is very finely ground using a method that preserves the high gluten content, which makes for a pliable dough and light, silky smooth pasta.

Ingredients (makes about 1 1/2 lbs fresh dough; serves 6)*

4 cups (approx 20 oz) Caputo Antico Molino "00" pasta flour (or substitute all-purpose flour)

5 large eggs

1 T olive oil

1/2 t salt

Directions

1. For best results, the flour must be incorporated into the eggs a little at a time. The typical way to do this is to mound the flour onto your work surface (e.g., a large cutting board or granite counter top) and then make a well in the middle with your fingers.
2. Add the eggs, salt and olive oil into the well and beat with a fork.
3. Working outward from the well, gradually incorporate flour into the eggs with your fork, mixing well as you go.
4. Eventually, enough flour will be incorporated so that a sticky dough is formed.
5. Using your hands, continue to incorporate flour until a firm dough is achieved. You may or may not need the entire amount of flour.
6. Continue kneading the dough ball on a lightly floured work surface using the palms of your hands, pushing against the work surface, for about 5 minutes. At this point, the dough should be only slightly sticky.
7. Wrap the dough in plastic wrap and let rest at room temperature for 20-30 minutes. This step is essential to allow the glutens to fully hydrate to produce a pliable dough.
8. The dough is ready to be rolled and cut, or shaped into the desired pasta shape with the aid of a pasta-making machine.
9. Toss the final pasta lightly in flour and keep at room temperature until ready to cook.

*Note: This ratio of flour to egg works well for me. If you need to scale in half, you can go with 2 cups of flour and 3 MEDIUM eggs (photo at right). That's enough for, say, 24 medium-sized ravioli.

Above: Pasta dough ingredients

Right: A thin sheet of rolled out pasta dough

Below: Jenna helped out from a very young age

Left: Ball of pasta dough resting

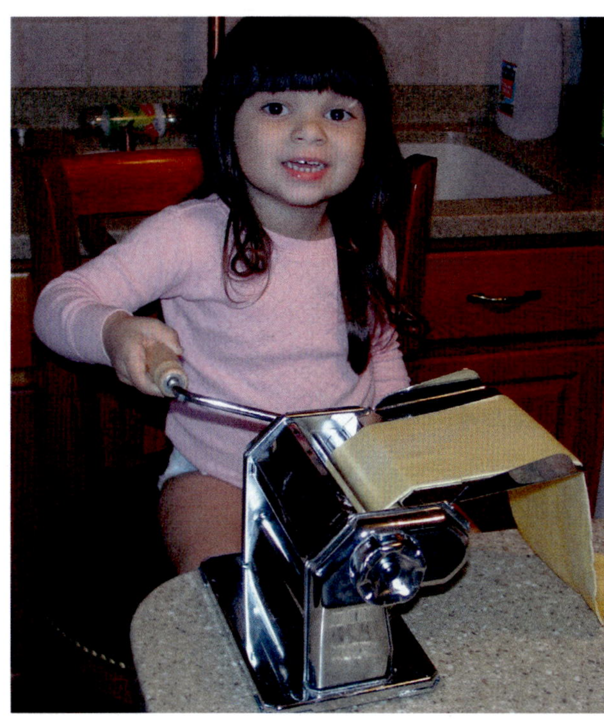

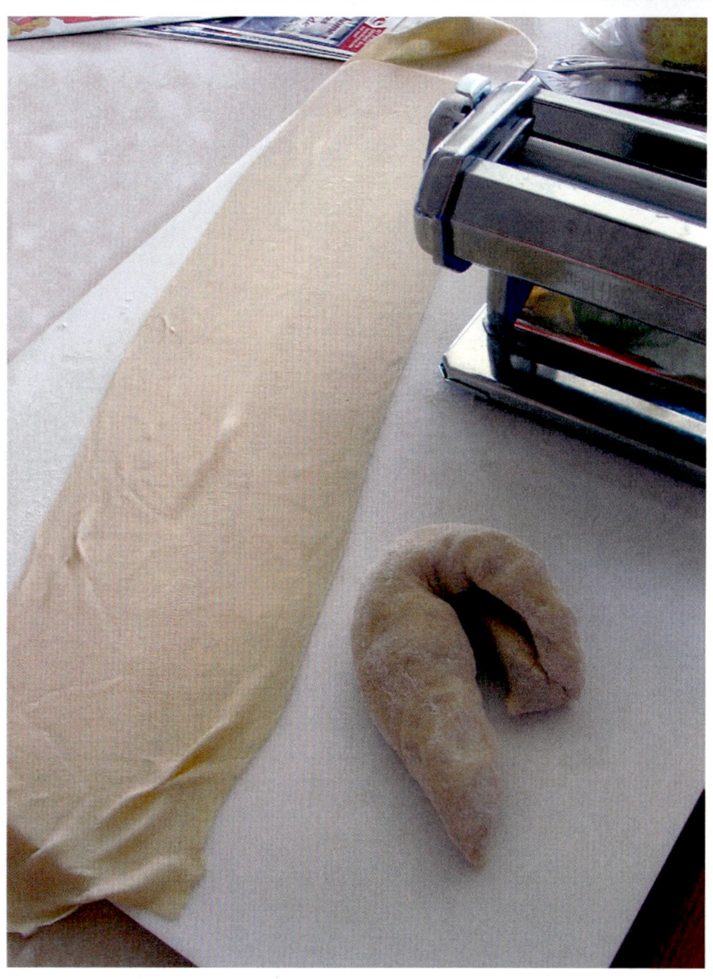

Fresh Mozzerella

Making cheese at home is both fun and rewarding. Some fresh cheeses, like mozzerella or ricotta, are very quick and easy to make, while others are a bit more challenging and require some attention and patience while the cheese ages.

You can make mozzerella with just about any kind of milk, but I prefer whole milk for the extra creaminess it gives to the cheese. One very important point, however, is to avoid milk that has been pasteurized by ultra-high temperature - sometimes labeled as "UHT." The high temperature denatures (i.e., breaks down) the milk proteins such that they are unable to form proper curds, which is essential for cheese-making. I get my milk from a local dairy market where they pasteurize fresh milk using a low-temperature process.

Ingredients (makes about 1 lb of fresh mozzerella)

1 gallon whole milk; low-temperature pasteurized

1 1/4 cup cool, bottled water

1 1/2 t citric acid (see note)

1/4 t liquid rennet (or 1/4 rennet tablet - see note)

1 t non-iodized salt

Equipment

Stainless steel 8-quart stock pot

Knife long enough to reach the bottom of the stock pot

Slotted spoon or hand strainer

Instant-read thermometer

Rubber gloves

Directions:

1. Dissolve rennet tablet in 1/4 cup water
2. Dissolve the citric acid in 1 cup water
3. Add milk to pot, then add citric acid solution while stirring vigorously
4. Heat milk to 90ºF with gentle stirring
5. Remove pot from heat and add rennet solution, and stir gently, but well, for 30 seconds; cover the pot and leave undisturbed for 5 minutes. At this point, the milk should appear as a custard. You should be able to gently press on the custard and see good separation from the clear liquid whey
6. Cut the curd at an angle in two directions to produce small "cubes"
7. Heat the pot to 110ºF while you gently stir the curds. Remove from heat and continue stirring for 3-4 minutes
8. Pour off as much of the liquid whey as possible, and then ladle the curds into a colander, gently folding them to drain off the remaining whey
9. At this point, heating the curds in a microwave is doable, but I prefer the more traditionally method. Bring another pot of water to 185ºF. The pot should be large enough to accommodate the colander and there should be enough water to submerge the curds
10. Dip the curds into the hot water several times, folding them gently until they begin to become elastic (this is where the rubber gloves come in)
11. The curds will be fully stretchable when they reach approximately 135ºF.
12. Add the salt and work into the cheese as you continue to stretch, dipping it in and out of the water to maintain the temperature of the cheese
13. Shape the cheese into a ball and place in cool water to cool

Above left: slicing the curds
Above right: fresh mozzerella
Right: cooked and separated curds

Note: Citric acid may sound scary, but it's actually an essential component of cellular metabolism in all aerobic organisms (yes, that includes humans) - look up the Krebs cycle if you're interested. Citric acid is what makes your lips pucker when you bite into a lemon or other "citrus" fruit.

Rennet is a mixture of enzymes, the main one being chymosin. Not to get too scientific here, but caseins (the principal proteins in milk) exist as micelles (microscopic globules). One component of casein, called kappa casein, is a negatively charged molecule on the outside of the micelles. The negatively charged micelles repel each other, keeping the milk proteins soluble (i.e., in liquid form). Chymosin removes the negative charge on the kappa casein. The result is that the micelles can no longer repel each other and the milk curdles.

Natural animal rennet comes from the lining of a calf's stomach, where it helps in the digestion of milk. There are vegetable sources of rennet as well; just make sure you get rennet "for cheese making." Don't use "Junket," which has relatively little of the necessary chymosin enzyme.

Ricotta

Making homemade ricotta couldn't be more simple. Ricotta (literally, "re-cooked" in Italian) is, of course, an unripened, soft cheese produced when milk proteins are heated in the presence of a mild acid. Traditionally, the acidity comes from the addition of lemon juice to heated milk. While that is still the tried and true method on Italian farms, I like to be more precise, for consistency purposes - must be the scientist in me!

Ricotta can be made from whole milk, reduced fat milk, or even whey left over from other cheese-making processes. Just avoid ultra high pasteurized milk, as this pasteurization process alters the structure of milk proteins such that curds are difficult to form.

Finally, I like using fresh, "raw" milk (i.e., unpasteurized) for my ricotta, which I get from a local dairy farm. I think it makes for an exceptionally creamy ricotta. Don't worry - the heating process during ricotta-making is more than sufficient to kill any bacteria that may be present in the raw milk.

Ingredients

1 gallon whole milk

2 t food-grade citric acid

1 t salt

Equipment

Food thermometer

Directions

1. Dissolve citric acid in 1 cup water; set aside.
2. If you happen to have a pH meter lying around the house (like who doesn't?), add the citric acid solution until the pH of the milk drops to 6.0. Alternatively, add half of the citric acid solution, for now, and stir to mix.
3. Add the salt to the milk and slowly heat (medium/low) with stirring, until the temperature reaches 170ºF. At this point, if the pH is sufficiently low, you should see small curds, or flakes, starting to form in the milk. If not, add more of the citric acid solution in small amounts (1 tablespoon at a time) until the milk begins to curdle.
4. At this point, very gentle stirring is important to avoid breaking up the curds into tiny bits. Continue heating to a temperature of 190ºF and then turn the heat off. The curds will float - gentle move them to the center of the pot and then let them rest, undisturbed for 15 minutes.
5. Ladle the curds onto a colander lined with food-grade cheesecloth and allow to drain for 30 minutes; transfer to a container to chill.

Ricotta science:

The proteins in milk are either curd proteins or whey proteins. The curd proteins are caseins, which make up about 80% of total milk protein. Milk caseins exist alongside milk fat in tiny globules called "micelles." The caseins on the surface of each micelle expose a negative charge, which prevents the micelles from coming together - think of trying to push together the same pole of two magnets. The addition of acid masks the negative charges on the micelle surface, allowing them to clump together to form curds - behold, RICOTTA!

Whole milk, by virtue of its lactic acid content, has a slightly acidic pH of around 6.6. The addition of citric acid further reduces that pH to around 6.0, which is required for curd formation.

Above: Ricotta

Below left to right:

Citric acid

Heating milk to 170ºF; note the start of curd formation

Straining the curd through a fine-mesh food strainer

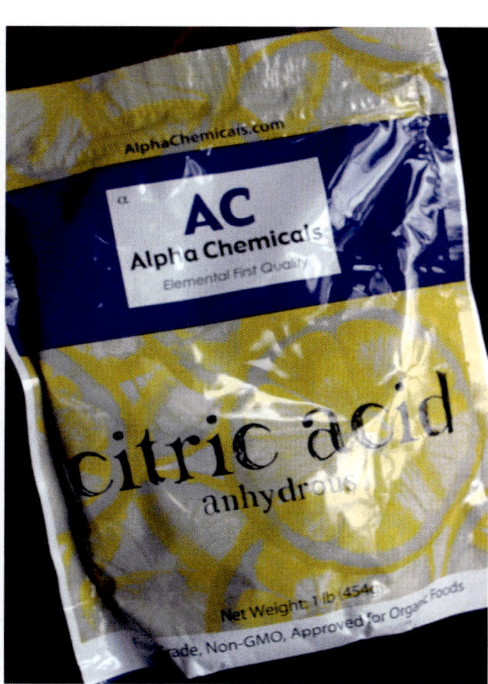

Jarred Tomatoes

For many years, I have grown my own vegetables and omato plants make up a good portion of my vegetable garden. Each summer, I home-jar fresh tomatoes to get me through the rest of the year until the following year's crop is available. I also end up jarring some homemade tomato sauce - just for use on those days when I'm feeling particularly lazy - but the bulk of my tomatoes are jarred fresh. This is mainly because fresh tomatoes are much more versatile; I can use them for the traditional, slow-cooked tomato sauce or a quick, fresh marinara. I can use them for pizza sauce, homemade salsa, in soups and stews, or even puree them for fantastic Bloody Marys!

For the most part, I jar different types of tomatoes separately over the main course of the growing season, San Marzano tomatoes being the variety I prefer for sauce. At the end of the season, however, I would pool together the remaining vine-ripened fruit and just jar them all together.

Jarring tomatoes is very easy, but vine-ripened tomatoes are a must. So if you don't grow your own, seek out the freshest and most ripe tomatoes you can find, perhaps from a local farm.

Ingredients (makes about 12 quart jars)

Approximately 25 - 30 lbs vine-ripened tomatoes

8 t kosher salt

Small bunch of fresh basil

Equipment:

Pressure canner

Caning equipment (jar lifter, canning funnel, small rubber spatula)

Quart-size canning jars, lids and rims

8-quart pot for blanching tomatoes

Large plastic bowls

Paring knife

Large slotted spoon

Large ladle

Directions:

1. Wash and rinse jars thoroughly
2. Fill the 8-quart pot halfway with water and bring to a simmer.
3. Fill a large plastic bowl halfway with ice cold water.
4. Working with a few pounds of tomatoes at a time, drop them into the simmering water bath for 1-2 minutes. Remove and place in ice water to cool.
5. With the paring knife, cut around a discard where the stem attached to the tomato. Grasp the skin between the paring knife and your thumb and peel off. You can make a slit in the skin to make the peeling easier. If the skin doesn't come off very easily, allow the tomatoes to stay a bit longer in the hot water.
6. When all the tomatoes are peeled, they should fill two large plastic bowls with about 12-15 lbs tomatoes in each (see photo).
7. To each bowl, add 4 t salt and a generous handful of torn basil leaves; mix well.
8. Using the canning funnel and ladle, fill each jar with the peeled tomatoes to about a half inch below the neck of the jar. Run the rubber spatula around the inside of the jar to remove any trapped air.
9. Thoroughly dry the rim of each jar and cover with a lid cover. Place a rim over the cover and finger tighten just to the point where there is some resistance.
10. Place the jars into the pressure canner and process as per the canner directions. I typically process tomatoes for 30 minutes once the internal pressure reaches 15 psi.

Counterclockwise from left:

Jarred tomatoes

San Marzano tomatoes

Peeled tomatoes ready for processing

12-quart pressure canner

Processed tomatoes cooling

Slow-cooked Tomato Sauce

The best homemade tomato sauce requires only two things - the freshest ingredients possible and patience. Some of he best food memories I have from my childhood include those early Sunday mornings when my mother would begin the ritual of preparing Sunday dinner, which invariably included some type of pasta and tomato sauce that was cooked for hours upon hours - the longer the better. The aroma that permeated our home was incredible and filled me with such anticipation that I would intentionally starve myself during the day, saving my appetite for what I knew was coming. Sadly, there was no point in trying to rush my mother to get dinner on the table sooner - that would just never happen - she would just give you that "What, are you crazy?" look. Thankfully, however, Sunday dinner was always around 3:00 PM, much earlier that our typical dinner hour. There was just something about sitting around the dinner table with bright sunshine coming through the window, bathing the platters of piping hot pasta, meatballs, sausage and crusty Italian bread that made Sunday dinner special for me.

To this day, the best way to spend a Sunday for me is to relax and make a nice batch of tomato sauce. There's a saying in Italian - *non invecchi mentre cucini* - "you don't age while cooking." It's so true.

As you probably know by now, I grow my own San Marzano tomatoes for sauce - there are none better. Each season, I jar a dozen or so cases of fresh tomatoes for use in various recipes throughout the year, but mostly to be able to make fresh tomato sauce in the dead of winter. This recipe is for the classic, slow-cooked sauce with meatballs and sausage. If you prefer, you can make a vegetarian version by omitting the meat, but it really gives the sauce a deep, rich flavor. Most folks, understandably, don't grow their own tomatoes. The next best option, then, is to use canned tomatoes. Look for imported, Italian, whole, peeled, San Marzano tomatoes.

I typically make a rather large batch of sauce. This recipe is easily enough for 8 people and 2 lbs of pasta. The sauce stores well for up to a week refrigerated and can be reheated as needed. Alternatively, the sauce can be frozen in plastic containers.

Ingredients

8-10 meatballs (pg 137)

6-8 links sweet Italian sausage, preferably homemade (pg 247)

1/2 cup extra virgin olive oil

4 28-oz jars (or cans) of whole San Marzano tomatoes in their juice

2 6-oz cans tomato paste

1 medium onion, chopped

6 fresh basil leaves, torn

Several springs of parsley, chopped

Salt

Directions:

1. Heat olive oil in a large sauce pot and brown meatballs. Remove from pot and set aside. Add sausage links, brown and then remove and set aside.
2. Add the onion and cook until translucent.
3. Add the tomatoes, paste, parsley and basil. Stir to blend and then taste for seasoning. Add salt to taste.
4. Return the meatballs and sausage to the pot and simmer on low for at least 3 hrs, stirring occasionally.

Above: Homemade tomato sauce simmering

Right: Meatballs and sausage cooked in sauce

Below left: Jarred fresh tomatoes

Below right: Jarred homemade sauce for those days when I'm not up to making a large batch

Marinara Sauce

Classic marinara sauce is pure simplicity. Very different from the classic slow-cooked tomato sauce (previous page), marinara should take you no longer than 20 minutes, start to finish, or you're doing it wrong! The ingredients are few, but should be the freshest that you can find - vine-ripened Italian tomatoes, fresh garlic and high quality olive oil, kissed with a little hot pepper, basil and salt - that's it. Ignore marinara recipes that call for onions, tomato paste, wine, butter (ugh), or anything else - they have no place in marinara sauce. You want the fresh, sweet tomato flavor to be the star of this sauce.

When I make marinara in the summertime, I use vine-ripened San Marzano tomatoes from my garden - there's nothing better - but I also jar those tomatoes for use throughout the rest of the year. Jarring fresh (uncooked) tomatoes provides some versatility, in that you can use them directly out of the jar for marinara or you can slow-cook them for the traditional tomato sauce. The recipe below uses jarred San Marzano tomatoes from my garden. If you must use canned tomatoes, just make sure you use genuine, imported, San Marzano tomatoes.

Fresh, "loose" sauces, like marinara, pair better with spaghetti or linguine than with other pasta shapes; the spaces between the individual pasta pieces maximizes the amount of sauce you'll get with each bite.

Ingredients

1/3 cup olive oil

2 quarts of jarred tomatoes or substitute two 32-oz can of premium imported Italian plum tomatoes

2 cloves garlic, chopped

4 fresh basil leaves, coarsely torn

Pinch of crushed red pepper

Salt to taste

Directions:

1. Heat oil in a sauce pan and sauté garlic for 30 seconds.
2. Add the tomatoes and crush them in the pan with a potato masher. Don't overdo it - you want to see chunks of fresh tomato.
3. Add the basil, red pepper and salt to taste (approximately 1/2 t).
4. Cover sauce pan and cook on medium low heat for 15 minutes. The fresh tomato marinara is ready for your favorite pasta. Don't forget the crusty Italian bread.

"Sun Dried" Tomatoes

Yes, you can actually dry your tomatoes in the sun, if you happen to live in a climate that's hot and dry for most of the year. Sun drying takes some time (several days) and a little ingenuity to protect the tomatoes from bugs, critters and the occasional storm. A second options is to dry tomatoes in the oven at a relatively low temperature (e.g., 170°F). That method has disadvantages as well - it requires the better part of a full day, and you will have to keep your oven door cracked open to allow for moisture to escape.

After having tried various methods, with mixed success, I have found that a food dehydrator produces consistent results in a relatively short time. It's worth investing in a decent dehydrator if you plan to go this route. I make a relatively large batch of "sun dried" tomatoes each summer from my vine-ripened San Marzano tomatoes. For the past 10 seasons or so, I have used a stainless steel, forced hot air convection dehydrator that has independent controls for heat and air flow; it can easily accommodate the 15 lbs or so of tomatoes that I make in a batch.

Once properly dried, tomatoes can be stored almost indefinitely. The method that I have landed on is to vacuum seal them in smaller batches and then keep them in my freezer. All you have to do, then, is to thaw a bag and allow them to soak in some good extra virgin alive oil - fresh as the day they were dried!

Ingredients

15 lbs vine-ripened San Marzano or Roma tomatoes (for drying and storage)

Salt to taste

For a single batch of prepared sun dried tomatoes:

1 lb dried tomatoes

Extra virgin olive oil

1 clove garlic, chopped

5 or 6 fresh basil leaves, coarsely chopped

1 T grated Pecorino Romano cheese

Directions:

1. To dry tomatoes in a food dehydrator, slice them in half lengthwise and give them a light sprinkle of salt.
2. Arrange them on the dehydrator racks and dry according to equipment directions. This takes about 8 hrs in the unit that I have, with the heat on medium and low air flow. Dry tomatoes until most of the moisture is gone, but don't over-dry. The tomatoes should still be a bit soft and pliable.
3. Vacuum seal dried tomatoes in quart bags and keep in freezer.
4. When you're ready to make a finished batch, thaw a bag of dried tomatoes and place them in a container just large enough to hold them.
5. Add the garlic, basil and grated cheese.
6. Add enough olive oil so that all the tomatoes are well-coated. Mix and allow tomatoes to soften in the oil for several hours or, preferably, overnight.
7. Add more olive oil, if needed, and serve with crusty Italian bread.

Note: Should you happen to over-dry your tomatoes, fear not. You can rehydrate them in a steamer basket before proceeding with step 4 above.

Above: “Sun dried” tomatoes

Right: Dried tomatoes fresh from the dehydrator, ready for vacuum sealing

Below right: Halved tomatoes going into the dehydrator

Below left: A bowlful of vine-ripened San Marzano tomatoes

Pickling

My vegetable garden yields way more produce than my family can consume in a summer - even with the amounts that we typically give to relatives and friends. The solution, of course, is to preserve the harvest for use throughout the rest of the year. For me, most of that effort goes into jarring tomatoes (page 275). Pickling, however, is another way to preserve and enjoy home-grown vegetables after the garden shuts down for the season.

My daughters love to grow their own pickling cucumbers in my garden, and then use them to make dill pickles. Just about any vegetable can be pickled, but crisp vegetables like banana peppers, seem to be better suited for pickling than, say, tomatoes, Also, freshness is the key to the best pickled vegetables. Avoid vegetables that are bruised, soft or over-ripe.

You can buy a pickling spice mix, or you can make a custom mix of your own liking. I prefer the latter because I can alter the spice components to suit the particular vegetable.

Finally, the pickling method described here is for what is sometimes referred to as "quick pickling." That it, there is no pressure canning involved, so the pickled vegetables should be kept refrigerated. I do employ a bit of a trick (described below) to better seal the lid to maintain freshness for longer periods. However, these vegetables seem to disappear so fast that long-term storage is never really an issue!

Ingredients

1-quart wide-mouth Mason jars with lids and bands

Fresh vegetables for as many quart jars as you plan to fill.

For each quart jar:

1 t Kosher salt

1/2 t calcium chloride (sold as Pickle Crisp™)

1 t whole black peppercorns

1 clove garlic, chopped

1 T pickling mix (see below)

Apple cider vinegar

Hot (not boiling) water

Directions:

1. Wash and dry Mason jars; always use new lids.
2. Rinse vegetables and place them into the Mason jars. They should fill the jars without packing too tightly. Vegetables can be left whole or sliced.
3. To each jar add the salt, Pickle Crisp™, peppercorns, garlic and pickling mix.
4. Fill each jar halfway with vinegar, and then to the neck of the jar with hot water, leaving abut a half inch of air to the lip of the jar.
5. Make sure the lip of the jar is dry and immediately seal the jar with a lid and band. Hand tighten and invert the jars several times to mix. Refrigerate the jars.
6. The hot water will help dissolve the salt and when the jars cool, the lids will seal as pressure drops in the jars (it's not "weird science," it's the Combined Gas Law). Between the salt, acidity and refrigeration temperature, the pickled vegetables will last quite a long time - that is, if you can resist devouring them!

Note: My basic pickling mix consist of crushed bay leaves along with whole seeds of coriander, mustard, fennel and allspice. I also use dried hot chili peppers and fresh garlic for some pickled vegetables.

Above: Various pickled vegetables; hot banana pepper rings, whole cherry bomb peppers and whole orange banana peppers

Right: Dill pickles

Below: Pickling mix

Fresh Olives

Home-curing of fresh or "raw" olives is very rewarding, but requires a tremendous amount of patience, as the process from start to finish can take up to a year, depending on the curing method.

If you've ever bitten into a fresh olive picked from a tree, you'd quickly realize that they're completely inedible. This is principally due to a chemical known as oleuropein. The principal goal of the curing process is to remove the bitter oleuropein from the olives. Curing can be accomplished in a number of different ways; lye curing is the quickest method, but it requires great care to handle and dispose of the caustic lye. The more time-consuming (but much safer) method is the brine cure, which is what I use for curing olives.

Olives are typically harvested from late summer through the end of the year. They go through a maturation process in which green (immature) olives become purple/black (mature) olives. There is actually an Olive Maturation Index (OMI) that growers use, principally for selecting olives for processing into olive oil. For brine curing, I specifically purchase olives with an OMI of 2.0, a stage in which the olives have changed from green to yellow-green with about 20% in "veraison transition," the point at which olives start to take on a purple-ish hue (see photo).

Oleuropein is slowly leached from the olives during the brining process. The slow fermentation that takes place during curing breaks down the oleuropein and eliminates the bitterness. Olives prepared in this manner can be safely stored in brine for a year or more, developing flavor with time.

Ingredients

Raw olives

Pickling salt

Whole fennel seed

Fresh garlic, chopped

Apple cider vinegar

Directions

1. Rinse olives in water, discarding any that are bruised or scarred.
2. Fill a large container (I use a food-grade plastic lug) with cold water.
3. With a sharp knife, make 2 or 3 slits in each olive, cutting down to the pit, and immediately drop them in the water. Cover the container and allow olives to soak for 24 hrs. Drain the olives and replenish with fresh water. Do this daily for 7 days.
4. Prepare a brine with 1 1/2 cups pickling salt per gallon of water. Remove olives from their final rinse and place them in containers. I use half gallon food-grade plastic containers or mason jars. To each container, add a tablespoon each of fennel seed and chopped garlic. At this point, you can also add in some optional ingredients. like a few pieces of chopped celery, cauliflower, pearl onions, lemon rind, hot pepper, etc.
5. Fill each container about a third full with vinegar, and then to the top with the brine, covering the olives completely; you just have to eyeball this step.
6. Cover the containers loosely and store at room temperature for about 2 months, checking occasionally to top off with additional brine, if necessary. After this period, you might see some surface yeast present as a result of fermentation; this is perfectly fine.
7. At this point, you can firmly seal the containers and store them in a cool place for at least 4 additional months to develop flavor. When I crack open a jar, I transfer a few scoops of olives to a serving bowl and drizzle them with a little olive oil. Worth the wait!

Above: Freshly-picked, raw olives

Left: Olives in brine/vinegar solution in a half-gallon mason jar; about 9 months in storage

Below: A small bowl of finished olives - perfect for snacking

About the Author

James Desiderio isn't a restaurateur, professional chef, food blogger, or anything of the sort. He is, however, a Ph.D. scientist with a 35-year career in the pharmaceutical/ biotechnology industry. To him, cooking is "an art form but also part science; every dish involving some aspect of physics, chemistry and/or biology." Tinkering with recipes is, by definition, a science experiment in which the scientist (aka "chef") starts with a hypothesis, designs an experiment to test that hypothesis, records the data at the end the experiment, and then draws a conclusion that ties back to the original hypothesis. That's basically "cooking" through the eyes of a scientist!

James is also the lucky member of an extended Italian family whose roots are in southern Italy. His direct relatives are from the Naples region and various in-laws are from Calabria and Sicily. As with most Italian families, food is held in high esteem. Treasured recipes, part of the rustic culture of southern Italy, have been preserved and passed on through generations of the Desiderio family. A small sample of those family recipes - including some of James' favorites - are presented in this book.

To feed his passion for cooking with fresh, authentic ingredients, James maintains a rather large and unique vegetable garden, which in his own words, is "larger than the home in which I grew up in New York." Besides gardening and preserving the harvest, James makes homemade wine, cheeses, pasta and cured artisan meats, all following the time-honored techniques of life in southern Italy.

James currently lives in rural Massachusetts, with his family; Lori, Amanda, Jenna and the family dog, Pepper.

Index

Made in the USA
Middletown, DE
19 February 2019